American Dominion

American Dominion

The Rise and Radicalization of a New Christendom

Keri Ladner

BLOOMSBURY ACADEMIC
NEW YORK • LONDON • OXFORD • NEW DELHI • SYDNEY

BLOOMSBURY ACADEMIC

Bloomsbury Publishing Inc, 1359 Broadway, New York, NY 10018, USA
Bloomsbury Publishing Plc, 50 Bedford Square, London, WC1B 3DP, UK
Bloomsbury Publishing Ireland, 29 Earlsfort Terrace, Dublin 2, D02 AY28, Ireland

BLOOMSBURY, BLOOMSBURY ACADEMIC and the Diana logo are
trademarks of Bloomsbury Publishing Plc

First published in the United States of America 2026

Copyright © Keri Ladner, 2026

Cover design by Jen Huppert
Cover image © iStock.com/hidesy

Scripture quotations taken from the (NASB®) New American Standard Bible®,
Copyright © 1960, 1971, 1977, 1995, 2020 by The Lockman Foundation.
Used by permission. All rights reserved. lockman.org

All rights reserved. No part of this publication may be: i) reproduced or transmitted in any form, electronic or mechanical, including photocopying, recording or by means of any information storage or retrieval system without prior permission in writing from the publishers; or ii) used or reproduced in any way for the training, development or operation of artificial intelligence (AI) technologies including generative AI technologies. The rights holders expressly reserve this publication from the text and data mining exception as per Article 4(3) of the Digital Single Market Directive (EU) 2019/790.

Bloomsbury Publishing Inc does not have any control over, or responsibility for,
any third-party websites referred to or in this book. All internet addresses given
in this book were correct at the time of going to press. The author and publisher regret
any inconvenience caused if addresses have changed or sites have ceased to exist,
but can accept no responsibility for any such changes.

Library of Congress Cataloging-in-Publication Data
Names: Ladner, Keri author
Title: American dominion : the rise and radicalization of a new Christendom / Keri Ladner.
Description: New York : Bloomsbury Academic, 2026. |
Includes bibliographical references and index.
Identifiers: LCCN 2025037468 | ISBN 9798216275763 HB |
ISBN 9798216275787 ePDF | ISBN 9798216275770 eBook
Subjects: LCSH: Dominion theology–United States |
Evangelicalism–Political aspects–United States | Radicalization–United States |
Radicalism–Religious aspects–Christianity | Christianity and politics–United States
Classification: LCC BT82.25.L33 2026
LC record available at https://lccn.loc.gov/2025037468

ISBN:	HB:	979-8-216-27576-3
	ePDF:	979-8-216-27578-7
	eBook:	979-8-216-27577-0

Typeset by Integra Software Services Pvt. Ltd.
Printed and bound in the United States of America

For product safety related questions contact productsafety@bloomsbury.com.

To find out more about our authors and books visit www.bloomsbury.com
and sign up for our newsletters.

Thanks, Wally.
Thanks for everything.

But Jesus called them to himself and said,
You know that the rulers of the Gentiles domineer over them, and those in high position exercise authority over them. ***It is not this way among you,*** but whoever wants to become prominent among you shall be your servant, and whoever desires to be first among you shall be your slave; just as the Son of Man did not come to be served, but to serve, and to give his life as a ransom for many.

Matthew 20:25–28, NASB (emphasis added)

Contents

Foreword xi
Preface: Wake Up, Olive xiv

Introduction: An Appeal to Heaven 1

Part 1 The New Apostolic Reformation 17

1 Manifest Sons of God 19

2 The Latter Rain 31

3 Joel's Army 45

4 The Seven Mountain Mandate 59

Part 2 Building a Kingdom 71

5 The Columbine Martyrs 73

6 Demons on the Map 85

7 The Seven Mountain Mandate in Africa 99

Part 3 America's New Culture Wars 111

8 Lights, Camera, Dominion! 113

9 Paleo-Confederates 125

10 From Homeschool to the Secular Academy 137

Part 4 Post-Democratic America 149

11 Tea Party Dominionists 151

12 The Trump Prophecies 163

13 The Battle over Public Schools 173

14 Let Us Worship 185

15 January 6 195

16 The Election of Mike Johnson 207

17 Project 2025 217

Conclusion 227

Notes 232
Sources 245
Index 259
About the Author 265

Foreword

Christian nationalism is a serious threat to our democracy, and, at its center, is the concept of dominionism.

Rooted in a reading of the book of *Genesis* in which God tells Adam and Eve to exercise dominion over the earth, dominionism is understood by some Christians to be the purpose for which God created humans. For these Christians, what they call "the dominion mandate" means it is their job to build the Kingdom of God on Earth.

Until recently, work on dominionism and the various components of the movement we call Christian nationalism was scarce due to a dismissive attitude in the media and the academy; everyone thought they were "too fringe" to warrant serious attention. Those attempting to write about it were brushed off as alarmists.

Now that dominionists have captured seats of power, there has been something of an explosion of interest. To date, a few have drilled deep on individual segments of Christian nationalism, often with a focus on the concept of dominion, but none have integrated the various dimensions and factions of Christian nationalism into a coherent narrative. None have traced its origins and explained how such divergent groups have made common cause despite their significant differences.

This book does that, and beautifully so.

In the middle of the twentieth century, dominionism was the driving force of a movement called Christian Reconstructionism. Reconstructionists sought to make all of life and culture conform to "Biblical Law." R.J. Rushdoony, the architect of that vision for a biblical society, drew on pre-Civil War Southern Presbyterianism and, in many ways, replicated that patriarchal, agrarian culture and authority structure, and early Christian Reconstructionism appealed to many in Neo-Confederate circles. The twenty-first-century expression of this form of evangelicalism can be found in Moscow, Idaho, where the network of institutions that Doug Wilson has built has more explicit ties to the Neo-Confederate world. This is an important part of the history Ladner traces, with webs of connections to the far right and more mainstream American evangelicalism.

Through the twentieth century the charismatic/Pentecostal movement exploded in popularity, in no small measure due to their faith-healing practices. Here also, Ladner shows the fluid interactions among loosely associated leaders, documenting ties, sometimes explicit and sometimes more hidden, to the far right; specifically, the Ku Klux Klan and British Israelism.

By the end of the century, while Doug Wilson was building his empire in Idaho, the charismatics/Pentecostals had developed their own variation of dominionism that was both similar and different from what had come before. What became the New Apostolic Reformation's dominionism called it the Seven Mountains Mandate.

Observers often missed the alignment between the two versions of dominionism because Christian Reconstructionists and those part of the New Apostolic Reformation hold contradictory views on a number of other issues, especially their theologies about the end of times.

The point that is illustrative here is that, in the long run, the fantastical visions about the time between now and the establishment of the Kingdom of God matter less than a framework that helps people organize the day-to-day aspects of their lives. Dominionism "works."

Ladner understands that the world isn't neatly compartmentalized into a typology of distinct belief systems with clear lines between different versions of Christianity. Yet the way we think about religion leads us to think it is. The story told in *American Dominion* contributes to the way we understand dominionism and the rise of Christian nationalism and defies this oversimplification.

There is a third source of influence that shapes today's Christian nationalism: a form of Catholicism called Integralism. Integralist Catholics might not talk about "dominionism"; they don't use the label. But like the other groups discussed above, they would replace a democratic system that relies on a commitment to equality with a hierarchical system that unites church and state with a God-appointed leader at the head.

Early in the book, Ladner notes that Reconstructionists and others are not concerned about the preservation of democracy. Indeed, Reconstructionists are deeply critical of "social equality" and think other forms of government are more biblical. The NAR looks for leaders to be "anointed by God," rather than democratically elected. And Integralist Catholics echo the "divine right of Kings," holding that some people are equipped, destined in some way, to lead while others are to follow.

All three of these intertwined movements reject the Declaration of Independence's claims that "all men are created equal" and that legitimate government rests on the "consent of the governed." All three flirt with the idea that we should have a king.

American Dominion is groundbreaking in that it offers a more integrated understanding of the diverse factions of Christianity that make up Christian nationalism. Seeing specific constituencies of Christian nationalism in relationship to each other, and in the context of their historical development, is crucially important to better understand this phenomenon now and in the future.

Julie Ingersoll, Professor of Religious
Studies at the University of North Florida

Preface: Wake Up, Olive

Olive, come out of that grave!

Andrew Heilegenthal held the microphone and sang, surrounded by his wife, Kalley, and their closest friends, with whom they sang every week at Bethel Church in Redding, California. In front of them, thousands of worshipers sang in unison, hearts and voices aimed toward heaven, attempting to bring its power down to earth. Behind Andrew and Kalley, Christmas trees, adorned simply with golden-white lights, surrounded the stage. No gifts lay beneath these trees, but surely boxes and boxes of lovingly wrapped presents waited at home for two-year-old Olive Heilegenthal, Andrew and Kalley's daughter.

Come out of that grave, in Jesus's name!

On December 14, 2019, Olive had stopped breathing and was pronounced dead. A few hours later, her mother posted on Instagram a picture of a vivacious toddler running through a pile of leaves, a cardigan hanging off her shoulders. The photo's caption read, "We are asking for bold, unified prayers from the global church to stand with us in belief that [Jesus] will raise this little girl back to life. Her time here is not done, and it is our time to believe boldly, and with confidence wield what King Jesus paid for. It's time for her to come to life." That night, members of the Bethel congregation came together at the church to declare in faith what they believed—knew—to be true: that God had given them the power to raise the dead. Unified as the body of Christ, with their prayers rising to heaven like incense, they could decree life into Olive's body so that the toddler would begin to breathe again.

Olive, come out of that grave!
Come out of that grave, in Jesus's name!

Kalley pounded the floor next to her husband, whose right hand was lifted toward heaven as his left hand held the microphone. He swayed, gently at first, then rocked back and forth, declaring the power of Jesus over his child and telling her to arise. Soon, everyone on stage was jumping, dancing, lifting high the name of Jesus, and claiming what they were so certain belonged to them: life for Olive. Resurrected life that could only come through the victory over death that Jesus Christ had bought with his own blood. With that victory, he had given dominion over all things, even death itself, to those who would follow him.

So Andrew, Kalley, the Bethel congregation, and like-minded Christians all over the world prayed boldly, with declarations of their authority over death, claiming the power of heaven into a two-year-old's lifeless body that lay in the county morgue. Through their faith-filled declarations and unified worship, they were wielding the dominion that Christ had given them to bring Olive back to life. After all, the gospels record him telling a child who had died, "Little girl, I say to you, arise!" (Mark 5:41, NKJV) Should not his followers be able to do the same?

Bethel Church sits at the top of a hill overlooking the mid-sized city of Redding, California. The building itself bears no resemblance to the stone cathedrals of Europe, the steepled chapels of New England, or the multi-million-dollar megachurches of Houston, Dallas, Chicago, and Orlando. Without the words "Bethel Church" branded onto the plain brown building, it might be mistaken for a warehouse, office complex, or conference center. On all sides, Northern California's Shasta Mountains rise thousands of feet into the sky, providing a stunning backdrop to an otherwise simple building that, every year, draws in tens of thousands of people from across the United States and countries around the world. The proverbial city—church—on a hill, shining in such a way that all are drawn to it.

The senior pastor, Bill Johnson, has a similarly unremarkable appearance, yet has spent decades transforming Bethel from a mid-sized church in a mid-sized city into the epicenter of a global movement that declares the Christian's dominion over all things. He has tanned and weathered skin, graying hair, soft eyes, glasses, a pleasant smile. Though Johnson never attended college and has no theological training, he has written prolifically on what he calls the "normal Christian life"—the ability of everyday Christians to speak in tongues, heal the sick, cast out demons, even raise the dead. "If [Jesus] did [miracles] as a man," Johnson wrote in his manifesto *When Heaven Invades Earth*, "I am responsible to pursue His lifestyle."[1] Because Christ has given dominion to his followers, they can—and should—manifest power over the forces of darkness, everything from demonic possession to poverty to sickness and even death, in their daily lives. And like the church that he pastors, Johnson is remarkably influential all over the world. Though largely unknown outside of charismatic circles, he is one of the best-selling authors in America.

This book is not about faith-healing; it is about the intersection of religion and politics in an evangelical movement called dominionism. But before we get into that story, we need to understand the appeal of the dominionist movement. People do not usually come to Bethel Church for politics. They come to this church, and so many others like it, to be part of a powerful work of God, one that replaces the sometimes-vague, by-and-by promises of traditional religious movements with promises of real healing, real prosperity, and real power—all delivered through a life-changing encounter with the divine. The community is infused with love, hope, and some of the most popular worship songs written in the era of Christian contemporary music.

Bethel Church is an epicenter of one of the fastest-growing religious movements in the world: the Pentecostal-charismatic movement. Begun in the early twentieth century but with deliberate efforts to recall the first-century roots of Christianity, this movement promises its followers a kind of direct access to God through speaking in tongues and other "signs and wonders." And it has often promised a kind of power flowing from that encounter that goes beyond ecstatic expression. Faith healers, for example, have found a home in the Pentecostal-charismatic movement, with promises of healing that can circumvent costly and complicated medical interventions. The so-called prosperity gospel took root in the movement, as well, promising followers divine intervention over their finances.

More recently, those promises of divine intervention have been brought into American politics. Those promises appear under different labels, such as "dominionism" and "New Apostolic Reformation," but at their heart they are about supernatural engagement with the political system to bring about an idealized future in which believers are not at the periphery of political power, but at its very center. Donald Trump has surrounded himself with evangelical leaders who claim these promises. He gave them access to political power, and they in turn helped deliver him the White House. When Paula White said, "As his pastor I put a hedge of protection around him,"[2] she may have sounded bizarre to many Americans, but millions heard in her words something familiar. They might have prayed those words to protect a vulnerable child, or to try to ward off sickness or financial ruin. So it made perfect sense to bring such claims of divine power into other areas of life—including politics. Christians, of course, have always been active in politics, and there should be nothing scary about believers bringing their beliefs and values into the voting booth with them. If this book were simply about that, the story would not be terribly important or interesting.

But what has emerged with the rise of dominionism is more troubling, as became clear on January 6. Prophetic claims about Donald Trump's "anointing"—that God had divinely chosen him to lead America—ran head-on into clear evidence that he had lost the 2020 election, producing a kind of religious disconnect with historic norms around democracy. As a result, thousands of people stormed the capital armed not only with their own understanding of patriotism but with a sense that they had been called by God to take extreme measures to undermine those norms. And leaders have used everyday fears, alongside convictions about God, to keep dominionists standing by, ready to do battle, using increasingly apocalyptic language to stir deep passions and convince more and more people that something very undemocratic needs to happen.

As such, this book tells the story of how ideas and beliefs that spent decades on the fringes of American public life have, in recent years, moved into the mainstream. The once-settled terms of our engagement with American democracy are, in fact, up for negotiation and are being renegotiated. In other words, this book is about the long process of radicalization, the movement of fringe ideas toward the mainstream, and the fundamental restructuring of our social contracts with both a faith that calls on believers to love the unlovable and a democratic system that promises voting rights and equal protection under the law. This process of radicalization did not begin with Trump, nor will it end with him, as the ideas and beliefs that fuel it have deep histories that are interwoven into some of the most critical moments of American history. But something happened when dominionist leaders surrounded Donald Trump in his rise to the Oval Office and assured him that he had been put in this place by God. Fringe belief systems suddenly became not only palatable but articles of faith for the millions of evangelical believers who would come to endorse the legitimacy of political violence.

◆

If all of that sounds like an effort to install a theocratic government, that is exactly what the leaders of this movement have aimed to do. But we oversimplify the story if we then make dominion-minded evangelicals out to be villains plotting in dark webs of conspiracy the ruin of American democracy, to be replaced with a theocratic government. The picture is more complicated. This new understanding of God's relationship to the political order does not need a political structure, and it does not live in a particular party. It is used by politically conservative organizations to marshal power, but it does not live in those organizations, either. It lives in churches—places where believers seek powerful encounters with transcendence and desire to live their lives in accordance with it. These churches are joyful places, often with bookstores and coffee shops and ministries of support, full of real community, led by charismatic (in more than one sense) leaders and often very talented musicians, leading services full of promise and hope. They are places where that hope even tries sometimes to stand up to death itself, especially the senseless death of a small child.

In the story told over this book, you will meet a lot of bad actors—power-hungry charlatans and hucksters, people who accumulate power and money far beyond their needs and gaslight thousands of people to do so. At the core of their movements are the words they use and the organizations they create, leading to the power they have to enact all sorts of harm.

But you will also meet a lot of well-meaning people who truly desire to live according to divine wisdom and be in community with those in need, in a place where their own real needs are also met. They are afraid, in a world that provides plenty of reasons to be afraid, and sometimes their fear mixes with, and is fed by, a joyful religious fervor. This is their very human story, too, messy and complicated, as life always is. After all, Americans from all backgrounds have become more comfortable with demonizing those who do not share the same priorities or values, and nothing erodes democracy faster than the sense that those we disagree with—left, right, or center—are simply beyond the pale.

◆

"Day 3 is a really good day for resurrection," Kalley Heilegenthal posted on Instagram after the first night of worship did not bring Olive back. "We are overwhelmed with gratitude by your outpouring of love for us and faith for Olive. Jesus is Faithful and True and He's riding in with the victory He bought for Olive." In agreement with the child's prophetic destiny, Kalley continued, "Olive Alayne means 'victorious awakening'. We call on the mighty all-sufficient name of Jesus and we call you back by name, sweet girl. You will live."

Nothing could be more tragic, or more heartfelt, than a mother whose lifeless toddler has not yet been buried to refuse to acknowledge her death. And the people who surrounded her in prayer and worship wanted Olive to be raised from the dead, too, not for political reasons but for very human ones: parents should not have to place a two-year-old in a coffin and then try to find a way to live the rest of their lives with an enormous hole where a child should have been. They should not have to wake up every day awaiting their own deaths so they can be reunited with their daughter in heaven.

The worship services to resurrect Olive continued not for one evening, or two, or three, but for five.

"Olive hasn't been raised," came a church announcement on December 20, nearly a full week after her sudden death. "The breakthrough we sought hasn't come." The family decided to stop praying for her resurrection and would proceed with plans to celebrate a beautiful life that ended far too soon, a life that her parents will carry until the end of theirs. "The joy of our faith is that, though we haven't seen the miracle of Olive being raised, she is alive in the presence of God."[3]

The story of dominionism has consistently had far-reaching political overtones, but what continues to draw evangelicals into the movement is the same thing that led the people of Bethel Church to spend nearly a week praying for the resurrection of a very young child. Not an effort to take over the government, but the desire to live in the presence of God and experience the wholeness of heart and even power over death that their leaders promise.

Introduction:
An Appeal to Heaven

"By closing these bedroom doors, they have opened Pandora's box,"[1] a young lawyer for the Alliance Defense Fund (ADF, now Alliance Defending Freedom) named Mike Johnson wrote in 2003. The US Supreme Court had recently ruled in the landmark case *Lawrence v. Texas* that sodomy laws, which prohibit intimate contact between consenting adults of the same sex, violate the Constitution's implied right to privacy. Johnson was then building a legal career defending what he and his ADF colleagues called "religious liberty," and this defense of liberty meant the prosecution of same-sex couples under criminal law. In the 2016 case, *Ark Encounter LLC v. Parkinson*, Johnson successfully argued that the Ark Encounter, a Kentucky-based attraction which promotes the view that God created the earth approximately 6000 years ago, should receive state tax credits, even though employees had to agree to a religious creed that includes young-earth creationism. Johnson has, for decades, promoted the idea that privileging his version of Christianity is essential to American freedom.

Before becoming Speaker of the House—and third in line to the presidency of the United States—Louisiana Representative Mike Johnson and his wife, Kelly, traveled the country to teach seminars on what the Bible says about government. America was founded as a Christian nation but has lost its moorings, due to the decline in church membership and rise in liberal politics. The Johnsons have been on a decades-long mission to reclaim Christian America with their hard-right conservatism, regularly casting "the liberals" as enemies of God while insisting that the political fight that conservatives are waging is really about implementing biblical truths in America's government.

◆

In August 2012, the up-and-coming politician Ted Cruz stood on the stage at New Beginnings Church in the Fort Worth community of Bedford. The 1954 Johnson Amendment has kept churches from endorsing political candidates, on danger of losing their tax-exempt status; however, Cruz's father, Rafael Cruz, has insisted that the Johnson Amendment is a violation of the Constitution's Establishment Clause and advocated for the law's complete repeal. So Ted stood on the stage to receive an unofficial endorsement from Pastor Larry Huch, who claimed over the soon-to-be senator that the year 2012

> will begin what we call the End-Time transfer of wealth. And when these Gentiles begin to receive this blessing, they will never go back financially through the valley again. They will grow and grow and grow. It's said this way: that God is looking at the church and everyone in it and deciding in the next three and a half years who will be his bankers. And the ones that say, "Here I am, Lord; you can trust me," we will become so blessed that we will usher in the coming of the Messiah.

Huch prophesied that Ted Cruz was to become a leader in the End-Times transfer of wealth, a movement that modern charismatic prophets have foretold. They teach that God will soon cause material and financial resources to flow away from the ungodly and toward the righteous so that they will be able to build his kingdom here on earth. Rafael followed Huch's bold declaration over his son by claiming that Ted was destined to be a king, who would serve God not from the pulpit but rather from within the halls of government. Soon after, Texans elected him as their junior senator to the US Congress.

Long before Ted Cruz and Mike Johnson were elected to Congress, Sarah Palin was a local politician in Alaska's growing town of Wasilla. She had served as a member of the City Council from 1992 until 1996 before being elected mayor, an office she held from 1996 until 2002. An active member of the Wasilla Assemblies of God, Palin had been part of a local prayer network from the time she first began her forays into city politics. Plenty of American politicians at all levels have espoused prayer, beginning with the seventeenth-century Puritans, but there was something different about what Palin and those in her network considered to be "prayer." Instead of humbly talking with God, they made declarations to call what rightfully belonged to them out of heaven and into their lives.

What's more, these declarations emphasized the demonic realm in ways that seemed to come straight from the Middle Ages. Palin and her prayer team were engaging in an angels-versus-demons spiritual warfare that was being enacted primarily in civil politics. When the Kenyan prophet and witch-hunter Thomas Muthee came to visit Wasilla Assemblies of God in 2005, he made declarations over Palin against the forces of witchcraft as she was beginning her campaign to become governor of Alaska.

Palin ignored the gender barriers of evangelicalism's more conservative wings when she became John McCain's running mate and the first woman on a major-party presidential ticket in 2008. She appealed easily to evangelical voters, who appreciated her commitment to economic conservatism, insistence on the dignity of human life, and unwillingness to be bought by "the establishment." But she represented even more to her nationwide network of angels-versus-demons prayer warriors, who were much more conservative than most evangelicals at the time. To these dominionists, Palin was more than a conservative politician; she was an apostle called by God to wage spiritual warfare in the US government.

In 2021, Palin ran for—and nearly won—Alaska's seat in the US House of Representatives. By that point, the spiritual-warfare movement that she had helped bring out of some fringe churches and into the halls of power had moved on without her.

◆

Before Jim Bob Duggar became the lead in TLC's most-watched show, *17 Kids and Counting* (which became *18 Kids and Counting*, and then *19 Kids and Counting*, followed by the spin-off *Counting On*), he was an elected member of the Arkansas State House of Representatives from 1999 until 2003. There, he promoted legislation that was consistent with the teachings of the Institute of Basic Life Principles (IBLP), a fundamentalist group that enforces among its members patriarchal families, a complete ban on birth control, female submission, debt-free living (affiliated families cannot even take out a mortgage or car loan), and homeschooling. Duggar has made other forays into elected office, including a 2002 run for the US Senate and 2006 and 2021 runs for the Arkansas State Senate. Though he lost these races, the cultural impact of his family's reality television show has far surpassed any legislation that he could have introduced.

Bill Gothard, the founder of the IBLP, was inspired by the work of Rousas John Rushdoony, whose teachings present an approach to Christian life and society known as Reconstructionism. Reconstructionism takes an uncompromising position on the belief that only Christians are qualified to hold any position of public leadership; further, government efforts at social engineering—most notoriously, via public schools—are attempts to play God and should be abolished in favor of a feudal society centered on patriarchal families and local churches. Reconstructionism is the hardest form of dominionism, a theological teaching and social movement espoused by some of the most conservative evangelicals who have taken an increasingly active role in American politics.

◆

"As his pastor I put a hedge of protection around him," Paula White said in a faith-filled declaration that was directed toward President Donald Trump. "I secure his purpose. I secure his destiny. I secure his life, God, and I thank you that he will walk in a holy boldness and a wisdom, God, and that you will go before him. You will be his rear guard, and you will go in front of him this day and every day, God."[2] A decade before, she had prayed with the future president at Trump Tower in Manhattan about whether he should run for the highest office in the land, but she advised him that the timing was not yet right. When he announced his candidacy in 2015, she was in full agreement that he should run. Trump has never attended church regularly, and White's own church has faced congressional scrutiny for misappropriating tax-exempt funds to pay for her waterfront mansion and private jet. But in the world of faith-filled declarations and spiritual warfare in civil government, the understanding of the relationship between church and state takes on different contours, such that a prosperity-preaching televangelist with a history of mishandling donated funds can be an unofficial advisor to the president of the United States.

In January 2020, White made the declaration,

> In the name of Jesus, we come against the marine kingdom, we come against the animal kingdom, the woman who rides upon the waters. We break the power, in the name of Jesus, and we declare that any strange winds, any strange winds that have been sent to hurt the church, sent against this nation, sent against our president, sent against myself, sent against others—we break it by the superior blood of Jesus right now.[3]

She went on to say, "We command all satanic pregnancies to miscarry right now. We declare that anything that's been conceived in satanic wombs, that it will miscarry. It will not be able to carry forth any plan of destruction, any plan of harm."[4]

Almost exactly one year later, on January 6, 2021, she was declaring over President Trump that she secured his purpose and his destiny, that he would "walk in a holy boldness and a wisdom," just minutes before he began the speech that incited the Capitol Riot.

◆

The End-Times transfer of wealth; casting "the liberals" as enemies of God's perfect order; faith-filled declarations to cast out demons and cancel curses of witchcraft; prosperity-style preaching just before an attempt to overthrow the US government; efforts to eradicate public schools in favor of homeschooling. None of these ideas represents a mainstream Christian teaching or even one with historical precedent. They all emerge from dominionism, which has many different branches but one common goal: to transform the American government, as well as that of all nations of the world, into the kingdom of

God on earth. The core belief bringing these ideas together is that God has called Christians to have dominion over all things.

Dominionism is not one single ideology, but rather a collection of varying, sometimes competing belief systems. Rushdoony founded Reconstructionism, while Palin adhered to the New Apostolic Reformation, a movement that White grafted herself into a few years before Donald Trump's election in 2016. Other forms of dominionism include Neo-Confederacy and the heavily racialized teachings of Identity theology. Leaders from these belief systems have come alongside each other to promote their shared goals, transforming dominionism from a disparate patchwork of extremists into a movement with the numbers and political capital to make the leap from the fringe and into the mainstream. Since the year 2000, waves of dominionism have been crashing against the shore of American public life, making ever-deeper impressions on political discourse, as radical concepts of what government is have reshaped churches while eroding their porous boundary with the state.

On January 6, 2021, crowds of charismatic Christians began arriving at the National Mall and Capitol Ellipse before the sun came up. They had come not for a riot but rather for a worship service and were armed with what they saw as their greatest weapons: prayer and praise, which combined—they believed—had the power to sway an election that had already been called for Joe Biden. Some carried shofars, rams' horns made into trumpet-like instruments that have been a feature of Jewish worship for millennia. These worshipping soon-to-be rioters marched, blowing their shofars at what they viewed as critical moments—when a particularly moving prayer was prayed, in the middle of a worship song that bore witness to the day's significance, after making a ritual march around the Capitol. Some of the shofars blown that day were decorated with the American flag.

One person carried a poster depicting Christ wearing a red MAGA hat, while others walked around with signs proclaiming, "Jesus Saves!" Dozens waved white flags that depicted an outline of a pine tree and the words "An Appeal to Heaven." A few draped themselves with the flag while singing worship songs, aiming their worship and prayers at the space between heaven and the US Capitol. Others stood defiantly against the biting January wind, holding the flag like revolutionary stalwarts. And when the attack on the Capitol began, at least one person brought an Appeal to Heaven flag inside the Rotunda, two corners tied together around his neck and the rest of the banner billowing behind him, like a cape. These ecstatic votaries, who believed that their acts of worship necessitated a certain kind of political action, were taking their cues from a firebrand preacher named Dutch Sheets.

"Lord, we just come into agreement with those on the ground there in Washington," Sheets declared on January 6. Not physically present at the Capitol Ellipse, he phoned in to a portion of the rally and prayed, his staticky voice coming through a loudspeaker as the crowd's low-boil rage was beginning to turn aggressive. "Lord, we pray for all of our friends there … Thank you, Lord, for covering them, protecting them … This violence, and the spirit of violence, and the spirit of wrath does not produce righteousness. We take authority over it now. Be there over the Capitol crowds in Jesus' name. Amen."[5]

◆

The 2021 Capitol Riot was far from Sheets's first foray into the world of electoral politics. When the contested 2000 presidential race hung in the balance, with neither George W. Bush nor Al Gore being officially declared the winner for over a month, Sheets went to Washington to declare in the physical realm what he knew to be true in the spiritual: God had given victory to Bush. "Agreeing with the prayers of millions of people," Sheets began, "we simply made the declaration that turned out to be the final release." To show the real-world impact that his declaration made, he went on, "A few days later, the Supreme Court made its decisive ruling and Vice President Gore conceded."[6]

Inspired by what he believed was his role in deciding the election, in 2002, Sheets and a ministry colleague named Chuck Pierce began a fifty-state tour to call America back to God. "We realized we were to take the spiritual keys we had been given and 'ride' across this nation with the Lord," Sheets wrote in a 2024 book that he coauthored with Pierce, "striking the ground and trumpeting the message of revival."[7] Ride they did, crisscrossing the country and networking with both religious and political leaders who shared the same vision. Sheets slowly but surely developed a large following as he rode "across the nation with the Lord," igniting fires of revival that burned right through the people who listened to his messages.

About a decade after the fifty-state tour, Sheets was introduced to the flag that would become emblematic of the Capitol Riot and the rise of a radical form of Christian nationalism. In his telling, he was presiding over the 2013 spring commencement ceremony for a training center where he was serving as executive director, Christ for the Nations Institute in Dallas, Texas. A former Green Beret whom Sheets called his spiritual son unfurled an Appeal to Heaven flag during the ceremony and presented it to him. "I sensed its weighty significance," Sheets said of this moment. "Little did I know, however, this flag would also represent God's next great assignment for my life, searing upon my heart the same cry He birthed within the Revolutionaries at the founding of our great nation."[8] His national profile soared in the years after Trump's 2016 election, with his national tours turning into pro-Trump rallies for tens of thousands of charismatic evangelicals. There he would ceremonially unfurl the Appeal to Heaven flag and implore his followers to call the nation to revival.

The Appeal to Heaven flag has a deep history that predates American independence, having been commissioned by General George Washington in 1775. The simple outline of a pine tree alludes to the little-known 1772 Pine Tree Riot, a local rebellion in New Hampshire against a British policy that prevented colonists from harvesting mature pine trees; instead, they were reserved for use by the king, and colonists chafed at this restriction on what they saw as their own resources. The phrase that Washington used on the flag, "An Appeal to Heaven," came from *The Second Treatise of Government* by the political philosopher John Locke (1632–1704). Far from a Christian nationalist, Locke defended secularism, and his writings helped lay the foundation for America's liberal tradition. In an early form of separation of church and state, he promoted the then-revolutionary belief that the church should not have any control over people or governmental processes. This concept became enshrined in the US Constitution.

Sheets, on the other hand, has claimed that God gave him the assignment of tearing down the wall that separates the church from the state. "Today, the future of this great Christian nation, formed under this banner [the Appeal to Heaven flag], symbolizing eternal covenant, liberty and the power of prayer, is in jeopardy," he wrote for *Charisma* magazine, a flagship of the Independent Charismatic movement, the year before Donald Trump's 2016 election. "Yet my conviction is strong: there is still hope for America! We can emulate the strategy of our Founding Fathers and make 'An Appeal to Heaven!' If we do, we, too, will experience God's supernatural intervention."[9]

◆

Throughout American history, evangelicals have had varying relationships with authority. On one hand, many of America's democratic norms were born in evangelical churches. Roger Williams (1603–83) was a Puritan leader who took significant strides in the long and difficult process of severing the church's formal ties to the state. He believed that if church and civil society were not separated as much as possible, each would taint the other so that both would be corrupted. In the first half of the nineteenth century, during a time known as the Second Great Awakening, the revivalist Charles Finney (1792–1875) broke down church barriers that had separated men from women and African Americans from whites. Processes such as this one paved the way for American citizenship and democratic participation to be opened to people who were not white males. More than a century later, Martin Luther King, Jr. (1929–68) followed evangelicalism's tradition of advocating for the poor against the powers that be by using faith-based language to call out the legal oppression inflicted on people of color. These evangelicals challenged authority and power structures while developing new norms around democratic participation, beginning inside the church and spreading to civil society.

Other evangelical leaders, however, have used their influence to sway their congregants, as well as civil leaders and elected politicians, in directions that look much more autocratic. The infamous Salem witch trials of 1692 showed how horribly awry both church and civil society can go when the two spheres become too connected to each other. Puritans set important precedents in establishing the separation of church and state, but this tragic episode that saw the execution of twenty innocent people was a setback that showed the importance of their experiment. Though on at least one occasion Billy Graham (1918–2018) removed the stanchions separating the "white" section from the "colored" one at a revival crusade he held, he taught a troubling relationship between Christianity and America that helped pave the way for Jerry Falwell's movement. A central figure in organizing evangelicals into the conservative voting bloc known as the Religious Right, Falwell (1933–2007) had a direct line to President Ronald Reagan and influenced his policies around nuclear buildup and the dismantling of social welfare programs.

Then there was R. J. Rushdoony (1916–2001), the dominionist who developed the thought behind Reconstructionism. He advocated replacing the Constitution with the Bible and most of the government—federal, state, and local—with churches. At the center of this hypothetical power structure is the white landowning male, who exercises unlimited authority over his wife and children while functionally serving as a kind of local warlord. Preceding by half a century Mike Johnson's effort to revive sodomy laws, Rushdoony advocated the stoning of queer individuals, as well as of children who dishonored their parents. Reconstructionism is far from normative within evangelicalism. Yet Rushdoony was mentored by Cornelius Van Til (1895–1987), the same theologian who taught the widely read evangelical philosopher Francis Schaeffer (1912–84), and Rushdoony also worked alongside Falwell in organizing evangelical opposition to public schools.

Contrary to Roger Williams's belief that the church should be separate from civil government so that the church itself would not be corrupted, Sheets has taught—in a manner consistent with previous generations of Christian nationalists, including Falwell—that the government cannot control the church, but the church has every right to sway and influence the government. Yet Sheets has run farther than Falwell ever could have in his understanding of how far the church can—legally and, as seen on January 6, illegally—go to influence the government. Sheets and his fellow travelers claim a special connection with God that gives them insight into what God is doing in heaven and wants to do on earth, and they believe they have a divine mandate to pull the levers of power. When he wrote in 2024, "We declare the release of government angels to assist the Ekklesia [the 'true church'] to reign with Christ,"[10] he was making a literal statement about the church and political authority. Not entirely unlike Rushdoony, Sheets believes that the church itself is to rule.

◆

Dominionism—the belief that God has given Christians dominion over all things—includes an array of fellow travelers who have walked similar paths, sometimes disagreeing with each other, sometimes joining forces in spite of disagreements so as to create a sustainable movement. These travelers are fierce Christian nationalists who have crafted narratives of American history that, in one way or other, blend it into biblical history. With Sheets, this biblical narrative for America begins with a new kind of doyen, one who can easily blend faith and politics in ways that previous generations of evangelicals could not: the apostle.

The apostle brings what he or she claims are messages directly from God, along with all the power and resources of heaven that are needed to bring those messages to fruition. Those messages may say that God has chosen Trump to be president or that he wants a church to resurrect a two-year-old who recently died. Apostles may even claim that there are additional passages of the Bible that God has been waiting until now to reveal or that the true meaning of biblical texts has been hidden for millennia, as did the apostle Brian Simmons when he wrote *The Passion Translation* of the Bible. When Sheets declared to the crowd on January 6, "We take authority over it now," and when he traveled to Washington during a contested election to declare victory for Bush, he was invoking his apostolic role as someone who can call down from heaven what he claims God desires to do on the earth.

Apostles are more than influential authors, speakers, and—in the case of Simmons—Bible translators who have never studied the original biblical languages. In fact, many apostles never attended college or seminary, or if they did, they either did not graduate or earned an unaccredited degree. Sheets studied at the same school he later directed, Christ for the Nations Institute, an unaccredited ministry school.

Yet the apostle's credentials do not come from education but rather—as apostles claim—directly from God. No governing body, no denomination, no church body, and no school can determine whether God has called someone to be an apostle. And when God makes that call on someone, no institution on this earth can overrule it. Churches and individuals can only submit to the apostle, recognizing him (usually him but sometimes her) as a funnel to call down God's plan and blessings from heaven for them. And that is exactly what an apostle is: someone who oversees entire networks of churches while professing to serve as a mediator between God and those under his or her authority. Sometimes those networks consist of tens of thousands of churches—more than belong to most denominations—all submitting to one individual who claims to be the mouthpiece of God.

Sheets leads an apostolic network, which oversees numerous churches around the world, called Network Ekklesia International. *Ekklesia* is the Greek word used for "church" in the New Testament, and the term refers broadly to any kind of assembly, including the Jewish synagogues of the New Testament world. To Sheets, however, an *ekklesia* is a ruling body, not necessarily a democratic assembly but rather a colonizing force for an empire. And this empire that the *ekklesia*, the church, represents is the dominion of King Jesus because God has called Christians to rule. "This invitation to cross the threshold back into the sphere of governmental intercession has not only been extended to me, but to the entire Body of Christ,"[11] he wrote in 2015. God has given this body of Christ, the *ekklesia*, the keys to the government; Sheets went on to claim, "We must realize that we are God's governing force on the earth, which have been given keys of authority from Him to legislate from the spiritual realm."[12] Again, the church is not legislating here as a democratic assembly but rather as a body submitted to the authority of one person, an apostle (or, for some churches, multiple apostles and apostolic networks) who asserts to extend the dominion of King Jesus.

"I realize that the kind of government I am describing, in which there is a clear order of priority in the various roles, is difficult to understand and embrace in American culture," wrote Danny Silk, a senior pastor at Bethel Church in Redding, California. "Our American style of democratic government is designed to keep all its governing members in a system of checks and balances, where each branch of government must be accountable to another branch so that no one legislator, judge, or president can gain control of the whole government."¹³ Silk was referring specifically to the democratic norms of *church* government, which have historically provided the basis for democratic participation to be expanded to American civil society. Yet the form of church government that he and his dominionist colleagues at Bethel Church promote is led by apostles, who do not rely on the majority consensus of the church's membership and instead make unilateral, top-down decisions. Americans are used to democracy; modern-day apostles, such as Sheets, are autocrats.

And when apostles with the reach of Sheets spread a message claiming that God has called on the *ekklesia* to control the government, the concept of autocratic apostles ruling churches more and more easily slips into comfort with an autocratic president attempting to overturn an election—especially when he has the clear support of those apostles.

This leadership structure of modern-day apostles leading networks of sometimes thousands of churches with what they insist is supernatural authority reflects Sheets's understanding of leadership in ancient Israel, as recorded in the Old Testament. Moses, Joshua, and Daniel were three men who had the supernatural giftedness—the *anointing*—that is associated with modern-day apostles: divine wisdom, supernatural revelation, and insight into what God is doing in heaven so that they can call it down to earth. "So Daniel was able to be used by God to restore a nation not just because he was wise, not just because he was a dreamer, but because he had an anointing, and an impartation, and a heart to walk in both wisdom and revelation."¹⁴ The nation that Daniel restored was Israel, and the nation that Sheets aims to restore is the United States.

Sheets claims that America has a special relationship with God that goes back to the commissioning of the Appeal to Heaven flag. "The evergreen tree stands for eternal covenant," he preached during the build-up to the 2016 election.¹⁵ "The concept of this covenant goes all the way back to Abraham," he continued, tying the biblical patriarch of the Jewish people to the founding of America. In other words, the promise made between God and the American nation is no different than the biblical promise he made with the ancient Jewish patriarch millennia ago; to Sheets, just as Israel was chosen by God, America has been chosen by God and has a place in the biblical story that continues unfolding today. And just as Israel was led by charismatic, apostolic leaders, so America is to be governed by apostles overseeing the *ekklesia*. "God ordained from the foundation of the world the founding and establishment of the United States of America. And he's not finished with her."[16]

And his message is being heard. Not only were dozens, possibly hundreds, of Appeal to Heaven flags present at the Capitol Riot, but in 2023, House Speaker Mike Johnson flew the Appeal to Heaven flag at his congressional office. And the following year, Supreme Court Justice Samuel Alito flew one at his beach house.

Within this dominionist, apostolic paradigm, modern-day America becomes almost conflated with the ancient Israel of the Old Testament. Comparisons between America and Israel are nothing new and can be traced back to the earliest Puritan settlers, who saw themselves as metaphorically crossing through the wilderness and into the new Promised Land of Israel, or the New World. Referencing ancient Israel to describe America has long been one means of describing American exceptionalism, the idea that America is uniquely great within the history of all the nations of the earth. America is *like* Israel because it has been chosen by God to receive divine blessings and, in return, to be a blessing to the rest of the world. America is *like* Israel because it has a greatness that it must live up to, and just like the ancient nation, regularly fails to do so.

But what happens when modern-day apostles begin using language that suggests not that America is *like* ancient Israel, but that America *is* Israel? That God established a covenant with America not at the time of the founding, but in the very first book of the Bible? When a flag drawn from secular ideals is repurposed into a Christian nationalist symbol by an apostle who claims it represents America's biblical origins? When shofars that were used in ancient worship practices are decorated with American flags and used in an attempt to overthrow the government?

Perhaps the most important question is,

Where did all of this come from?

A Note on Terms

This book describes numerous religious movements that defy easy categorization, and I consistently use two terms that are somewhat problematic in explaining these movements. The first is "evangelical" (alongside "evangelicalism"). The definition of what "evangelicalism" is was thought to be settled with the brilliant scholarship of David Bebbington and his famous quadrilateral: evangelicalism refers to a religious movement that is focused on the cross, the Bible, conversion, and social activism. This quadrilateral has helped scholars and journalists for decades arrive at a common understanding of what they mean when they say "evangelical" or "evangelicalism." As a result, research on evangelicalism has thrived.

What became apparent when 80 percent of white evangelicals cast their votes for Donald Trump in November 2016, and again in November 2020, and yet again in November 2024, is that much of what we thought we understood about evangelicalism in America is inadequate. A flurry of scholarship rushed to fill this void, while journalists wracked their brains for an explanation of why a thrice-married libertine who violently castigated women, people with disabilities, even former prisoners of war (notably John McCain) would have such an appeal among people who are focused on the Bible, the cross, conversion, and social activism.

Evangelicalism is far from a monolith. It is a collection of various movements, some of which are fundamentally incompatible with each other, all vying for a claim on the "correct" evangelicalism. Any term that can encompass Jim Wallis's Sojourners organization, Reconstructionists who wish to execute queer people, dispensationalists who see the Bible as full of prophecy for the End Times that we currently live in, and the faith-based impetus of Martin Luther King, Jr., is problematic at best. Yet we can speak of *evangelicalisms*, some of which have little to do with the politically dominant strain examined in this book.

But the term still works, for the same reason that the Bebbington quadrilateral has worked in describing evangelicalism: it gives us a common reference point to describe a movement that we agree does exist and plays a prominent role in American public life. Fraught as the "evangelicalism" label may be, we continue to use it, so I use it in this book.

The second term is "cult," a term that fell out of favor after the 1978 Jonestown massacre. I recognize that there is much scholarly discourse about the helpfulness of referring to a particular movement as a cult. While plenty of new religious movements self-identify as evangelical, none would claim to be a cult. As such, the label is always one that an outside observer applies to a group that he or she sees as fundamentally aberrant. The lines become even more blurred when our ideas of a cult focus on extreme authoritarianism, when similar authoritarianism can be found in the military, which we do not consider to be a cult. Is the term itself useless? Some would argue that it is, and there is scholarship to support that position.

I chose to use the term "cult" in describing some of the religious movements in this book because I believe that it is a helpful, though inexact, reference point. These are movements that began far outside of the evangelical mainstream yet had connections to aspects of evangelical theology, especially the Keswick movement that shaped Billy Graham. All such movements described in this book were either part of the progression toward Jonestown or derivatives from the same root that produced Jim Jones's movement. I believe that the connections to the archetype of the authoritarian, heterodox cult leader do make the term useful. The interconnectedness alone may render the "cult" label obsolete, but for the purposes of this book, it provides a starting point, if not an ending one. The term's imprecision can be seen in how moderated, diluted versions of what these cults promoted have long thrived in megachurches that have thousands of attendees and international reach. I do not refer to these massive global movements that come from the same tree as Jonestown as cults.

Perhaps our understanding of what evangelicalism is should be expanded to include the various heterodox, authoritarian movements that have proliferated to the extent that they now comprise the mainstream. That is a task for another day. For now, the urgency is to understand the dominionist movement, how it transformed evangelicalism and now threatens to end American democracy.

Part One

The New Apostolic Reformation

1
Manifest Sons of God

In the small town of Durham, Maine, in 1896, a preacher named Frank Sandford followed what he claimed was the prompting of God to build a Bible school that would become known as Shiloh. Sandford was a faith healer who insisted that not only had he commanded illnesses such as typhoid, tuberculosis, pneumonia, and cancer to leave the sick person's body, but he had also resurrected a 45-year-old woman, coincidentally named Olive, who had supposedly died of meningitis. Despite preaching sermons that seminary-trained pastors denounced as heretical, a string of miracles credited to him enabled Sandford to quickly amass a large cadre of followers.

"If the Divine Master only had a band of workers such as this, there would be no limit to what He might do with them," Sandford had read in the writings of Hannah Whitall Smith. "May God raise such an army speedily!"[1]

Having only three cents to his name, Sandford called on his followers—the "band of workers"—to work for free as they built a commune that, at its height, would house six hundred people. They handed over all of their earthly possessions; Sandford, in turn, taught them how to live fully under the guidance of the Holy Spirit. Or so he claimed. At Shiloh, starvation was rampant, and deadly disease outbreaks tore through the community despite Sandford's claims to work miraculous healings. Those who failed to adequately submit to his authority risked being expelled from the community, sometimes with no home or family to return to. By the time he was arrested in 1911, at least seven of his followers had died as a direct result of following his demands. Possibly dozens, including infants and young children, had met the same fate.

Not that Sandford has ever been a particularly significant figure within the scope of American religious history, or even evangelical history. By most measures, Sandford was merely a cult leader who demanded from his followers submission unto death. And cult leaders do not tend to take their place in a grand narrative of how religion in America has unfolded over decades or even centuries. Cult leaders are seen as aberrations, singular figures who rise and, before falling, amass a gathering of sometimes dozens, sometimes hundreds of followers who will die for a set of beliefs that are entirely at odds with mainstream religious norms.

Jim Jones, who ordered nearly 1000 followers to drink grape Flavor Aid laced with cyanide.

David Koresh, the leader of the Branch Davidians outside of Waco, Texas, who died, with dozens of his followers, in a fiery blaze following a nearly two-month standoff with federal authorities.

John Alexander Dowie, the mail-order faith healer who refused to allow his followers to seek medical treatment.

And Frank Sandford, whose followers fasted so intensely that deadly disease outbreaks became common occurrences at Shiloh.

Perhaps some cult leaders are mere aberrations whose stories can be told neatly, as if they are pimples on the grand narrative of American religious history rather than a critical (if not underestimated) part of the narrative itself: the cult is an isolated religious group that can be distinguished by members' unquestioning dedication to the leader. As with other hollowed-out groups whose existence depends upon one singular individual, one who often becomes increasingly erratic as power is consolidated, cults collapse when that leader is arrested, or dies, or forces his followers into mass suicide. These cults then exist simply as sidenotes in history books or as case studies for lawyers and judges seeking to understand how far really is too far for a religious leader to go before First Amendment protections no longer apply.

But never as part of a bigger story that began long before and outlasted the cult. And never as a meta-movement that saw its core doctrines become part of mainstream religious discourse and even America's electoral politics.

Except with Frank Sandford and his Shiloh commune in rural Maine, that is exactly what happened.

◆

Sandford gave the different sites at Shiloh names that came directly from the Bible. Near the entrance was the Street Called Straight, alluding to the locale in Damascus where the Apostle Paul stayed after encountering the divine and becoming blinded. There was Hephzibah, a meadow-like expanse named for an Old Testament queen, and a hospital, Bethesda, for both physical and spiritual infirmities. A garden and children's area called Olivet, after the Mount of Olives where Jesus prayed the night before his crucifixion, stood in front of a cemetery where victims of Shiloh were buried. And in the main building stood David's Tower, the highest point in Shiloh, named for the greatest king of Old Testament Israel. And Shiloh itself referred to a prophesied ruler that would come from Israel's tribe of Judah:

> *The scepter will not depart from Judah,*
> *Nor the ruler's staff from between his feet,*
> *Until Shiloh comes,*
> *And to him shall be the obedience of the peoples.*
>
> Genesis 49:10, NASB

In using biblical names, Sandford was doing more than showing the symbolic purpose of the different sites at Shiloh. Rather, he believed that Shiloh itself was to be the New Jerusalem, in a very literal sense, that Christ—the "Shiloh" of Genesis 49:10—would return to rule and reign from this outpost in rural Maine. Consistent with his belief that he was at the center of God's plan for God's people that began in the Old Testament, Sandford attempted to recreate the worship of that period by observing Jewish feasts—Passover, Pentecost, and Tabernacles—and holding services on Saturday, the Jewish Sabbath, instead of on Sunday. And not unlike the followers of Dutch Sheets who gathered outside the US Capitol on January 6, 2021, Sandford and his followers regularly blew shofars as acts of worship.

Sandford was a British Israelist, part of a contingency that held to the pseudohistorical belief that white Europeans are, in a very literal sense, the Israel spoken of in the Old Testament. In 1840, a Scottish writer named John Wilson published a book called *Our Israelitish Origins* to answer a theological and historical conundrum: What had happened to the 10 Lost Tribes of ancient Israel? After being exiled to Assyria in approximately 732 BCE, the ten tribes that had been taken into foreign captivity disappeared from the biblical record and became lost to history.

In *Our Israelitish Origins,* Wilson used highly speculative evidence to show that the 10 Lost Tribes had emigrated out of Assyria, across the Caucasus Mountains, and into Western Europe, where they ultimately settled. As such, according to British Israelism, the white people of Europe, particularly the British, are actually the true Israel whose history is recorded in the Bible. What's more, all of the *prophecies* in the Bible that apply to Israel actually apply to modern white people. In other words, biblical history never ended; it is still occurring, and white people are at the center of it—including those gathered at Shiloh.

"Humanity does not know where they all are,"[2] Sandford preached in a sermon about the identity of Israel. But human knowledge mattered little, because "God knows where the twelve tribes are today." Sandford, who did not doubt his identity as a true, ethnic Israelite, went on to claim, "God made me know ... that I myself was that Jew." He was of the Israelite tribe of Judah, but more than that, he was a leader of Judah, one who took directions from God and had to be obeyed by his followers. Followed to the point of death, as some of the faithful gathered at Shiloh learned too late.

Yet Sandford was not Jewish in any ethnic, anthropologic, or religious sense; he believed himself to be Jewish as a British Israelist who claimed that, as a member of the white race, he was of true Israel. To be clear, British Israelism is an entirely pseudohistorical belief. There is no credible evidence that the 10 Lost Tribes of Israel migrated into Europe and settled in Britain.

Historical facts set aside, what was the role of British Israel, and particularly of *that Jew* whom Sandford declared himself to be? British Israel, and especially Sandford, was to rule. "The sceptre shall not depart from Judah," he quoted from the Genesis verse that references Shiloh, believing this to be a literal prophecy that would be fulfilled through white Europeans. Sandford, like many other British Israelists, believed that Britain's Queen Victoria was a direct descendant of the biblical King David, Israel's great monarch who, supposedly like Sandford himself, hailed from the tribe of Judah. In other words, the prophecy about the scepter not departing from Judah was being partially fulfilled through Queen Victoria ruling much of the globe as head of the British Empire. White people, as the true Israel, were destined to rule the world.

Sandford went on to quote from the Bible, "A lawgiver shall not depart from between his feet." He then explained this "lawgiver" refers to,

> One that is so close to God that he can get the words of God, and give out the laws of God to humanity ... a lawgiver, the last character described in the Old Testament is here today speaking to you, and calling you up to the very things that my father [Jacob, also known as Israel] said back there [in the Bible].[3]

Sandford, in his own words, was the lawgiver prophesied in the first book of the Bible. Like Queen Victoria, he was to rule in accordance with biblical prophecy, but with an even greater role: as the one who brings "the words of God ... the laws of God to humanity." Until Shiloh, Christ himself, comes.

This is British Israelism. Not merely the pseudohistorical belief that the 10 "Lost Tribes" migrated until they reached Western Europe and the British Isles, but also that leaders from these tribes—Queen Victoria and Frank Sandford, to name only two—are to rule the world as God's own emissaries.

At Shiloh, the faithful who obeyed Sandford as God's own lawgiver prayed for hours at a time and fasted for days on end, sometimes to the point of starvation. Fourteen-year-old Leander Bartlett died of diphtheria in 1903 after extensive fasting led to an outbreak of the disease. Sandford was arrested and convicted of manslaughter and cruelty to children, but when the Maine Supreme Court overturned his conviction in 1905, he returned to leading Shiloh.

He and his most devoted followers then set sail for Jerusalem, not the New Jerusalem that he believed Shiloh to be, but the holy city of ancient Israel, then part of the British Empire as the Mandate of Palestine. They took a series of "missionary" voyages during which, rather than disembarking and attempting to start new churches or engage in humanitarian work, they blew shofars from the ship and then continued sailing. They were engaging in spiritual warfare, another component of Sandford's teachings that would emerge as a force in American politics a century later.

After one ship, the *Kingdom*, ran aground off the coast of Africa in 1911, Sandford had all of his followers board another ship, the *Coronet*, which was already full. He set sail knowing that the ship was overloaded and woefully undersupplied. Six of his followers became sick with scurvy and died, leading to his arrest when he returned to Maine.

The most faithful remained at Shiloh, along with those who had nothing in the outside world to go back to. For a while, they even followed Sandford's directives from prison. In 1920, the Children's Protection Society of Maine urged that all children be removed from the deplorable conditions that existed at Shiloh, and the community collapsed. The remnant of the movement that Sandford began has continued to exist to the present day, under different leadership and now known as Kingdom Christian Ministries. Sandford himself died in obscurity, but what he began refused to die with him. Because before the Shiloh community disbanded, it was visited by a British Israelist who would bring Sandford's teachings out of rural Maine and into a budding movement within American evangelicalism.

Prior to visiting Shiloh, Charles Fox Parham (1873–1929) preached to large crowds in Kansas that Christ was the healer. At one revival meeting, claims were made that a woman with dropsy (now referred to as edema) and given three days to live was miraculously healed when Parham prayed for her. In another instance, someone claimed that Parham healed a seventeen-year-old girl who was at the throes of death because of heart trouble; instead of calling the doctor, the family called Parham. Another story says that someone was healed of deafness as soon as Parham baptized her. All along, he urged his followers to refuse medical treatment in favor of the prayer lifted up in faith.

The miracles credited to Parham confirmed what he believed to be true and likewise taught his followers: that not only should modern medicine be rejected, but so should Christian denominations. Parham had grown up as a Methodist and, before beginning his healing and preaching ministry, studied at the Methodist school Southwestern College to become a pastor. He left before graduating, however, disillusioned with how he perceived the Methodist denomination to be organized in such a way that prevented the spontaneous work of the Holy Spirit. To him, denominational pastors were unable to let the Spirit's healing power flow through them, leaving parishioners who desperately needed their bodies to be made whole clinging instead to church tradition and staid formalities.

In Parham's view, pastors who had to undergo an ordination process were unable to preach under the direct inspiration of the Holy Spirit because of how much denominations constrained them to preach only accepted teachings. Rather than becoming ordained, Parham abandoned the Methodist denomination to become an itinerant preacher and faith healer. He called his teachings the *apostolic faith*, referring to the apostles of the New Testament and suggesting that what he taught was authentic Christianity, as practiced in the first century. In performing miracles consistent with those of Christ during his earthly ministry, Parham suggested that he had recovered the true Christian lifestyle from centuries of denominations, man-made traditions, gaudy church buildings, and formal preaching—all of which lacked the healing that people's bodies and souls needed.

In 1898, shortly after Frank Sandford founded Shiloh, Parham began the Bethel Healing Home in Topeka. In search of inspiration for how to build the ideal Christian community, centered on Christ alone and the miracle-working power of the Holy Spirit, he traveled to Shiloh in 1900 to learn directly from Sandford. There, he witnessed something astounding: worshippers speaking in unknown languages as they praised God.

Sandford was not the first Christian in the modern era to promote the practice of *glossolalia*, or speaking in tongues. This can be seen at least as far back as the 1820s with a British sect known as the Irvingites, founded by Edward Irving. Like Sandford and later Parham, the Irvingites engaged in ecstatic utterances during worship services; they also emphasized miraculous healings and saw themselves as recreating the first-century apostolic church. Sandford may well have encountered Irvingite practices and beliefs before he founded Shiloh, and he added to them a new feature that Parham would come to adopt, as well: British Israelism. Perhaps just as consequently, Parham was inspired by Sandford's interpretation of Hannah Whitall Smith's words: "If the

Divine Master only had a band of workers such as this, there would be no limit to what He might do with them ... May God raise such an army speedily!"[4]

The teachings of British Israelism must have suited Parham well, as he was a lifelong segregationist. At the turn of the twentieth century, segregation was not merely a social norm adhered to on both sides of the colored line but was the law of the land in Kansas. Parham went far beyond the stipulations of the law by writing in his manifesto *A Voice Crying in the Wilderness*, published less than two years after his visit to Shiloh, "No one who has not Israelitish [Anglo-Saxon] blood in their veins will have any part or lot in the ride [sic] of Christ."[5]

Parham allowed that people of all races may, in fact, have a part in Christ, given his claim that intermarriage has spread Israelitish blood throughout the world. Yet he was sympathetic to the Ku Klux Klan that tore through the South in the years following the Civil War; after the Klan was reconstituted in 1915, he preached to crowds of men, women, and children wearing white hoods. In other words, filtered through the British Israelism of Sandford and then Parham, Whitall Smith's "band of workers" had become an Anglo-Saxon elite. Parham referred to his teachings about this Anglo-Saxon elite as the "Man-Child."

According to Parham, the "bride of Christ," spoken of in the New Testament and especially the book of Revelation, has a unique interpretation. Just as Adam's wife, Eve, came out of his body, so the bride of Christ must come out of Jesus's own body, or Anglo-Saxon Israel. Because the true Israel of the Bible consists (supposedly) of white people, the bride of Christ must be white, albeit some may be of other races because intermarriage gave them a few drops of white blood.

Revelation 12:5 says, "And she brought forth a man child, who was to rule all nations with a rod of iron" (KJV). Many interpreters have understood the woman in this verse as a representation of Israel or Mary and the man-child as Christ. Parham, however, taught that the woman is the bride of Christ—a collection of white Christians—and this bride will give birth to a "man child." The "man child" was not a single individual but rather an elite cadre of Christians who had attained the miracle-working powers of Christ himself. Not only will they be able to heal all the sick and even raise the dead; they will also, just as the gospels record Christ as doing after his resurrection, "like Jesus, have power to appear and disappear at will."[6] And in accordance with Revelation 12:5, they will "rule all nations with a rod of iron."

Like British Israelism, this doctrine of the "Man Child" has been obscure at best throughout the century-plus history of what became known as Pentecostalism. It has not been taught in most Pentecostal Bible schools and seminaries or preached from most Pentecostal pulpits. One place where both British Israelism and the "Man Child" doctrine survived, however, is in the movement that Parham championed: the Ku Klux Klan. In the years after the Second World War, a group of Pentecostal Klansmen would rename the "Man Child" teaching "the Manifest Sons of God" and make it central to a British-Israelist movement known as the Latter Rain. And the influence of the Latter Rain would fundamentally shape the ministry of none other than Dutch Sheets.

◆

These ideas about the "Man Child" would not become Parham's most well-known teachings, or even what his movement became famous for. After visiting Shiloh for six weeks, Parham returned to Topeka, having been filled with the message of speaking in tongues and British Israelism. Yet he found his Healing Home in disarray. His associates had taken over leadership, and rather than wrest back control, he left to found Bethel Bible College. It opened its doors to students in October of 1900.

Two months later, in December, Parham conducted a short-term Bible school and urged his students to discern what had led the first-century apostles, those who had followed Christ during his earthly ministry, to turn the world upside-down. The conclusion was that when the apostles and the earliest Christians were baptized with the Holy Spirit on the feast of Pentecost, fifty days after the crucifixion, they began to spontaneously speak in different languages. Parham and his students concluded that this act of *xenolalia*, or speaking in a language that one has not previously studied, was the evidence of baptism with the Holy Spirit. They immediately began pursuing this baptism and the concomitant xenolalia—the sure evidence that God had sent his Spirit down on them and commissioned them to change the world.

And then it happened. On January 1, 1901, a student named Agnes Ozman began uttering words and phrases in an unknown language. Other students and Parham himself soon followed suit, spontaneously speaking words that seemed unintelligible but surely belonged to some people group as a language. Just like the early Christians who had received the ability to speak in foreign languages on Pentecost, Parham's followers immediately planned to use their newfound gift of language to travel to countries around the world and spread the Christian gospel.

The problem—at least one of many problems—was that the utterances that Parham and his followers made were not actual languages. These early Pentecostals had not spontaneously received the ability to speak in a language that they had never studied. What they were engaging in was not *xenolalia*—the ability to speak in a foreign language—but rather *glossolalia*, what contemporary Christians sometimes refer to as "speaking in tongues." These "tongues" do not represent actual languages, and they lack any discernible structure or meaning. Many Pentecostal and charismatic Christians today find the practice of glossolalia to be a particularly powerful act of worship, something that occurs only between the worshipper and God. To Parham, however, glossolalia was a far cry from his and his students' intent of spontaneously speaking in actual, known languages—xenolalia—as recorded in the book of Acts on the Day of Pentecost.

◆

British Israelism was never mainstream within Pentecostalism, not even at the movement's inception. Parham taught his followers that speaking in tongues is the evidence that one has received the baptism of the Holy Spirit, that a Christian has been so filled with the Spirit that supernatural outpourings become daily occurrences. This teaching became central to the Pentecostal movement that he is often credited with founding.

Yet multiple revival movements that spanned the globe and became part of the fabric of Pentecostalism began as far back as the late 1800s, with one in India beginning as early as 1860. Similar revivals erupted in Chile, Madagascar, Korea, and especially Wales. The origins of Pentecostalism are perhaps best viewed as a constellation rather than the workings of one star shining brightly.

And today, Pentecostalism is one of the largest segments of Christianity and the fastest-growing religious movement in the world.

Ironically, for the white-supremacist Klan sympathizer, glossolalia helped give Pentecostalism a strong egalitarian impulse that quickly transcended racial lines. Parham's most well-known student was William Seymour, an African American man whose parents had been born into chattel slavery in Louisiana. Seymour studied under Parham for about six weeks and was taken with his teachings about the baptism of the Holy Spirit and glossolalia. But he may have been more influenced by a concurrent proto-Pentecostal movement, the Welsh Revival, than he was by Parham. The Welsh Revival saw an explosion of charismatic fervor among the working poor of Wales, especially coal miners, for a ten-month period in 1904–5.

Seymour traveled to Los Angeles in 1906, where he met with ministers who had participated in the Welsh Revival and were attempting to replicate it on the West Coast. His teachings in Los Angeles led to the Azusa Street Revival (1906–9), which included bursts of glossolalia, energetic dancing, and shaking—worship practices that the African Americans present may have found compatible with their cultural heritage. And for this reason, Parham rejected the Azusa Street Revival; to him, it reeked of "Africanism."

But from Azusa Street, Pentecostal missionaries traveled across the world, spreading a populist approach to Christianity that emphasized the believer's relationship with God over church hierarchies, tradition, and formality. Any Christian could become filled with the Holy Spirit, with or without attending seminary and becoming ordained into full-time ministry. This populism would enable Pentecostalism to one day become the fastest-growing religious movement in the world, in spite of Parham's overtly racist teachings.

Though Parham rejected the Azusa Street Revival, it caused Pentecostalism—both Parham's version that emphasized the "Man Child" teaching and Seymour's that empowered ordinary Christians to experience the power of the Holy Spirit—to spread on the West Coast, particularly in Los Angeles. Fewer than three miles from 312 Azusa Street, the most famous preacher in America, Aimee Semple McPherson, would open the country's first megachurch in 1923, Angelus Temple. And here, the Pentecostalism of Parham, which used British Israelism to promote the idea of an elite group of white, totally perfected Christians, would take a decidedly dark turn.

2

The Latter Rain

During the Chicago World's Fair in 1893, a Scottish minister named John Alexander Dowie (1847–1907) rented a space across the street from the antics of Buffalo Bill. He raised a flag that declared, "Christ is all," atop a wooden chapel and spent the year urging people away from Buffalo Bill's showmanship to instead find in Christ healing for their bodies and souls.

Dowie claimed that his last name was actually MacDhui, writing in his weekly periodical two years after the fair, "I want to say this; that I am an Anglo-Israelite. The blood of the Hebrews is in my veins. My fathers in the Roman age were Hebrews. They came from the ancient Israelites; and before the Romans settled in Scotland, our family gathered under the mountain of Ben MacDhui, which is my name in Scotch." He went on to emphasize, "Not Dowie, but Dhui."[1] An Israelitish name, befitting the alleged Israelitish origins of the Scottish people.

Having left the constraints of denominational preaching over a decade previously, Dowie claimed to have recovered the authentic Christianity as practiced by the early church in the first century. This authentic Christianity included the recognition of Israel's true identity as the white Anglo-Saxon people, as well as the ability to experience complete healing of one's soul and body. Like other proto-Pentecostal leaders at the turn of the twentieth century—notably Sandford and Parham—Dowie's insistence on faith-healing seems to have been an outgrowth of his belief that the true identity of Israel is being restored to the church. Though arrested 100 times in a single year by Chicago police for practicing medicine without a license, Dowie insisted on urging all who would listen to him to refuse the medical care of doctors and surgeons; instead, they should pray to Christ for their healing.

And at the 1893 Chicago World's Fair, he claimed to have healed Sadie Cody, the niece of Buffalo Bill. According to testimony published in his weekly *Leaves of Healing*, she had an abscess and tumor that caused her so much pain that she could scarcely be touched. She learned about Dowie and went to Chicago so that he could pray for her, and she immediately became whole. Dowie wrote of the experience, "And so I have had my revenge on Buffalo Bill in a very nice way, through the healing of one of his relatives, Sadie Cody."[2]

Yet there are no sources outside of Dowie's own supporters indicating that such a healing occurred. In fact, investigative reporters found that Dowie had planted people in his audience at the Chicago World's Fair who would come onto the stage and claim that they had been healed of ailments that had never actually plagued them.

To his followers, Dowie was the reincarnation of the Old Testament prophet Elijah, come to restore the true faith. To his critics, he was a charlatan who earned money by praying for people and insisting that, if their healing did not occur, the problem was a lack of faith on their part. As his fame grew, he began urging people to write to him their healing needs, along with a sum of money, making him a mail-order faith healer.

In 1900, the year that Parham visited Sandford's Shiloh commune in Maine, Dowie began construction on a utopian community called Zion, 40 miles away from Chicago. Zion would be 10 times larger than Shiloh, ultimately housing 6000 people, complete with its own church, school, places of business, and bank. In fact, Dowie owned the bank, an unincorporated entity into which residents of Zion had to deposit their funds. He also owned the church and declared that he was an apostle, a Christian leader with the same authority that had been vested in Christ's original disciples (minus Judas). The entire city of Zion was founded as a theocratic polity, wholly owned by Dowie and functioning as a massive securities fraud.

When it crashed a few years later, his followers lost all their money and material goods. Two of these followers were Thomas and Effie Lindsay, who had a son, Gordon, just before the collapse of Zion wiped out all of their assets.

Despite the hardship that this turn of events inflicted on his family while he was growing up, Gordon Lindsay (1906–73) became dedicated to the teachings of Dowie, particularly regarding the restoration of authentic Christianity via apostles, divine healing, and the recognition of British Israel. His ministry's periodical, known as *Voice of Healing* (after Dowie's *Leaves of Healing*), helped organize a group of Pentecostal faith healers, many of them British Israelists, into a mid-century movement that became known as the Latter Rain. And after the Latter Rain dwindled, he rebranded *Voice of Healing* as a ministry called Christ for the Nations. He founded Christ for the Nations Institute in 1970, and a few years later none other than Dutch Sheets would begin his training for ministry there.

Before any of those things could happen, however, Dowie took inspiration from a book written by a Quaker woman—the same book that inspired Frank Sandford.

◆

"Let go and let God."

Many American evangelicals have heard this phrase, so oft-repeated as to have lost all meaning. The deep history of the trite aphorism betrays its simplicity, to let go and let God. In the words of Hannah Whitall Smith, "Man's part is to trust and God's part is to work."[3] She wrote these words in the same book in which she declared, "If the Divine Master only had a band of workers such as this, there would be no limit to what He might do with them," inspiring Frank Sandford to a radicalized form of Christianity.

Whitall Smith's book that fell into Sandford's hand was called *The Christian's Secret to a Happy Life*, published in 1875 and hugely influential among evangelicals in both America and the UK. In the book, she promoted the idea of a faith that abandons all cares, instead trusting God to do the work that would generate results. *The Christian's Secret to a Happy Life* can be summed up in the phrase, "Let go and let God."

This idea contrasted sharply with the Puritan legacy of hard work and diligent study of the Bible. Not that Whitall Smith and her followers rejected the Bible; quite the opposite. What many of them rejected were the church denominations, hierarchies, and theological minutiae that they saw as creating a formal, rigid Christianity that left the believer longing for joy. Whitall Smith's solution to this disease of joyless Christianity was unquestioning obedience to the promptings of the Holy Spirit—to let go and let God.

But how does one know whether one is truly being led by the urgings of the Holy Spirit, rather than by one's ego, a passing whim, or even a mental illness? This question becomes a real problem when figures such as Sandford and Dowie fill the vacuum left by church denominations and seminary-trained ministers; they instead promise divine healing (with spurious results) as evidence that the Holy Spirit has gifted them to be apostles, to be obeyed just as a Christian would obey God himself.

Sandford and Dowie—and by extension, Parham and Lindsay—followed a theological tradition that was heavily shaped by Whitall Smith. This tradition was known as the Keswick Movement or the Higher Life Movement. Keswick is a small town in England where, beginning in 1875, crowds of evangelicals from both America and the UK gathered for an annual convention. Many of the names associated with Keswick resonate to this day with evangelicals, showing just how influential the theology that spread from the yearly convention was: Hudson Taylor, Amy Carmichael, Dwight Moody, R.A. Torrey, even Billy Graham. Not that these individuals were British Israelists, faith healers, or cult leaders; Keswick theology was just one ingredient—albeit a significant one—in shaping the movement that would become dominionism.

Keswick created a theological hybrid that held space for the Calvinism that had shaped Puritan life and teachings, as well as the more nebulous ideas of obedience to the Holy Spirit promoted by Whitall Smith. Teachings at the annual convention centered on the idea of sanctification by faith, that one becomes righteous before God through the inner life of belief rather than outward expressions of piety. Some Calvinist ministers chafed at the idea, even while recognizing that the people at their churches who worked most tirelessly for the social betterment of others were Keswickians. Believing their faith made them righteous, they engaged in acts of great faith that went beyond traditional markers of piety; serving those on the margins of society took precedence, sometimes even over attending church services.

The annual Keswick conventions and the theology propagated from them did not belong to one particular denomination, such as Baptists, Methodists, Lutherans, Episcopalians, or Presbyterians. People from all denominations came, while critics from all denominations likewise rejected Keswick teachings. Several Keswickians—including Hudson Taylor, Amy Carmichael, and eventually Billy Graham—chose, at varying times, cooperation across denominations or rejected denominations altogether. This antiestablishment ethos that craved obedience to God rather than the preservation of church formalities became fertile soil for the cult leaders who, without attending the annual conventions, still adopted bits and pieces of Keswick theology—and especially the book that inspired it, *The Christian's Secret to a Happy Life*.

Though Gordon Lindsay may have been altogether unaware of the annual Keswick convention, he was certainly affected by the more radicalized versions of its teachings. That one should *let go and let God* was taken to extremes by faith healers such as he and his predecessor, Dowie, as well as Sandford and Parham. Christians should let go of their reliance on doctors and modern medicine in favor of trusting God to heal their bodies as well as their souls. Failure to do so would mean a lack of faith. In Lindsay's words regarding an illness he faced, "I thank the Lord for my physician friends, but I must testify. God has revealed Himself to me as my Great Physician, so I always felt that I must lean upon Him alone."[4] In his telling, as a young man he fell deathly ill from food poisoning but refused to see a doctor, even though this choice meant that the friends caring for him in their home would not allow him to stay. He went to stay with the British-Israelist missionary and faith healer John G. Lake, also a disciple of Dowie and Parham; according to the story, there Lindsay found the faith to get out of bed and put on his clothes. He immediately became better.

This emphasis on letting go and letting God so that one could experience miraculous healings for physical ailments was not limited to extremists on the cult fringes of Pentecostalism. One person influenced by the Keswick meetings was the Canadian preacher A.B. Simpson. Simpson founded the Christian Alliance and Evangelical Missionary Alliance in 1887 in Old Orchard Beach, Maine, a mere 40 miles from where Frank Sandford would establish the community of Shiloh. The sect that became known as the Christian and

Missionary Alliance promoted what Simpson called the fourfold gospel: Christ as Savior, Christ as Sanctifier, Christ as Healer, and Christ as Soon Coming King. This approach would greatly influence yet another faith-healing pastor who would found the Foursquare Church and become one of the most famous people in America from the 1920s until her death in 1944: Aimee Semple McPherson.

> *What is my task? First of all, my task is to be pleasing to Christ. To be empty of self and be filled with Himself. To be filled with the Holy Spirit; to be led by the Holy Spirit.*[5]

Sister Aimee (1890–1944), as she came to be known by her many followers, grew up preaching to her toys in a winsome foreshadowing of how she would become one of the first people to preach across the airwaves. In 1908, she married Robert Semple, an Irish preacher who had converted to the Pentecostal message that was spreading rapidly in the early years of the twentieth century. Sister Aimee also converted to the Pentecostal message and, over the next three decades, would transform it into a force that would shape much of American public life.

She and her husband traveled to China as missionaries, but when he died of malaria, the soon-to-be mother became a widow. Sister Aimee gave birth to a daughter, Roberta, before returning to the United States to live with her mother. She worked for the Salvation Army until she married Harold McPherson in 1912, gaining much-needed stability for herself and Roberta. Yet at a time when women were overwhelmingly confined to domestic life, she decided that the duties of a stay-at-home wife and mother were not for her. She defied the standards of conservative evangelicalism by leaving her husband so that she could travel across America with her two young children and preach the gospel to anyone who would listen.

As her popularity grew, her demeanor changed from that of a Canadian farm girl and former missionary into a mesmerizing cultural icon. Conservative women, especially evangelicals, did not adhere to contemporary fashions, but Sister Aimee wore make-up and curled her short hair in a way that resembled the flapper style of the Roaring Twenties. Conservative evangelicals saw her as a scandal, but she promised something that even some straitlaced fundamentalists of the era desperately wanted: divine healing. Under the motto of "Christ as Healer," Sister Aimee claimed to heal thousands of people during her lifetime, not by medicine but by prayer and faith.

Massive crowds attended the meetings she held as she crisscrossed the country with her mother and two children. She offered prayers for healing, laying hands on people one by one and refusing to stop praying until she felt the anointing of God leave her hands. Then, the matter of healing rested between the sick individual and the Holy Spirit. Hundreds at every meeting claimed to experience miraculous cures for deafness, paralysis, and all other afflictions for which modern medicine could not remedy. Critics attributed any alleviation of symptoms to hysteria, the mob mentality, or the placebo effect. Even Sister Aimee insisted that when one is healed by God, the healing is only temporary, never permanent. Still, the draw of faith-healing compelled crowds to flock to her wherever she traveled.

Through faith-healing revivals held all across America, she raised the money needed to construct a 5300-seat megachurch in Los Angeles, Angelus Temple, with additional funds contributed by none other than the California branch of the Ku Klux Klan. Sister Aimee had a friendly relationship with the Klan, and on at least one occasion, she preached to a crowd of white hoods. Though she strove to include people of different racial backgrounds in her church, the presence of Klansmen undoubtedly kept many away.

Angelus Temple was, and remains, an architectural marvel that seems custom-made for putting the gospel on display to thousands of people at a time. The unconventional revivalist and faith healer who graced the stage put on theatrical performances that told and retold the gospel story, sometimes with Hollywood's elite in the audience. And every week, miracles. At least claims of them, as people with cerebral palsy, multiple sclerosis, cancer, and tuberculosis came from all across the country to be healed by Sister Aimee.

But beneath the showboating and claims of numerous miracles occurring, something much darker was taking place at Angelus Temple. Sister Aimee publicly denounced British Israelism, but at least one of her staff members, Wesley Swift, was a British Israelist and fierce antisemite. In July of 1938, as anti-Jewish tensions were reaching a fever pitch in Europe and especially Germany, she invited the antisemite Gerald Burton Winrod to preach. This event may have introduced Swift to the more extreme teachings of British Israelism, teachings that were more consistent with the Ku Klux Klan that Sister Aimee had a friendly relationship with. Swift had studied at Angelus Temple's LIFE Bible College and became a minister at the church during the 1930s and 1940s. While there, he began ruminating on an idea called Serpent Seed.

Serpent Seed claims that when Adam and Eve were in the Garden of Eden, Eve had sex with the serpent—interpreted by many Christians, including Swift, to be Satan—and became pregnant with Cain. Cain then became the father of the Jewish people, making Jews the literal children of Satan. As such, those who call themselves Jews are not of true Israel; they are liars and the enemy in the cosmic war being waged between the forces of darkness and the forces of light. Serpent Seed teaches that true Israel—British Israel, or the white church—finds itself in a perpetual struggle with the Jewish people, and they must be defeated.

Lindsay, who had deep connections to Angelus Temple and the Foursquare denomination, seems to have rejected Serpent Seed. However, at least until the 1940s, he traveled in circles that included proponents of Serpent Seed and even leading figures of the Ku Klux Klan. He organized meetings of British Israelists along the West Coast, many of whom had turned to the antisemitic form of British Israelism that was now taking root both on the fringes of Pentecostalism and at the hub of Angelus Temple. Whether or not he accepted any form of Serpent Seed, Lindsay's ministry among British Israelists gave it a platform that allowed the teaching to thrive.

Serpent Seed became the organizing principle of an altogether different sect of British Israelists, a movement known as Identity. Identity theology is a violently racist belief system that has long underpinned white-supremacist groups such as the Ku Klux Klan and Aryan Nations.

Angelus Temple, and Sister Aimee's Foursquare denomination, quietly became a hub for extremist ideas that included the Ku Klux Klan, British Israelism, violent antisemitism, and faith-healing. Uniting these ideas was Parham's concept of the Man-Child—something that did not feature in Sister Aimee's preaching but was central to other Foursquare ministers.

◆

At the time, the prevailing belief system among both Pentecostals and fundamentalists was dispensationalism, which teaches that the earth is on the cusp of facing a cataclysmic judgment from God. "True Christians"—those who believe this End-Times schema—would soon be spontaneously "raptured" into heaven so that they could be spared the succession of fires, earthquakes, and diseases that would imminently decimate the world. In August of 1945, the United States detonated the atomic bomb on the Japanese cities of Hiroshima and Nagasaki. With the advent of the nuclear age, prophecy belief went into overdrive as zealous fundamentalists and Pentecostals scoured the Bible for evidence that the atomic bomb had been divinely foretold thousands of years ago.

But among a small group of Pentecostal ministers, a different interpretation of current events emerged. Was there possibly a spiritual component, an atomic power that could be harnessed for Christians to do God's work? Franklin Hall, a minister in Southern California, published *Atomic Power with God Through Fasting and Prayer* in 1946 to show Christians that fasting—the spiritual practice of going without food—could be harnessed in such a way that everyday Christians could perform miracles.

In the book and to his audiences, Hall taught that Christians could go on extended fasts, sometimes a month or longer, and then experience the supernatural breakthrough that they had been seeking. He taught an extreme version of the "let go and let God" theology that spread from Keswick by urging Christians to let go of their physical needs—in this case, by fasting for extended amounts of time—and let God operate miraculously in their lives. *Atomic Power with God Through Fasting and Prayer* became a centerpiece of two parallel revivals that broke out in the postwar era. These revivals, both organized heavily by Lindsay, disrupted the prevailing notion that Christians will soon be raptured into heaven in favor of something much more militant and activist in American politics: the idea that the church was to be victorious over sin, wickedness, disease, and even the devil himself. Instead of a rapture into heaven, Lindsay and his cohort began preaching that Jesus Christ had given dominion of the planet to his followers—an approach to the gospel known as *dominion theology*.

Beginning in 1947, the healing revival barnstormed the world of Pentecostalism, which had by then become (in no small part because of Sister Aimee) a respectable institution that was appealing to not only struggling laborers but also the middle class. Faith-healing revivalists such as Hall, Lindsay, Jack Coe, A. A. Allen, and Oral Roberts (who founded Oral Roberts University) toured the United States, Canada, parts of Europe, and even Africa, filling stadiums with thousands of people desperate for healing, just as Sister Aimee had done a generation before.

Soon Lindsay encountered another faith healer named William Branham. Branham (1909–65) was not only a British Israelist but had actually been ordained into ministry by Roy Davis, the National Imperial Wizard of the Knights of the Ku Klux Klan. Additionally, Branham had held ties to the Nazis during the Second World War. But on the North American scene during the postwar years, Branham rose to fame for altogether different reasons: his seeming ability to cure anyone of anything that ailed them through the power of God. Though a slight man with frail nerves, Branham could command an audience with tens of thousands of people, using illusionist tricks to make them think he was causing objects to hang suspended in midair simply through his faith.

While Sandford and Dowie had proclaimed themselves apostles, men who oversaw the church with God's own authority, Branham (1909–65) declared himself a prophet, one who speaks the very words of God to his followers. These words did not have to come from the Bible, which evangelicals have long regarded as the authoritative word of God. Though Branham's words never became official scripture and sometimes contradicted the Bible, his followers did not question him because, as a prophet, he could speak what God wanted the people of this generation to know. Not the generations of Noah, Moses, Paul, or other figures from the Bible, but those living in postwar North America. In this movement, the words of a prophet were tantamount to scripture itself.

In the fall of 1947, Branham led a healing revival in Vancouver, Canada. This revival was attended by a group of Foursquare ministers, many of them British Israelists, who were running an orphanage and Bible college in the remote prairie town of North Battleford, Saskatchewan. George Warnock, George and Ern Hawtin, and Herrick Holt were so amazed by what they experienced under Branham's ministry that they urged their students to fast and pray to God for revival to fall on them.

Then, on February 11, 1948, a woman who was studying at their Sharon Bible School uttered a prophecy that claimed they were standing at the door of a great revival and need only enter into it. The next day, a new revival began to pour down—the Latter Rain. Students and faculty alike reported that they were physically knocked over by the raw power of God. The gifts of the Spirit were being fully restored to the church—glossolalia, divine healing, prophecy—as were the biblical offices of church leadership. No longer were churches to be led by pastors and Bible teachers. Instead, according to the doctrines that emerged out of the Latter Rain, they should be led by apostles and prophets. This teaching is known as the Fivefold Ministry and is embraced by dominionist churches today: the order of authority in church governance is apostle, prophet, evangelist, pastor, and teacher. Seminary training is not required and often frowned upon.

One prophecy that was spoken in those early days of the Latter Rain at the Sharon Orphanage and Bible School was that the recipients of the divine outpouring should not tell their loved ones about what was happening. Yet the news spread rapidly through print media and the Foursquare Church, and within weeks, Christians began pouring in from across North America and even parts of Europe.

In May of 1948, just three months into the revival, something happened that the British Israelists who were leading the movement saw as nothing short of miraculous: the Jewish people had reconstituted in the Middle East, and Israel was declared a state. Nineteen centuries of diaspora had ended in what had to have been, according to the Latter-Rain revivalists, a fulfillment of biblical prophecy. Believing that the Western church of Europe and North America *also* represented Israel—literally, as British Israelism's underlying thesis is that the 10 "Lost Tribes" are actually the white people of today—Latter-Rain leaders saw their revival as a counterpart to the restored nation of Israel.

Like so many other Pentecostals, these ministers used the current events around Israel to talk about the End Times, but with a twist. Instead of seeing the reconstitution of the Jewish people as a sign of God's impending judgment, they saw it as a sign of the impending Manifestation of the Sons of God—a reformulation of Parham's teaching about the Man-Child.

In Parham's reading, the Man-Child would defeat the "dragon," presumably the devil, spoken of in Revelation. To Warnock, the Manifest Sons of God would take dominion back from Satan, "the rising up of the Sons of God in the power of the Spirit, to take the Kingdom which Satan has usurped and occupied for so long."[6] And what was this kingdom of Satan? Virtually everything, as he took the dominion that God had given to humanity, beginning in the Garden of Eden, when he convinced Adam and Eve to disobey God by eating from the Tree of the Knowledge of Good and Evil.

Satan was defeated at the Feast of Passover, when Christ died for the sins of the world, and would soon be stripped of all power at the fulfillment of the Feast of Tabernacles, when the Manifest Sons of God would destroy him completely. In other words, the Manifest Sons of God were engaged in a cosmic war, fought metaphorically against demonic powers and principalities but acted out in the real-time arena of human affairs. In fact, the term "Latter Rain" comes from Joel 2, which declares, "He will cause the rain to come down for you—the former rain, and the latter rain" (Joel 2:23, NKJV). The same chapter speaks of a locust invasion that decimates everything in its path; Manifest Sons of God proponents teach that this is a metaphor for a great army that engages in scorched-earth warfare, burning and razing everything in its path. While this passage has historically been interpreted as having a metaphorical or allegorical meaning, or even literally referring to an actual locust invasion that led to a famine, to the Latter-Rain revivalists, this army of God was a literal horde of Manifest Sons of God who would arise in the End Times.

And soon, the dominion over the world that has long belonged to Satan would come to belong to them. The Manifest Sons of God would rule and reign with God over all the affairs of humankind.

◆

Though not present with the North Battleford group, Branham greatly influenced the Latter Rain through his teachings and healing revivals. Lindsay was awed by Branham, so much so that he turned his entire ministry toward promoting Branham through his magazine, *Voice of Healing*. When Branham suddenly dropped off the revival circuit owing to personal health concerns, Lindsay pivoted and used his platform to promote other healing revivalists who had similar messages.

Branham went on to connect Manifest Sons of God theology to the Serpent Seed teachings of Identity, which he promoted in his later years. In his variation, the Manifest Sons of God will arise during the End Times to defeat the children of Satan, the Jews. While this is certainly a troubling idea, what is also deeply disturbing is his connection to one of the most notorious cult leaders in history. Decades after the Latter-Rain revival began, one of Branham's protégés from Indiana would reject the virulent racism of Serpent Seed and break with Branham over his racist teachings. Jim Jones would build his People's Temple around Manifest Sons of God theology, with his own variations added to it, while, following in the footsteps of Sandford and Dowie, attempting to create a utopian community. In the early 1970s, over nine hundred people followed Jones to a commune called Jonestown in the South American country of Guyana. On November 18, 1978, 918 people died after drinking grape Flavor Aid that had been laced with cyanide.

Still, the teaching of Manifest Sons of God persists. Kris Vallotton, the prophet of Bethel Church, wrote in his 2016 book *Heavy Rain*, "Christians who were a part of these movements [the Latter Rain and Manifest Sons of God] had some real insights into the true identity of believers." The problem was not the teachings of Manifest Sons of God, but rather the attitudes of the leaders who promoted it: "But many of the movement leaders began using their insights to promote spiritual elitism, and the entire revelation was branded as heretical."[7] In other words, many of today's dominionist prophets and apostles are the heirs of the Latter Rain and still teach the ideas associated with Manifest Sons of God.

Furthermore, Bill Johnson, the apostle of Bethel Church who works alongside Vallotton, is one of a number of dominionist leaders who greatly revere William Branham, with no qualifications made for his association with the Ku Klux Klan or his promotion of Serpent Seed. In fact, the Latter-Rain revival, which was spearheaded by Branham's teachings and organized by Lindsay's promotion, was the forerunner of the New Apostolic Reformation.

3
Joel's Army

I will change the understanding and expression of Christianity in the earth in one generation.[1]

Mike Bickle was born in 1955, by which time the Latter Rain and Healing Revivals were beginning to falter. Gordon Lindsay was parting ways with William Branham as his racist teachings moved from run-of-the-mill British Israelism to the virulent Serpent Seed teachings of Identity theology. Paul Cain, Branham's protégé who regularly held healing crusades at packed-out stadiums around the world, would soon leave public ministry altogether. Branham himself died following a car accident in 1965, bringing an end to the era of faith-healing revivalists crisscrossing the country to hold massive rallies.

But the revivals never went away completely. As a teenager and young adult, Bickle imbibed Latter-Rain books, including Franklin Hall's *The Atomic Power of Fasting and Prayer*. "If the unleashing of atomic energy is the prelude to the end of the earth (as is mentioned in Luke 21); and the seals, trumpets, and vial judgments of the Revelation of Jesus Christ," Bickle read in Hall's book, probably numerous times, "then the few who know and experience the saving power of God would do well to protect themselves against the day of His Coming by a last great awakening through fasting and prayer."[2] Those were the keys: fasting and prayer. And the raising up of prophets to speak the very words of God to the church.

In 1999, Bickle and a group of Latter-Rain prophets—including Paul Cain—opened the International House of Prayer in Kansas City, Missouri

(IHOP-KC). Housed in a converted strip mall in the suburb of Grandview, IHOP-KC hardly looked like a place to spark an End-Times revival. There was nothing spectacular about the plain brown, one-story building that wrapped around an oversized parking lot, flanked by a gas station and fast-food joint. Where signs once announced the names of now-defunct stores, gilded letters read, "International House of Prayer"; below, "Exalting Jesus, 24/7 Worship & Prayer Since 1999, Great Commission."

Despite its more than ordinary appearances, at IHOP-KC's peak, tens of thousands of people traveled to Kansas City each year to spend time immersed in the presence of God. Some of the most talented evangelical musicians in the world trained at International House of Prayer University, which boasted top-of-the-line equipment and state-of-the-art facilities. Others trained for ministry there by learning how to be what Bickle called a Forerunner, someone uniquely called by God and trained to bring about the End Times and the return of Christ. Their jobs were "proclaiming prophetic scriptures, worshiping, celebrating Communion, witnessing, preaching the gospel, casting out demons, healing the sick, being peacemakers, and functioning as forerunners who prepare the church for His coming."[3] Not that the school was accredited, but many evangelicals have long cared less about academic qualifications than about making God their only priority.

Some of the young adults who called IHOP-KC their home, if only for a season, had left behind staid, dusty churches that were full of formality and tradition but lacked supernatural engagement with the divine. They craved an authentic encounter with God and the chance to be in a community with others who were not satisfied with merely doing church. Others had left behind difficult families, tainted by divorce or abuse or just not ever being truly seen. At IHOP-KC, they could spend hours each day away from these traumas, basking in the presence of God in the Prayer Room. And they could be part of something greater than the misery that had once been theirs: 24/7 prayer that would usher in the return of Christ, and their very own chance to be a Forerunner.

Never mind that these teachings about Forerunners conflicted with more established evangelical views about the return of Christ. And the fasting was intense—members were expected to fast at least one day per week and regularly went on extended fasts of ten days or longer. But Bickle's long teaching sessions about modern-day prophets and flights that he had taken to heaven were unlike anything that people gathered at IHOP-KC had ever heard. He was raw, powerful, like he had actually seen God face-to-face.

Sure, there were some questionable goings-on, like the apparent suicide of Bethany Deaton and the homoerotic group that her husband led, even after their wedding. Parents back home expressed concern that their adult children were cutting them off the more time they spent at IHOP-KC. And people would get expelled from the community over simple disagreements regarding how to interpret a passage in the Bible.

But on the whole, what new interns at IHOP-KC regularly saw was that Bickle and his fellow prophets had created a joyous place. And the *intensity*. These people were serious about 24/7 prayer, to the point of neglecting their personal lives. Instead of simply ministering to the poor, they were ministering to God himself by keeping the altar burning, sometimes sarcastically joking that the fire burned with their bodies. People walked around with shirts saying, "Revival is Family"; what they needed was IHOP-KC, not relationships back home that cut them off from what God was doing. And Bickle was careful to make sure of this. In one of the prophecies that he constantly reminded his followers of, IHOP-KC was a white horse in a refreshing stream of water, and rabid dogs— Christians who did not understand prophecy, prayer, and fasting—wanted to attack the horse. Members of the community had the responsibility of making sure that did not happen, even if they had to cut all ties with their families.

But why should relationships back home matter? Here, they could meet with friends at the coffee shop/bookstore just outside the Prayer Room and have deep conversations about friendship with Jesus and the struggles of young adulthood. And inside the Prayer Room, the music was hypnotic, bringing those gathered out of their bodies and into the presence of God. Their churches back home seemed like rusted artifacts compared to the improvised dancing, rhythms, and lyrics that burned on the altar of nonstop prayer. And this metaphorical altar—24/7 prayer that had not stopped since September 1999—would usher in the second coming of Christ.

Of course, this was before Bickle was deposed from ministry when a woman stepped forward in October 2023 with allegations that he had sexually groomed her when she was a teenager. Then, as so often happens when one victim steps forward, more women spoke up about similar experiences, with Bickle grooming them from the time they were as young as fourteen. The allegations were deemed credible; Bickle had, for decades, used his spiritual authority as clergy to sexually abuse children.

IHOP-KC imploded as former devotees publicly shared their experiences of waking up from what they realized had all the trappings of a cult. A charismatic leader, attempts to isolate people from their family, strange teachings that do not fit into categories of historical Christian thought. And the curious statement that Bickle made repeatedly that more than hinted at his cult-leader narcissism, that God would change the understanding and expression of Christianity around the world in one generation.

But IHOP-KC was more than its cult-like trappings. It was a movement that goes back to the Latter Rain and the attempt to raise up a generation of End-Times Christian warriors. What Parham called the Man-Child and Branham referred to as the Manifest Sons of God was, to Mike Bickle, Forerunners.[4] And in the years before he founded IHOP-KC, he referred to this teaching as something more militant and destructive: Joel's Army.

Prior to the founding of IHOP-KC in 1999, Bickle and his teachings about Joel's Army stood at the center of a fissure within Pentecostalism, in which proponents of the Latter Rain faced off against moderates who believed he was going too far. And within a decade of IHOP-KC's founding, Joel's Army would be prime-time news.

◆

While the Latter Rain and healing revivals were continuing among small networks of Latter-Rain prophets and apostles, throughout the late 1960s and into the 1970s, the revivals were subsiding into something that would penetrate much of denominational evangelicalism: the Jesus Movement. The Jesus Movement began in San Francisco's Haight-Ashbury district, a place to which hippies were flocking after leaving their jobs, their homes, and everything that connected them to "the establishment." Drug-addicted, hungry, and often homeless, hippies became the bane of California's more respectable evangelicals, but during the 1967 "summer of love," a group of pastors and laypeople defied those sophisticated tastes and began outreaches to hippies in the Haight-Ashbury. Soon, churches across California and eventually the rest of the country were opening their doors to hippies. These churches even sang new worship music and restructured their services in order to reach more hippies with the Christian message. In turn, these revitalized and more entertaining styles of worship attracted evangelical youth and young adults—a critical demographic, given that most leave the church, sometimes for good, once they leave their parents' homes.

One of the more influential of the Jesus Movement churches was Calvary Chapel in Costa Mesa, California, pastored by Chuck Smith. Smith grew up in the Foursquare Church and even attended Sister Aimee's LIFE Bible College for his ministry training, placing him and Calvary Chapel firmly in the Pentecostal fold. Calvary Chapel exploded under Smith's leadership, from a failing church on the verge of closing to a vibrant community that could not keep up with all of the hippies converting to Christianity.

In 1974, Kenn Gulliksen began a sister church of Calvary Chapel; this first Vineyard church had in its congregation the likes of Bob Dylan and Keith Green, immediately thrusting the Vineyard into a kind of evangelical superstardom. As the number of churches affiliated with the Vineyard grew, a charismatic musician took over leadership as someone who would provide direction for the movement, helping it span the gap between the establishment evangelicalism of denominations—the Baptists, Methodists, Lutherans, and Presbyterians who had set ways of doing things but wanted to experience this new move of God—and the free-wheeling world of Pentecostalism. John Wimber was committed to invoking the Holy Spirit and teaching evangelical Christians to "do the stuff" of the Bible: praying for healing and even casting out demons. And, of course, speaking in tongues.

Wimber, who had written songs and even played keyboard for the band that later became the Righteous Brothers, did more than lead a movement that attracted mainstream evangelicals who desired charismatic experiences. He brought Pentecostalism right into evangelical churches through music. Talented songwriters and musicians who were affiliated with the Vineyard wrote many of the worship songs that denominational churches used in their services. Calvary Chapel had started the award-winning music label Maranatha back in 1971, and evangelical kids all across the country could recognize Maranatha's

"Psalty the Psalter" as a cartoon representation of the Psalms. In a similar vein, Wimber formed Vineyard Worship in 1985 to distribute the songs written in Vineyard churches. Unlike the hymns that have long been sung by evangelicals, music by Vineyard Worship and Maranatha was light on classical systematic theology and instead turned worship into a powerful encounter with God. This idea of experiential worship—singing songs that made the Christian feel directly connected to God—flooded evangelical churches, even as they rejected the more Pentecostal aspects of the Vineyard.

The Vineyard would intersect with the still-glowing embers of more radical Latter-Rain teachings when Wimber met Bickle in 1985. At the time, Bickle and his fellow prophets were leading a Latter-Rain church called Kansas City Fellowship. Wimber wanted to "do the stuff" of the Bible, and Bickle introduced him to the idea that the prophetic giftings spoken of in the Bible are very much for the church today. By the fall of 1988, Wimber was giving Bickle's Latter-Rain ideas a platform within the Vineyard—and by extension, throughout the world of establishment evangelicalism—by having him speak at Vineyard conferences, sometimes to thousands of people at a time.

The addition of Bickle's Kansas City Fellowship into the Vineyard brought a new apocalyptic fervor. In keeping with its roots in Calvary Chapel and, more distantly, the Foursquare Church, the Vineyard taught that Jesus would return at any moment for his church. Bickle and his fellow prophets turned the fire up on this belief by proclaiming—constantly—that an unprecedented move of God's power would soon fall, leading to a billion souls converting to Christianity in the End Times. Intermingled with the zeal surrounding these prophecies was a spate of Vineyard leadership coming to accept other teachings that come directly from the Latter Rain, especially that the End Times church would be governed by apostles and prophets. Some even adopted the militant language of Joel's Army.

It was truly awesome, the Holy Spirit or Jesus, standing there with sword drawn.

By this time, Bickle was working with none other than Paul Cain, the man who had not only learned directly from Branham but who had also filled in for him at healing crusades he was unable to attend. Wimber saw Cain as a true prophet, in spite of "thus saith the Lord" prophecies Cain made that were never fulfilled. Still, he taught of a victorious church that would be unparalleled in power. For Wimber and some other Vineyard leaders, this concept of a victorious church scratched right where they itched. For others, though, the new focus on bold declarations from prophetic leaders, instead of centering the everyday Christians who attended Vineyard churches, represented a departure from what the Vineyard had been. The Vineyard lost a fair number of pastors and churches at about the same time that Bickle and Cain's Kansas City Fellowship became Metro Vineyard Church.

And he was pointing to this sign that was brilliantly lighted.

Wimber believed that by bringing the prophets into the Vineyard, he could provide oversight and accountability to a raw and immature expression of Christian faith. The prophets did not just teach the dominion theology of the Latter Rain; their church ran a school that taught children to ascend into the third heaven instead of learning fractions and how to write paragraphs. Worst of all, Bickle's colleague, Bob Jones, had used his position as a prophet to command women who came into his office to undress and stand naked before the Lord. Bickle acknowledged that there had been some excesses to the prophetic movement and instated some regulations when he and the other prophets joined the Vineyard. Ultimately, though, the Kansas City prophets could not be governed. They could only be given a wider audience—and this is exactly what they gained through their partnership with Wimber and the Vineyard. With time, their influence penetrated far outside of Latter-Rain and even Vineyard circles and into establishment evangelicalism.

It read, "Joel's Army, Now in Training."[5]

Joel's Army was not some kind of metaphor for waging a righteous struggle against evil. Bickle taught that Joel's Army was a breed of Christians who would arise during the End Times and actually pray down the plagues of God that are enumerated in the book of Revelation. Taken literally (as opposed to a metaphorical approach embraced by many biblical scholars), these plagues of darkness, blood, fire, disease, and earthquake amount to a global genocide—effected by supernaturally empowered Christians whose prayers are heard by a wrathful, vengeful deity. This is what he spent his ministerial career striving to raise up: training Christians to pray the wrath of God out of heaven. This was the center of his numerous prophecies that were splitting the Vineyard.

Then something happened that, to true believers, could only be described as divine fulfillment of prophecy. On January 20, 1994, a revivalist named Randy Clark preached a sermon at the Toronto Airport Vineyard Church. He had come from St. Louis, Missouri, to preach for four nights, but instead stayed for two months because of what happened at the end of the sermon. According to reports, all of the 160 or so people there that evening fell over backwards and began laughing. Hysterically, for hours. Thus began a global convergence on the mid-sized church, as people from all across the world traveled to Toronto to take part in what came to be a twelve-year revival known as the Toronto Blessing.

Within a couple of weeks, up to 1000 people were at the Toronto Airport Vineyard Church each night to attend a service. Dozens of local pastors also attended the services, and they brought the revival back with them to their own churches. As word rapidly spread about what was happening in Toronto, people began flying from other countries to experience the revival; it simultaneously grew as other local churches began seeing similar manifestations—speaking in tongues, "holy laughter," and falling over backward. By the next year, thousands of people were at the Toronto Airport Vineyard Church each night, and the revival became one of the tourism highlights for the city.

John Wimber, who was still leading the Vineyard in the 1990s, tried to guide the Toronto Blessing away from the focus on manifestations and toward sound biblical teaching. Hysterical laughing frequently got in the way of preaching, which, at the Toronto church, had become increasingly light on biblical doctrine and was instead merely circulating stories about the revival. Wimber urged the pastors of churches affected by the revival to bring order to their services so that attendees would still get biblical preaching, but this rarely happened.

Five months into the Toronto Blessing, a Latter-Rain pastor from Vancouver named Gideon Chiu erupted in a lion's roar. Soon, people making animal noises at the meetings became a common occurrence. Then came the gold dust and the gold teeth. People claimed that gold dust fell on them during the revival services or that they would open their Bibles and shake gold dust out of the pages. Some people claimed to have received gold teeth in their mouths, though not a single spontaneous gold tooth was confirmed by a dentist.

Wimber was concerned that the revival was moving away from the heart of God—sound biblical teaching and care for the poor—and into an infatuation with increasingly bizarre manifestations. He made numerous efforts to rein in the focus on manifestations and bring the attention back to Christ, the Bible, and care for the poor, but the train had already left the station.

So in December 1995, nearly two years into the revival, Wimber traveled to Toronto to disaffiliate the church from the Vineyard. The Toronto Airport Vineyard Church became the Toronto Airport Christian Fellowship. The Vineyard had never really been a true denomination, so this change did not necessarily cause a denominational church to become nondenominational—a pattern in the history of Pentecostalism that has created fertile ground for cult leaders. But the church hosting the Toronto Blessing, and the revival itself, lost all accountability when Wimber removed it from the Vineyard.

Not everyone in the Vineyard was pleased with Wimber's decision to disaffiliate the Toronto church, especially not Mike Bickle. In the months after Toronto Airport Vineyard Church became Toronto Airport Christian Fellowship, Bickle requested that the Vineyard make more of an effort to adopt his model of prophesying and praying for the End Times; he had felt that, ever since joining the Vineyard, the move had been only about reining him in, not adopting any of his Latter-Rain theology. Wimber refused to revisit the question of the Toronto Blessing, and in August of 1996, Bickle and his Metro Vineyard Fellowship left the Vineyard. Three years later, as the Toronto Blessing was still running, he and his prophetic associates opened the International House of Prayer. For twenty-four years, it would serve as a cult-like hub of Latter-Rain teachings and narcissistic abuse.

The abuse went far beyond Bickle's grooming of teenagers and young women and Jones' using his spiritual authority to get women to undress for him. There were also numerous reports of alleged predatory behavior by Paul Cain.

Wimber took the abuse seriously and even called the police when specific incidents came to his attention. Ultimately, though, abuse stood at the center of everything that IHOP-KC represented, from the grandiose statements about trips to heaven and encounters with God to claims of faith-healing. This stage persona that the Kansas City Prophets created, of being specially called by God to create an End Times army of Forerunners, empowered them to manipulate and prey upon their followers. Perhaps this culture of abuse was part of the reason why Wimber and Bickle split.

The Toronto Blessing came to an end in 2006. At least that is when the Toronto Airport Christian Fellowship stopped hosting meetings six nights a week, as it had done for twelve years straight. By that time, similar revivals—albeit on a smaller scale—had erupted in churches around the world, such as the Pensacola Revival at the Brownsville Assembly of God, which ran from 1995 until 2000. Additionally, the Latter-Rain preachers who had gathered at Toronto during the years of the revival had begun developing vast networks of churches that submitted to their authority.

One Vineyard pastor who took issue with the disaffiliation of the Toronto church was Che Ahn, who moved his Pasadena, California, church out of the Vineyard to become nondenominational. He wrote in his 2009 book, *When Heaven Comes Down*, "The 1994 revival in Toronto restored the office of the apostle with the birth of many apostolic networks, including John and Carol Arnott's Partners in Harvest, Rick Joyner's MorningStar, Bill Johnson's Global Legacy, Heidi and Rolland Baker's Iris Ministries, and our church's own Harvest International Ministry."[6]

The dominionist leaders that Ahn mentioned as having birthed their ministries out of the Toronto Blessing are just a few of the myriad that had gathered there and networked with each other. Many attended the Toronto Blessing before Wimber disaffiliated the church from the Vineyard and, like Bickle and Ahn, believed that Wimber cut off from the Vineyard the most important move of God since the 1906 Azusa Street Revival. A fair number of these dominionist leaders were already aligned with Latter-Rain theology, making them sympathetic to Bickle's thundering prophetic declarations. When Wimber disaffiliated the Toronto church, these dominionist leaders were left with no accountability as they pressed more deeply into the Latter-Rain ideas of apostles and prophets.

In other words, when Wimber began experimenting with the Latter-Rain ministries of Bickle and his fellow prophets, he opened the floodgates for Latter-Rain leaders to make their home in the Vineyard. They saw the Toronto Blessing differently than he did and, when forced to choose between the Vineyard and the Toronto Blessing, chose the Toronto Blessing. Leaving the Vineyard, these apostles networked with each other in Toronto, turning the church into a hub for implementing, on an international scale, the Latter-Rain ideas of apostles and prophets.

This loose confederation of prophets and apostles who were deeply influenced by Latter-Rain teachings and their experiences at Toronto has been labeled—somewhat contentiously—the New Apostolic Reformation, or NAR. While the NAR term has become somewhat pejorative, what matters here is that these prophets and apostles were able to network together at the Toronto Blessing and share their similar dominionist visions. At the heart of those visions were the End-Times Christians who would be the Manifest Sons of God.

Che Ahn began Harvest International Ministry (HIM) in 1996 and was soon overseeing thousands of churches. John Arnott, the pastor of the Toronto church, formed Catch the Fire Ministries, which is smaller than HIM but likewise oversees thousands of churches. Randy Clark, the faith healer who preached the initial service that catalyzed the revival, formed Global Awakening. It now has its own school of supernatural ministry, where charismatically inclined Christians can learn how to become faith-healing revivalists. Global Awakening also has an unaccredited college and seminary, making it comparable to a denomination in its influence but lacking the accountability that denominations provide.

Perhaps the most well-known of the Toronto-influenced churches is the one that attempted to resurrect two-year-old Olive Heilegenthal before the eyes of the world. Bill Johnson first attended the Toronto Blessing in 1995, the year before he became the senior pastor at Bethel Church. He soon endeavored to replicate the culture that he discovered there by turning Bethel into a global center of revival that relentlessly pursued miracles. Today, thousands of young adults every year attend the Bethel School of Supernatural Ministry, and even more attend Bethel-led conferences in Redding, California, and around the world. In 2005, Bethel Church left the Assemblies of God denomination to pursue its own movement—away from the accountability that denominations provide.

Bethel Church has used its music to influence establishment evangelicalism with Latter-Rain teachings. Two music labels have come out of it, Jesus Culture and Bethel Music, and both have won numerous awards; their songs are used in worship at churches all over the world.

And then Mike Bickle. Unlike leaders such as Che Ahn and Bill Johnson, he never called himself an apostle. And unlike Bethel Church, the International House of Prayer never became the center of an apostolic network. But tens of thousands of young adults have spent six months to ten years or more of their lives at IHOP-KC and brought its Latter-Rain, dominionist teachings to their home churches. And Bickle did more than probably anyone else to bring Latter-Rain teachings into the Vineyard, leading to the transformation that came out of the Toronto Blessing.

◆

A new Toronto-style revival erupted in 2008 in Florida's city of Lakeland. The Lakeland Outpouring, as it came to be known, brought together all of these different elements of apostles and apostolic networks, faith-healing, manifestations of the Holy Spirit, and the central teaching that unites them into a singular theology of dominion: Joel's Army.

"No prophet or apostle who ever lived, equaled the power of these individuals in this great army of the Lord in these last days," Todd Bentley said, quoting from none other than Paul Cain. By all appearances, Bentley was a skinhead—tattooed, burly. He even had a conviction for sexually assaulting a young child back in his teenage years. Yet he had come to Lakeland, Florida, in 2008 for an outpouring of the Holy Spirit in a revival that would be broadcast on Christian stations around the world. "No one else enjoyed the power that is going to rest on this great army."[7]

If there was any question as to what this "great army" referred to, one could simply look at the dog tags that Bentley had tattooed onto his chest. They read, "Joel's Army."

"Joel's Army is the army of God,"[8] he wrote. Only by then, in 2008, this was no longer a fringe idea, relegated to a few iconoclasts who believed that church denominations were the mark that one was a follower of the devil. Bickle's influence had caused this idea to leap out of the small Latter-Rain circles where it had stayed for decades and into the Vineyard—and from there into mainstream evangelical circles. Though Bentley had no formal ministry training and was overwhelmingly rejected by seminary-trained ministers, hundreds of thousands of people traveled from all over the world and braved Florida's oppressive humidity so that they could participate in Bentley's revival during the spring and summer of 2008.

Not that the people who attended the Lakeland Outpouring were radicalized militants bent on being part of Joel's Army. Many were desperate for a miracle that they believed Bentley could provide. "I am a forerunner and one of many who will carry the healing anointing to the nations,"[9] Bentley wrote in 2008, referring to prophecies made by Bickle's disgraced colleague, Bob Jones. Bentley was a faith healer, steeped in Bickle's Latter-Rain theology and ready to share with a hurting world his gift of being able to work miracles. He wrote of his baptism in the Holy Spirit—when he first began to speak in tongues—"I had received not only tongues, but also an enduement of power from on high for miracles, signs, and wonders."[10]

When Bentley went to Lakeland, his intention was not merely to preach. He went there to make cancerous tumors explode in the name of Jesus. "I have prayed for the blind. And we have, right now, documentation of somebody that was blind and can see," he claimed. "I have prayed for people that have been deaf, and God has opened their ears."[11]

Parents brought children with life-threatening birth defects after the doctors had already done all that they could do. In an episode dedicated to the Lakeland Outpouring, ABC *Nightline* featured a father who had traveled across the country with his young daughter, a toddler who had been born with several organs outside of her body. "My daughter needs a miracle,"[12] he said. A teenage boy sought a miraculous healing for spina bifida, which had prevented him from walking without assistance.

The promise of miracles has long been the rocket fuel that has driven otherwise-fringe teachings about Manifest Sons of God and Joel's Army. But are miracles actually occurring? In the case of the Lakeland Outpouring, the answer was no. Though Bentley boasted that he had raised twenty-five people from the dead, investigations found that not a single "miracle" associated with Lakeland had been medically verified; in fact, the revival actually increased the stigma that people with disabilities already faced.

Bentley was a rogue preacher even by the standards of modern-day apostles and prophets. He was not part of a denomination or even of an apostolic network, and he did not claim to be an apostle. So on June 23, two months into the revival, a group of apostles who had come out of the Toronto Blessing—John Arnott, Che Ahn, Bill Johnson, and their leader, C. Peter Wager—gathered in Lakeland for a special service that would bring Bentley into "apostolic alignment." They would ceremonially make him one of their own within their movement, the New Apostolic Reformation.

Not that this ceremony brought Bentley any accountability. The revival abruptly ended in the middle of August when he was hit with yet another scandal. Apparently, the minister, who was already married, was separating from his wife because he was having an affair with one of his staffers. The church hosting the revival attempted to have other revivalists take his place, but the crowds and revival left with Bentley. He had been the main attraction, and now everyone was ready to go home.

But the Lakeland Outpouring had spread the ideas about Joel's Army far and wide. People had come for a miracle, and they left with a radicalizing theology of militancy and warfare. Pastors and laypeople alike took these ideas back to their home churches, where they quietly simmered for the next three years. Then, in August of 2011, Joel's Army would burst onto America's political scene.

4

The Seven Mountain Mandate

"Blow the trumpet in Zion, declare a holy fast, call a sacred assembly,"[1] Texas Governor Rick Perry declared before more than 30,000 evangelical Christians in August 2011. He was quoting from the book of Joel, specifically from the passage that, according to Latter-Rain teachings, describes Joel's Army. Flanking the governor on stage were two apostles, C.L. Jackson and Alice Patterson. Around him, the crowds that filled the stadium were worshipful, reverent, not toward the governor but toward the God that they had come to lift high.

A team of musicians had just led those gathered in a set of worship songs, setting the mood for when the governor would come to the stage. When he took to the podium, the hushed reverence turned into thunderous applause. "Even now, declares the Lord, 'return to me with all your heart with fasting, weeping, and mourning,'" Governor Perry read from Joel 2. "He relents from sending calamity. Who knows? He may turn and relent and leave behind a blessing."[2]

Shouts of "Hallelujah!" and "Amen!" reverberated across the stadium in response to an appeal directed not toward Washington, DC, but rather the courts of heaven.

A generation before, Jerry Falwell and a cohort of high-powered religious and political leaders had organized conservative Christians into a powerful voting bloc known as the Religious Right. The mission was simple: America had been overrun by feminists, environmentalists, nuclear peaceniks, and welfare advocates; Christians had to take their country back for God. But despite their decades of campaigning and near-religious presence at voting booths, they had made no meaningful legislative gains. Abortion remained legal at a federal level, queer individuals were progressing in civil rights, and increasingly greater numbers of women were building careers and holding positions of power. Engaging the country's democratic processes to try to enact a conservative Christian agenda in American government, as Falwell had spurred his movement to do, was proving to be insufficient.

But ever since the turn of the millennium, a previously unknown form of Christian nationalism had been gaining traction: dominionism. John McCain picked Sarah Palin as his running mate in the 2008 presidential election, not knowing that she was from a New Apostolic Reformation (NAR) church and had long promoted dominionist ideals in local and state government in Alaska. During the election cycle, the mainstream media picked up on this movement that was much more extreme than what Falwell had promoted from the 1970s until his death in 2007. What the media did not grasp was just how widespread dominionism already was, well before McCain introduced Palin to a national audience. Few realized that Todd Bentley's revival in Lakeland, which also occurred during 2008, was cut from the same cloth as Palin's far-right populism.

In fact, few evangelicals recognized the difference between the conservative activism that they had long championed and the agenda that apostles and prophets, including Mike Bickle, were now bringing to the center of the evangelical social conscience. Many of the evangelicals gathered at Governor Perry's prayer rally, and perhaps even Perry himself, had never heard of Joel's Army.

But partnering with the International House of Prayer, the apostle Lou Engle, and American Family Radio, Governor Perry had called for a massive gathering called The Response by announcing, "On August 6 of this year, 2011, we are going to have a day of prayer and fasting. And it's going to be the real deal... It's going to be people standing on that stage, projecting and proclaiming Jesus Christ as our Lord and Savior at Reliant Stadium in Houston." And when he took to the stage at The Response, surrounded by apostles who were leading the event, he read from the passage about Joel's Army.

"The NAR is definitely not a cult,"[3] wrote a retired professor from Fuller Seminary a few days after The Response. Mainstream news media had picked up on Governor Perry's rally and raised alarm at what seemed to be a blatant rejection of the separation of church and state. One show, *Fresh Air* on National Public Radio (NPR), aired a broadcast about the NAR's connection to The Response and highlighted the role of C. Peter Wagner. Wagner (1930–2016) had spent decades teaching at Fuller Seminary, a respectable evangelical institution in Los Angeles. Yet he was fond of referring to the school as "Fuller Cemetery" for its insistence on tradition and rejection of charismatic practices.

Fuller Seminary was a place for middle-of-the-road evangelicals, but Wagner was anything except middle of the road. He and his wife had spent sixteen years in Bolivia as missionaries before moving to Los Angeles, where Wagner would begin thirty years as a church-growth specialist at Fuller. To use a term that would emerge in Silicon Valley decades later, Wagner was more of a growth hacker than someone who promoted conventional methods for pastors to expand their congregations. "Structures that were originally developed to facilitate evangelism, Christian nurture, worship, social service and ministry in general"—in other words, long-standing means for building and growing churches—"are now considered by some as the *causes* of much inefficiency and ineffectiveness in these same areas," he wrote in 1999.[4]

Since at least the 1980s, Wagner had been toying with Latter-Rain ideas about apostles and prophets overseeing church governance, rather than bureaucratic denominations from above and democratic congregations from below. But he was no mere theoretician who liked ideas for the sake of ideas, nor was he a theologian who understood historical Christian teachings. He was a social scientist, and a very pragmatic one at that. He wanted ideas that could generate results, in this case, new ways of organizing churches so that they could grow rapidly.

What Wagner saw on a practical level, from sixteen years as a missionary and then thirty years as a church-growth specialist, was that the fastest-growing churches in the world were Pentecostal-charismatic ones governed by apostles. He dubbed this movement of apostle-led churches the NAR, indicating that he was envisioning something beyond a few outlier churches that applied Latter-Rain ideas. What he spent the rest of his life working toward was the complete reorganization of global Christendom, away from denominations and other structures that have historically provided accountability and prevented (some, albeit not all) abuses of authority, toward singularly gifted men and women who could hear directly from God and funnel God's blessings down from heaven and onto their followers.

Yet NAR politics went far beyond the governance of Latter-Rain, charismatic churches. Wagner spent the last decade of his life promoting an idea known as the Seven Mountain Mandate (7MM), which would bring this model of church governance to every other sphere of society. And the 7MM is what led NAR leaders, including Mike Bickle, to organize a prayer rally for Governor Rick Perry.

The 7MM is the NAR's plan for taking dominion over all of society. According to the 7MM, there are seven "mountains" of culture: family, religion, education, the arts, media and entertainment, business, and government. The church has historically focused only on the religion mountain by building and growing churches, causing the church to become isolated from the surrounding culture. The time has come for Christians to ascend to the tops of the six other mountains and claim them for the kingdom of God.

What became the 7MM began in the 1970s with two renegade evangelicals, Loren Cunningham and Bill Bright. Bright launched Campus Crusade for Christ in the early 1950s and, in 1979, produced the highly influential movie *The Jesus Film*. Cunningham started Youth with a Mission (YWAM) in 1960; YWAM has since become one of the largest missionary-sending organizations in world history. Both men were focusing their efforts on young adults—evangelical youth who had recently left home, as well as their peers who had never been to church nor had a personal encounter with God. Within one year, Campus Crusade had 250 members, not at an evangelical school such as Wheaton College or Bob Jones University, but at the University of California at Los Angeles. Campus Crusade rapidly grew across the country, primarily at secular colleges and universities, and soon thousands of young adults were converting to evangelicalism every year. In turn, the successes of Campus

Crusade fueled the aims of YWAM, as Cunningham used his organization to send out college-aged missionaries to countries all over the world.

Bright and Cunningham saw that, while they were bringing large numbers of young people into Christian circles, the mainstream culture that they lived in was filthy, contaminated by drugs and the sexual revolution. University professors taught that there is no God, while movies exalted sexual promiscuity and even glorified Satan. Bright bemoaned that he had to teach young adults what sin is because their professors insisted there is no such thing as right and wrong. Churches were being weakened as evangelicals left the evangelical subculture; as numbers dwindled and finances grew tight, Cunningham's young missionaries struggled to get funding for their overseas endeavors. Plenty of revivalists had sought to reinvigorate churches and increase the membership rolls, but Bright and Cunningham envisioned a different solution: No longer were evangelicals to avoid secular culture; they were to transform it. Meeting in 1975, they shared with each other that God had called them to equip young evangelicals to attain influence and authority over the "Seven Spheres" of culture. Cunningham referred to these spheres as "mind molders," and Bright called them "world kingdoms." Through the strategizing of NAR apostle Lance Wallnau in the early 2000s, their vision of training young leaders to take over the Seven Spheres eventually became known as the 7MM. Through fulfilling the 7MM, evangelicals could once again be the dominant cultural force in America—and with the ongoing success of YWAM, export that cultural power across the world.

Granted, Cunningham and Bright were not representative of evangelicalism when they began developing Campus Crusade, YWAM, and what became the 7MM. Cunningham was a Pentecostal, and many evangelicals—especially fundamentalists—looked down on Pentecostals for the practice of speaking in tongues. Even within his Assemblies of God denomination, Cunningham was considered a renegade for holding controversial beliefs and sending untrained, inexperienced young people to other countries. Bright had dropped out of Princeton Seminary and Fuller Seminary and was criticized by other evangelical institutions, including InterVarsity Christian Fellowship, which already had thriving ministries on college and university campuses. But what

Cunningham and Bright lacked in theological training and accountability, they made up for in fervor as they recruited thousands of young people into their organizations every year. Though it did not promote dominionist aims, Bright's 1979 *The Jesus Film* would set a Guinness world record for being the most-translated movie in history, as missionaries across the world showed it to audiences in every country. In turn, Campus Crusade and *The Jesus Film* made the seminary dropout a fixture of American evangelicalism.

◆

"In taking dominion," Wagner told Terry Gross, the host of NPR's *Fresh Air*, "our goal is to have as many kingdom-minded believers in positions of influence in the arts and entertainment mountain as possible."[5] He was trying to address what he saw as an unflattering depiction of the NAR on her show immediately after Governor Perry's The Response, but many listeners felt greater alarm at hearing this agenda from the NAR's chief protagonist. In this example, he used the arts and entertainment mountain, which may seem innocuous enough; The Response, however, was about apostles and prophets taking over the mountain of government.

Granted, the 7MM claim that the church has been ignoring the rest of culture is not entirely accurate. Catholics, in America and beyond, have a deep history of, and theological mandate for, engaging in social issues. Both evangelicals and mainline Protestants have long been deeply involved in social issues, including abolition in the nineteenth century, civil rights in the twentieth, and climate change in the twenty-first. And when the Religious Right burst onto the scene in the late 1970s and early 1980s, conservative evangelicals began making a concerted effort to place antiabortion, pro-capitalism, pro-Israel politicians in power. What makes this social and political action different from the 7MM is that it has consisted mostly of local, grassroots efforts alongside engaging the church's and the country's democratic processes.

The 7MM, on the other hand, took root in a movement that espouses apostles, not democracy, and top-down authority, not local action. Wagner emphasized the role of *workplace apostles*, individuals profoundly gifted by God to take control of each of the seven mountains. Church apostles were already beginning to lead the mountain of religion, but workplace apostles were also needed to take over the mountains of family, religion, education, the arts, media and entertainment, business, and government. They were to take *all* mountains of culture and transform them, with workplace apostles at the top getting directives from heaven. Lance Wallnau, an apostle and chief propagator of the 7MM, refers to the leaders of each of the mountains as kings. Not presidents, not representatives, but kings. "He who can take these mountains can take the harvest of nations."[6]

Some have suggested that the 7MM is merely about Christians gaining influence in culture outside of the church. However, from the time that Wallnau began developing the idea in the early 2000s and Wagner brought it into his NAR paradigm, the 7MM has been about something much more than influence. "Reformation from the top down is what has to happen in order to see a historic change in nations," Wallnau wrote in 2020. He then quoted the last words that Jesus gave to his disciples, as recorded in Matthew 28:19–20: *Go therefore and make disciples of all the nations, baptizing them in the name of the Father and of the Son and of the Holy Spirit, teaching them to observe all things that I have commanded you* [NKJV]. Wallnau went on to say how Christians can fulfill this high calling, "That cultural change comes from the top down and rarely, if ever, from the bottom up."[7] Though the gospels record Jesus seeking out the poor and outcast of society, Wallnau's 7MM model calls upon Christians to take control of government, education, media, business, family life, and the arts. The 7MM is about power that can be wielded—not influence, not service, not caring for those that society has rejected.

Bringing this apostolic model out of Latter-Rain churches and to civil government, as 7MM promoters such as Wallnau and Wagner have said is their goal, means government officials do not operate in a democratic capacity but rather as apostles who receive their authority from heaven. In other words, when NAR leaders endorse candidates for public office, they do not do so because they see that individual as a worthy *politician*. Rather, they see that person as capable of fulfilling the role of the apostle, not on the mountain of the church, but rather on the mountain of government. So-called workplace apostles—not politicians, not economists, not educators, not pastors—are to hold transformative authority over society by being placed at the top of each of the Seven Mountains.

At its core, the 7MM is a blueprint for taking theocratic control over society. Though Wagner balked at the idea that placing workplace apostles over American government would lead to theocracy, that would very much be the practical outcome of the program he and Wallnau advocated. Democracy cannot survive when "kingdom-minded" Christians are holding all of the levers of power, especially when they are led by apostles who claim to hear directly from God. But at a deeper level, the 7MM proposes a radical restructuring of America's political systems, such that the Seven Mountains no longer promote inclusive values and minority rights but rather reflect the values and power-wielding ambitions of dominionist churches. In this paradigm, democracy is no longer necessary because America is ruled by King Jesus through governing apostles—starting with Sarah Palin, Rick Perry, and moving on to Donald Trump. The 7MM is not about engaging democracy, as was Falwell's idea when he organized the Religious Right in the late 1970s and early 1980s. The 7MM is about ending democracy.

Governor Perry may not have held to this reasoning when he announced that an event called The Response would occur in August 2011. He may not have realized that the people who organized his prayer rally used the same text that he quoted from—Joel 2—to describe an End-Times army of militant Christians who will pray God's wrath out of heaven.

But the prophets and apostles who had been surrounding him did. They needed a king to take the mountain of government. And he gave the apostles and prophets a unique entrée into the world of political power when he partnered with them to organize his prayer rally.

In the weeks and months before The Response, Governor Perry had become increasingly comfortable with using biblical language to describe the moral state of America, as well as the judgment of God—earthquakes, financial collapse, terrorism—that would come if the country refused to repent. "As a nation, we must come together and call upon Jesus to guide us through unprecedented struggles,"[8] read a statement on his website. These kinds of statements are almost standard fare for the pastors and pundits of the Religious Right and could have come from the likes of Lance Wallnau, Mike Bickle, or even Jerry Falwell. But ... they came from the Texas governor, an elected official who is duty-bound to uphold a constitution that prohibits any kind of discrimination on the basis of religion. Three years prior, in 2008, he had published an autobiography, *On My Honor*, in which he wrote that the government should not privilege one faith over another and even suggested that the public square is a place for all faiths. Yet something changed in the years since the election of Barack Obama and the rise of the Tea Party, so much so that in June of 2011, he declared that August 6 would be a day of fasting and prayer at the event that would be The Response.

The Response was part megachurch service, part political rally, and part Billy Graham-style crusade. Evangelicals had traveled from across the country to participate in what they believed to be a concerted effort to turn America back to God—a regular occurrence in the world of evangelical populism. And the idea of filling up a stadium to pray for national repentance was nothing new, although such an event certainly provided high levels of expectation and excitement. Young musicians led the massive crowd in high-energy worship songs, as if to signal that the Christians gathered in Houston were there only to love Jesus, not to promote any kind of political agenda—especially not the upending of American democracy. At least The Response was marketed that way. The governor attempted to frame the event as nonpolitical, but it was replete with dominionist ideals.

Apostle Lou Engle, who was associated with IHOP-KC and whose organization, The Call, organized the event, had written earlier that year, "There are moments in history when a door for massive change opens, and great revolutions for good or evil spring up in the vacuum created by these openings." One such opening had been created in the sixties, when—according to Engle—hippie culture had brought drugs, the sexual revolution, and the Gay Rights Movement to the young people of America. This alleged revolution for evil had spiritually crippled the nation, but now a new vacuum was being opened that Christians could seize. Engle went on, "In these divine moments, key men and women and even entire generations risk everything to become the hinge of history, the pivotal point that determines which way the door will swing."[9] Despite Governor Perry's effort to brand The Response as a nonpolitical prayer rally, Engle had been at the forefront of an effort that veered from the Christian nationalism of Falwell into something that was blatantly theocratic. In other words, The Response represented a shift in evangelical activism, away from the old guard of the Religious Right and to a new model built on apostles seeking to implement the 7MM, specifically on the mountain of government.

"God is raising up an alternate government in the earth," Engle wrote.[10] Claiming that the country is in the grip of a demonic spirit, he said, "No more tolerance and no more compromise! … Enough of laws that remove God and the prophetic voice of the Church from the public arena!" Then, to ignite a radical fervor in those reading his words, "We will not run, we will not give in, we will not quit until all the altars to Baal [an ancient pagan deity that Engle believes is being worshipped in America] are removed from our land!"[1] While he did not preach this overtly theocratic message to the tens of thousands of Christians gathered at The Response, he may not have needed to. The apostle's books were being read by evangelicals across the country, and he had the ear of a growing number of politicians that now included a governor who, one week later, would announce his candidacy for president of the United States.

Though Governor Perry started his campaign for the 2012 Republican nomination for president with strong evangelical backing, having the support of dominionist leaders who could draw massive crowds to their political-not-political rallies was not enough. He flubbed in televised debates with other candidates, on one occasion so severely that a reporter wondered if he had suffered a stroke. But perhaps even more significantly, his shift toward dominionist politics came late in his political career, after he was already serving as the governor of Texas and had entrenched views; while he was willing to work with dominionist apostles to raise his political profile, his policies did not match. Governor Perry supported using public funds to educate the children of illegal immigrants and claimed that people who opposed this stance lacked compassion. He may have been standing on firm biblical ground here—the Old Testament is replete with calls to care for the foreigner who lives among you—but he was not dominionist enough. He was not an autocrat, and he was not a workplace apostle, whether or not dominionist apostles tried to make him one of their own. He was a democratically elected conservative politician who espoused Christian values and wanted to become president.

Dominionists had not found their man in time for the 2012 election. But they would find him in time for the next one, and their model of church governance—virtually unlimited authority held by an apostle, who is accountable to no one except God—would merge easily with the autocratic posture of Donald Trump.

Part Two

Building a Kingdom

5

The Columbine Martyrs

"He came into the library and shot everybody around me," a terrified girl told a news reporter. "Then he put a gun to my head and asked if we all wanted to die."

"We ran into houses, wherever we could go, any houses we could find," said another.

"You hear a shot, and a loud bang, and then we hear some guy go, 'Holy crap! There's a guy with a gun!'"

"People were getting shot all around me."

On April 20, 1999, tens of millions of Americans froze as they watched footage of students running out of Columbine High School. One iconic scene showed a line of students with their hands behind their heads—confirming that none had a weapon—rushing past an ambulance. Other news clips showed paramedics loading gurneys into ambulances, some with students bleeding from multiple gunshot wounds. But what news cameras captured outside the school could not bear witness to the carnage that lay inside. A total of fifteen people had died in what was, up until that time, the worst shooting at a K-12 school in American history.

SWAT teams stormed inside what had become a veritable war zone while reporters interviewed students who had fled. They had been sitting in class, eating lunch, or studying in the library when explosions started going off. Some thought the pops were nothing more than a senior prank, but the pipe bombs that the shooters lobbed at their peers and the guns that they pointed at students' heads were all too real.

Parents were reunited with their children at nearby Leawood Elementary School, but not all of the Columbine students got out alive. Mothers and fathers whose children were still missing kept hearing that another bus of students was coming, but despite their most heartfelt desires, the bereaved parents soon realized that there were no more buses. For now, their children were missing.

Columbine High School sits outside of Littleton, Colorado, in an unincorporated area of Jefferson County. Though part of Greater Denver, the area around Littleton seemed immune to the violent crime that plagued parts of the bigger city. Residents saw Littleton as one of the safest places in the country to raise children, and the culture at Columbine was overwhelmingly evangelical. In fact, just an hour's drive from Littleton is the evangelical mecca of Colorado Springs, home to international ministries that include Focus on the Family, Navigators, Young Life, Integrity Music, the Association of Christian Schools International, and Biblica.

C. Peter Wagner had also moved to Colorado Springs in 1996 to join a growing retinue of prophets and apostles in what was to become the NAR. One of these apostles was none other than Dutch Sheets, who had a personal connection to the tragedy that occurred at Columbine.

Rachel Scott's family was among the thirteen awaiting the news that they dreaded most. In the hours before the phone call came, Sheets went to Rachel's home and sat with her family. Her brother, Craig, had been in the library when the shooters came in. They shot his best friend, Matt Kechter, who had been hiding with him under the table, and called his other friend, Isaiah Shoels, a racial slur before shooting him in the head. Craig had lain in his friends' blood, pretending to be dead, until the shooters left the library. He then led the surviving students to safety, risking his own life by going back to help an injured girl. What he had survived is, by some measures, worse than live combat. And now, he did not know where his sister was.

So Dutch Sheets sat with the family, with Craig, with Rachel's parents and stepparents, her three other siblings who had not been present at Columbine High School that day. Away from the news cameras and reporters who were interviewing anyone willing to talk, they waited for the phone call that they knew would come.

And Americans all across the country asked,

How could this have happened?

In the immediate aftermath, a story began spreading that would answer this question for millions of evangelicals. In the library, where the worst of the carnage occurred, one of the gunmen asked a girl if she believed in God. She was identified as seventeen-year-old Cassie Bernall, who had been studying Shakespeare when the gunmen came in. In a story that has since become mythology, she was praying when her killer pointed his gun at her temple and asked the fateful question. She answered yes, firmly, powerfully, knowing that she would give her life for this answer.

Except that is not what actually occurred. According to the eyewitness who hid under the table with her, Cassie was not praying but crying and whispering that she wanted to go home. And the gunman did not ask her anything; instead, he banged on the table and said, "Peek-a-boo," before killing her. There was another girl, Valeen Schnurr, who was on the other side of the library. She was praying, "Oh my God, oh my God, please don't let me die," when the other gunman asked her if she believes in God. She said yes, and the gunman turned and left, sparing her life. Valeen said yes and lived. Cassie, glorified as a martyr for her bold faith at gunpoint, was not asked anything.

Still, the mythology around Cassie fed into a bigger cultural story that had been taking shape for decades. And her martyr's death gave a simplistic, and altogether incorrect, answer as to why the Columbine shooting occurred: the killers had gone into the school that day to hunt and kill Christians.

As the civil rights movement coalesced in the 1950s, the young firebrand Jerry Falwell was galvanizing a backlash against it. The 1954 Supreme Court decision in *Brown v. Board of Education* ruled that school segregation was inherently unequal and began the difficult process of integrating America's schools. Fearing that this would expose white Christian children to drugs, sex, and rock and roll, Falwell served as the chaplain to an organization that aimed to close down Virginia's public schools rather than have them integrate. When this effort failed, he opened a segregation academy, a church-run private school that only offered admission to white children. The church that sponsored the school, Thomas Road Baptist, would become ground zero for Falwell's organizing of conservative evangelicals into the Religious Right.

Two Supreme Court decisions that came down in the 1960s became the focus of his sermons as he began building the Religious Right in the 1970s. *Engel v. Vitale*, ruled in 1962, said that schools cannot hold prayers, as this practice violated the First Amendment's separation of church and state. *Abington School District v. Schempp*, ruled in 1963, said that schools cannot encourage Bible-reading or recitation of the Lord's Prayer. These rulings meant that public schools no longer privileged Christianity—or religion at all, for that matter. Combined with the integration of public schools, the new status quo could only mean, according to Falwell, that (white) Christian students would soon be persecuted for their faith.

In other words, American society was secularizing, beginning with public schools. Religion, and especially Christianity, no longer dictated the norms of social order. And to segregationists such as Falwell, the perils of Black culture encroaching into historically white spaces meant that drugs, sex, and rock and roll would become the new standard by which morality would be determined. The only possible outcome would be social breakdown—communism, anarchy, and teenage boys bringing guns, propane bombs, and pipe bombs into a mostly white, suburban school in one of America's evangelical strongholds so they could kill Christian students.

Though Falwell's views were embedded in a reaction to *Brown v. Board of Education*, he was able to pitch a big enough tent that a fair number of African American pastors participated in his Moral Majority; they, too, were concerned about the decline of religion in public life and what this meant for the moral standards of the communities that they served. And conservative evangelicals began to covet the power that they would need to restore the status quo—if not to resegregate public schools, then to at least have the *Abington* and *Engel* Supreme Court cases overturned.

They would take America back for God.

Not by implementing the Seven Mountain Mandate—this would come a generation later—but by engaging America's political processes. They would come together and democratically elect politicians who represented their interests. Gradually, the tide would turn until a conservative president could nominate justices to the Supreme Court who would support the return of prayer and Bible-reading in public schools.

Two decades after Falwell founded the Moral Majority, on May 27, 1999, Rachel Scott's father, Darrell, testified before a subcommittee of US Congress about his daughter's murder. The seventeen-year-old had been the sweetheart of Columbine's junior class and an unfailingly kind friend, loved by those around her for her gracious spirit. And she became the first victim of the Columbine shooting when one of the boys that she had tried to befriend shot her in the head. On this somber day on Capitol Hill, her father recited a poem that reflected on what he saw as the cause of her murder.

Your laws ignore our deepest needs
Your words are empty air
You've stripped away our heritage
You've outlawed simple prayer
Now gunshots fill our classrooms
And precious children die
You seek for answers everywhere
And ask the question, Why?
You regulate restrictive laws
Through legislative creed
And yet you fail to understand
That God is what we need.[1]

In his testimony, Scott placed the blame for the Columbine tragedy not on how easily the shooters were able to access guns, but on the waning role of religion in public life. The bereaved father claimed, "Spiritual influences were present within our educational systems for most of our nation's history. Many of our major colleges began as theological seminaries." He then bemoaned, "What has happened to us as a nation? We have refused to honor God, and in so doing, we open the doors to hatred and violence."

To Scott, as with Falwell and the millions of conservative evangelicals he led, America's declining spirituality was the cause of Rachel's murder. "And when something as terrible as Columbine's tragedy occurs, politicians immediately look for a scapegoat such as the NRA. They immediately seek to pass more restrictive laws that contribute to erode away our personal and private liberties." But these laws, which include the *Abington* and *Engle* Supreme Court decisions, as well as gun-safety laws, could not have prevented the shooting; in fact, according to Scott, they had *caused* it by replacing Christianity with secularism as the guiding force in America's public schools.

But Columbine had been a turning point. It had brought prayer back into public schools. "As my son Craig lay under that table in the school library and saw his two friends murdered before his very eyes, he did not hesitate to pray in school. I defy any law or politician to deny him that right!"[2]

The solution to the violence that had overtaken his children's high school that day was not gun-safety legislation but rather a repeal of the Supreme Court decisions that had formally secularized America's public schools. Prayer and Bible-reading had to become the order of the day again.

Scott was under no delusion that Congress would introduce legislation that privileged Christianity in public life, or that the Supreme Court would overturn the *Abington* and/or *Engel* decisions. Instead, he called on the youth of America to rise up and reclaim their schools—and their nation—for God.

> The young people of our nation hold the key. There is a spiritual awakening taking place that will not be squelched … I challenge every young person in America, and around the world, to realize that on April 20, 1999, at Columbine High School, prayer was brought back to our schools. Do not let the many prayers offered by those students be in vain.

Scott's message was heard far beyond his congressional testimony, in no small part because Dutch Sheets had sat with him while he waited for the call saying his child had died.

What would soon come is a more radicalized engagement between conservative evangelicals and right-wing politics, with Sheets leading the charge from Columbine to the Capitol Riot.

◆

Meanwhile, the story of Cassie's declaration of faith in God at gunpoint was changing youth culture all across America. Just three days after the Columbine shooting, Ron Luce's multi-million-dollar ministry, Teen Mania, held an Acquire the Fire youth conference outside of Detroit, Michigan, from April 23 to 24, 1999. He had not planned for such a tragedy to rattle the kids who would be present at the conference; the timing was purely coincidental. Still, upwards of 70,000 teenagers and young adults gathered to experience Teen Mania's pyrotechnics, high-powered worship songs, and all-star lineup of speakers. And there, everyone gathered learned about Cassie, how they should have a faith like hers, a faith that is stronger than even the fear of death.

Over the next few years, musicians wrote songs about Cassie. Michael W. Smith, one of the most-recognized Christian musicians of the 1990s and 2000s, wrote a song called "This Is Your Time." The music video to it begins with a clip of Cassie, recorded on an amateur camera, declaring that she would be willing to die for her faith in God. Rebecca St. James, another star in the world of contemporary Christian music, recorded "Yes, I Believe in God" to express her desire for a faith like Cassie's. Another group, The Kry, recorded "Cassie's Song."

Cassie's story did not merely fill the airwaves of Christian radio; it also filled Christian bookstores. Luce wrote *Columbine Courage* to urge Christian teenagers to defy laws preventing them from organizing prayer and Bible-reading in public schools. The band dcTalk, which had managed to break out of the confines of Christian music when its 1995 hit song "Jesus Freak" was played on secular radio stations, composed a book called *Jesus Freaks* to tell the stories of martyrs throughout Christian history. *Jesus Freaks* reads like a modern version of the sixteenth-century classic *Foxe's Book of Martyrs* and opened the fraught world of martyrdom to an entire generation of teenagers. The first story in the book tells of a seventeen-year-old girl who was in the school library when she was shot and killed for her faith. Though Cassie's name is not used directly, there was no question about who the writers were referring to.

By the fall of 1999, the story broke about how Cassie had actually not been asked anything by her killer before he shot her in the head. The Jefferson County Police Department and local newspapers had been sitting on the story for months, but they were hesitant to publish it because of how meaningful this version of events was to Cassie's family. Her parents, grandparents, brother, aunts, uncles, and cousins had not gained a cultural icon; they had lost a vivacious young woman with a penchant for adventure and dreams of attending the University of Oxford. The story of her courage and faith gave them something to hold onto; why rob them of this salve? Yet the story finally was published, as those right next to Cassie when she died cried for the true version of events to come out and people across America demanded answers about what had happened in the library.

Still, the myth of Cassie's martyrdom remained a cultural phenomenon as a memoir published by her mother, entitled *She Said Yes*, surged into the top ten of the *New York Times* bestseller lists. But the message that Misty Bernall brought to her readers was different than the martyr hysteria that had come to grip so much of America. While much of the rest of the country was celebrating Cassie's death and using it to find meaning in the face of the Columbine shooting, Misty was having to bury her only daughter and then sit at her gravesite so that, even in death, Cassie would not be alone.

Christian teenagers all across America fantasized about dying as martyrs. Misty, on the other hand, pleaded with parents and caregivers to spend time with the children whom they love and recognize the warning signs before a child becomes a killer, like the one who took Cassie's life. While she cherished the songs and books written to celebrate Cassie's bravery, she did not want her daughter to become a totem for a new cult of martyrdom. She wanted her child back. And she wanted the violence to end.

With time, Cassie's story faded, not into oblivion but more into the collective memory of how people came to talk about and somehow find meaning in the Columbine shooting. And another false claim of martyrdom would soon rise to prominence: the NAR's story of Rachel Scott.

◆

"The blood of these martyrs cries from the ground, 'Revival to this generation!'" Dutch Sheets wrote in a book released the year after the shooting. "The same ears that heard the blood-cry of righteous Abel hear those of righteous Cassie and Rachel. The fire of the torches they carried is spreading to other torches across this land." He went on to say something that reflected what his NAR colleagues in and around Colorado Springs were already galvanizing: "Once again, the blood of the martyrs will be the seeds of revival."[3]

There was no evidence—ever—that Rachel had died a martyr's death. Cassie's martyr story can be attributed to a mistaken identity: there was a girl in the library who said yes, and she lived to tell about it. In Rachel's case, however, there was only one eyewitness to her murder, a friend named Richard. He was the only person who could attest as to whether or not she had been asked about her faith in God before being shot in the head, but he was still in a coma from his own gunshot wounds when the story of her martyrdom began circulating.

Rachel's family attended a NAR church, led by a pastor named Bruce Porter. In a book entitled *The Martyr's Torch*, as well as on his website, Porter shared emails that he had exchanged with other local pastors, presumably those in the NAR networks that saturated the area around Colorado Springs and Denver. "Precious in the eyes of the Lord is the blood of His martyrs,"[4] read an email that he sent in the early morning hours of Saturday, April 24, 1999. Rachel's funeral would be held later on that day, with the entire country watching as CNN broadcast it with no interruptions.

"Rachel carried a torch that was stained by the blood of the martyrs from the very first day of the Church's existence in the world nearly 2000 years ago," Porter declared to the 2000 people gathered to celebrate Rachel's life and the televised audience across the country grappling with the Columbine shooting. "This warrior has now dropped that torch … Who will pick up the torch again?"[5]

The story of Rachel's martyrdom was slow to catch on nationally, despite Porter's televised statements. But one NAR leader, Lou Engle, latched onto it and turned it into the impetus for a gathering that would eerily foreshadow the Capitol Riot two decades later.

◆

"Out of Columbine, a massive gathering of kids would come to Washington, DC to pray and to fast and would change history," Engle declared on September 2, 2000. "I want you to lift your hands and begin to pray that martyrs' blood would begin to bring a revival to the youth of America." Behind him loomed the US Capitol. In front of him, as many as 400,000 young adults, teenagers, and their parents had answered his call for concerned evangelicals to gather and lift their voices to heaven. They would be heard, not only by God but also by the politicians who lined the halls of power just over on Capitol Hill.

"Lift your voices and begin to pray," he continued. "Father, remember Cassie. Remember Rachel, the ones that are still wounded ... Let this be the shot that was heard around the world for a new Jesus revolution, we pray." The throng of evangelicals had gathered in memory of the Columbine martyrs, recognizing that their deaths created a mandate for political change. In many ways, The Call DC looked like a political rally. Thirty-seven years before, hundreds of thousands had gathered in this same place, the National Mall, in an event known as the March on Washington, at which Martin Luther King, Jr., had delivered his famous "I Have a Dream" speech. A few years later came a similarly sized event, a protest against the Vietnam War. And there was no disguising that The Call DC was also a political rally, one that put the evangelical agenda in front of politicians in ways that Falwell could have only dreamed of.

"Father, your Word says that you would come, and you would turn the hearts of the fathers to the children and the children to the fathers so powerfully they could break the curse off of a nation."[6] Not that the nearly half a million evangelicals gathered understood who Engle was or knew anything about his fellow prophets and apostles, including his partner Dutch Sheets. The Call DC was the first major public foray that the NAR made, not only into political life but also into mainstream evangelicalism.

Up until then, evangelicals had largely rejected Pentecostalism—or had at least tried to. Their churches had been transformed by the Jesus Movement, and they welcomed in bits and pieces of Pentecostal theology by singing songs from the Vineyard and Calvary Chapel. Evangelical parents sent their kids to Teen Mania events, not fully understanding that Teen Mania was born right out of Pentecostalism. The Toronto Blessing and the revivals that erupted out of it were largely disparaged by the leadership of Southern Baptists, Methodists,

Lutherans, and other evangelical denominations—even while laypeople flocked to the revivals. Now, however, nearly half a million evangelicals had traveled all across the country and flooded the National Mall for a worship rally with a deep political bent that was led by some of the most extreme leaders in Pentecostalism's history. What had brought them here was not theology. It was the call to action created by the story of the Columbine martyrs.

On stage that day were dozens of members of the Columbine community, including the family of Rachel Scott. And the appeal that her father had made to a congressional subcommittee a month after her murder was echoed in the speeches made by the apostles and prophets who partnered with Engle in leading the event. Conservative Christian values—especially prayer and Bible-reading in public schools and the end of abortion—had to become normative in American public life in order to prevent the next Columbine.

In fact, the whole purpose of The Call was to raise up Joel's Army. Engle wrote the next year, "The Call is a massive solemn assembly of two generations … It is a response to the prophet Joel's resounding summons: 'Even now', declares the Lord, 'return to me with all your heart, with fasting and weeping and mourning.'"[7] Eleven years later, Rick Perry would partner with Engle to host a spin-off of The Call—The Response. And there, he would quote from the exact same passage in the book of Joel.

And the prophets and apostles there were prepared to enact political change on a level far surpassing Falwell's ambitions; they saw the gathering as having an effect on America's government structures, even though no legislation was passed as a result of The Call DC. The apostle Che Ahn wrote of the event, "Later, when the presidential election made history with its bizarre circumstances and final victory for President Bush, I felt assured that the prayer and fasting of those youth had made a real difference in the electoral outcome."[8]

The Call DC was not an aberration. It was a new way of doing evangelical politics. And many of the same leaders who were present that day, as well as others who were not present but still connected to Lou Engle, were part of the chaos that led up to the Capitol Riot two decades later.

But first, they had to figure out a way to make the NAR project work in politics. America was not prepared for this kind of extremism and was a decade away from welcoming the far-right populism that would bring Trump to power. Engle had to take The Call somewhere else to figure out how prophets and apostles can work with elected politicians in ways that can turn the NAR agenda into civil law.

6

Demons on the Map

Throughout the 1990s, before the Seven Mountain Mandate became the political theology for the NAR, C. Peter Wagner was building networks of prophets and apostles who were focused on prayer. Not prayer in a more conventional understanding—communing with God, petitioning for divine intervention in areas such as sickness and finance, or meditating on God's goodness. When Wagner referred to prayer, especially as he increasingly promoted Latter-Rain teachings, he usually meant one thing: spiritual warfare. Prayer was more than a conversation with God; it was a weapon to be wielded against the forces of darkness—demons and even the devil himself.

"The Master found a demon-possessed nation," Frank Sandford had written sixty years earlier. "He proceeded to break the bands [of possession] personally and then sent forth others equipped to free men—to continue and to carry on the work of liberation."[1] An entire nation in the grips of demonic possession is how Sandford viewed Judea at the time of Christ, this explanation revealing why so many demonized people came to Christ for physical and spiritual healing. Wagner had a term for dealing with entire nations in demonic bondage: *strategic-level spiritual warfare*. And Sandford provided the key for strategic-level spiritual warfare when he wrote, "It was not 'the prayer of faith' but the *command of faith* that was needed."[2] When Jesus and his earliest apostles encountered people who were ill, they knew that a demonic spirit was involved and that their response had to be to command the demon to leave. And when an entire nation was being tormented, a bigger strategy was needed.

In 1997, a team of about two dozen prayer warriors from Wagner's networks undertook one of the most arduous journeys on the planet: the ascent of Mount

Everest. Their intent was to engage in spiritual warfare against the Queen of Heaven, whom Wagner claimed was one of the most high-ranking demonic rulers on the planet. She was keeping a massive region that he referred to as the 10/40 Window—the area between 10 degrees north and 40 degrees north in the Eastern Hemisphere—in bondage to the forces of darkness.

In Wagner's telling, the rule of the Queen of Heaven can be traced back to at least the biblical record from the first century CE. The temple of the Roman goddess Diana was located in the city of Ephesus, in modern-day Turkey, and was considered one of the seven wonders of the ancient world. Wagner claimed that Diana was a literal spirit, saying, "The chief territorial spirit [high-ranking demonic power] over Ephesus and Asia Minor was the renowned Diana of the Ephesians (also known by her Greek name, Artemis)."[3] However, her hold on the region began to crack when the Apostle Paul began his missionary journeys, which included the city of Ephesus: "Before Paul arrived, she had things very well in hand in the greater Ephesus area and beyond."[4] Her legions of demons answered to her and wreaked havoc on the spiritual climate of the city, while influencing the larger Roman Empire. "But then, confusion set in. The demons, who were supposed to be under her authority, were being driven out of people they had oppressed for years by mere handkerchiefs!"[5]

Yet the Queen of Heaven was not finished. Diana may have been defeated, but the Queen of Heaven was able to find a new host. One of these new hosts was none other than Mary, whom Roman Catholics have long revered as the mother of God for her role in bearing the second figure of the Trinity, Jesus Christ. Wagner insisted that her title "Queen of Heaven" shows that this reverence for Mary is a reconfiguring of the cult of Diana, with all of the attendant demons.

Another host for the Queen of Heaven is the Japanese sun goddess. Shortly after Rick Perry's prayer rally in 2011, when Wagner went on NPR's *Fresh Air* to give his explanation of what the NAR is, he claimed that the earthquake and tsunami earlier that year, which killed 20,000 Japanese people, occurred as a result of the Queen of Heaven. In fact, the Japanese emperor was having sex with this demon and thereby keeping his nation under her dominion.

Back in the 1990s, when Wagner's ideas about demons and strategic level spiritual warfare were first being propagated, a prophet named Ana Mendez claimed that she knew where the throne of the Queen of Heaven was located. "One day, while in prayer in the 10/40 Window prayer tower," Wagner wrote in 1998, "God showed Ana that a major stronghold of darkness over the whole 10/40 Window was located on the highest of high places, Mt. Everest in the Himalaya Mountains."[6] Mendez knew that God was calling her to lead an expedition of prophetic and apostolic prayer warriors up the mountain to engage in spiritual warfare against the Queen of Heaven. The 1997 expedition was code-named Operation Ice Castle and required the team to traverse the most dangerous terrain on the planet to reach what appeared to be a castle made of ice—the throne of the Queen of Heaven.

The expedition took three weeks of perilous trekking over the notorious icefall, which had claimed the lives of dozens of sherpas, and abysses while braving subzero temperatures. Mendez and Wagner believed the idiosyncratic adventure was a remarkable success because the team of prayer warriors achieved their goal. Their spiritual warfare had brought down the Queen of Heaven and opened up the 10/40 Window.

Two decades previously, in the late 1970s, America was entering one of its most peculiar moments in modern history, an episode known as the Satanic Panic. Thousands upon thousands of people reported what became known as Satanic ritual abuse, a violently sadistic form of Satan worship in which children are sexually assaulted, babies are sacrificed on black altars, and young boys and girls are flayed alive. A decade later, investigations by the FBI revealed there actually is no such thing as Satanic ritual abuse. But in the moral panic of the 1980s, innocent playground rhymes that children sang became evidence that their daycare teachers were using them in pornography and even raping them. People went to prison when there was absolutely no evidence that a crime had even occurred, only a hysterical fear of the demonic.

Suddenly, demons were everywhere, and figuring out how to expel them became an imminent task for evangelical leaders. Enter C. Peter Wagner, by then an influential, if not controversial, professor of church growth at Fuller Seminary.

In 1982, Wagner and John Wimber, who had previously been his student, began co-teaching a Fuller Seminary course called MC510: Signs, Wonders, and Church Growth. The course blended Wagner's expertise as a church-growth specialist with Wimber's insistence that evangelicals "do the stuff" of the Bible—heal the sick, cast out demons, and even raise the dead. Wagner served as the teacher of record; however, Wimber did most of the teaching. "Teaching," however, might be a loose term here, especially in the context of a master's-level program at a well-respected seminary. Wimber would invite the presence of the Holy Spirit into the classroom and then guide students into understanding what the Spirit was doing. To say that Wagner was impressed is an understatement. He claimed that on the first night of the MC510 class, he was miraculously healed of high blood pressure and soon stopped needing medication for it. In fact, many of the students who attended MC510 encountered what they considered to be supernatural events, including miraculous healings.

Wagner developed a term for the new expression of charismatic revival that Wimber was leading: the Third Wave of the Holy Spirit. The first wave referred to the birth of Pentecostalism at the turn of the twentieth century, with Charles Fox Parham's Bethel Bible School and William Seymour's Azusa Street Revival. The second wave referred to the post-Second World War renewals—the Latter-Rain and healing revivals. And now God was doing something new by bringing what Wagner saw as the power of the Holy Spirit into the world of mainstream evangelicalism, in no small part through the work of Wimber. Not that Wimber espoused dominion theology, but he did—perhaps inadvertently—give a platform for individuals, including Wagner and later Bickle, to promote dominionist ideas from the Latter Rain.

MC510 became one of the most sought-after classes in the world of evangelicalism, with waiting lists hundreds of students long. Yet despite the appearance of success, not all was well behind the scenes. Wagner was experimenting with increasingly fringe ideas that he had encountered first as a missionary to Bolivia and second as a seminary professor embedded in Los Angeles' charismatic evangelicalism—albeit at a school that does not espouse charismatic theology. One of the ideas that he started experimenting with around the time of the MC510 course, the same time that the Satanic Panic was spreading, was strategic-level spiritual warfare. There were territorial spirits, he began teaching, that hold sway over vast geographic areas and keep the people in bondage. Missionaries experience immense difficulty trying to convert people in these areas because of the demonic powers over the region.

Wimber disagreed—profoundly. Not only was this concept foreign to the New Testament, but he saw it as a dangerous preoccupation for people who were new converts. Just how should one go about casting out high-ranking territorial spirits when what the Christians under his care really needed was to study the Bible and care for the poor? Wimber was comfortable with more conventional ideas of spiritual warfare, in which demons must be exorcised from individuals who are being tormented by the powers of hell. But here he stopped, whereas for Wagner, this concept served as the launching pad for a radical demonology.

The MC510 class came to an abrupt end in 1985, not over strategic-level spiritual warfare but rather a much more mundane problem. Hundreds of people still wanted to enroll each semester, but the Fuller faculty was increasingly concerned about the course's academic rigor. Many believed that a graduate-level course should not include a clinic for teaching students how to enact miracles; there could be value in such a clinic, but under the sponsorship of a church, not a respected institute of higher learning. By this point, a serious rift was developing between Wimber and Wagner. As he would do with Mike Bickle a few years later, Wimber wanted to rein in the more extreme teachings coming from his colleague. But at Fuller Seminary, Wagner was a faculty member, while Wimber was merely an adjunct.

Over the next decade or so, until his death in 1997, Wimber strove to position the Vineyard as a bridge between the mainstream evangelicalism that emphasized biblical teachings, and the charismatic revivalism that evangelicals found both distasteful and irresistible. Wagner, meanwhile, plunged into Latter-Rain teachings about prophets, apostles, and spiritual warfare. As a church-growth specialist, he came to see these teachings as supporting rapid church growth; in a form of circular reasoning, he suggested that anything that promotes church growth comes from God. Wagner insisted that because churches founded on Latter-Rain principles were growing, this field represented what God was doing. Whether or not the principles could be found in the Bible or historical Christian teachings mattered little; after all, during the Third Wave of the Holy Spirit, God was doing a brand-new thing that had not yet been seen in church history.

◆

All this time, Wagner was serving as a strategist for evangelical missions as part of the Lausanne movement. It began in 1974, when the famed evangelist Billy Graham brought together 2700 Christian leaders from 150 nations in the first-ever Lausanne Congress. Graham perceived a need for evangelists and missionaries to adapt their methods so that they could reach more people with the Christian gospel during a period of rapid global change. The civil rights movement in America had occurred alongside global decolonization, in which formerly colonized countries were obtaining independence from their colonizers. The Cold War, nuclear arms race, and space race had further transformed the global order and were changing the face of Christian mission work. Evangelicals, Graham reasoned, needed new strategies for missions.

In 1989, leaders convened Lausanne II in Manila, a sprawling city in the Philippines that has become ubiquitous with urban squalor. There, an associate of Wagner's named Luis Bush used the phrase "Resistant Belt" to describe a swathe of land across Europe, Africa, and Asia that experienced severe poverty, political corruption, and few converts to the Christian faith. Further, a sizable plurality of this population adhered to Islam. The next year, Bush used a new term to describe the same region, but in terms of opportunity for Christian missions rather than despair: the 10/40 Window. It refers to the area between 10 and 40 degrees north in the eastern hemisphere, containing countries such as India, China, Afghanistan, Iran, Iraq, Bangladesh, Pakistan, Cambodia, Morocco, and Ethiopia.

The concept, at least the face of it that was present at virtually every evangelical church throughout the 1990s, was anything but extreme. Christians should pray for the 10/40 Window and finance the work of missionaries there. This was the frontier of Christian missions, and a concentrated effort to reach this area with the gospel could transform the 10/40 Window into an oasis of thriving churches.

But with Wagner at the helm of the 10/40 Window prayer movement, it would be anything but simple. It would, in fact, be a platform to spread his ideas about spiritual warfare in ways that would gain widespread acceptance among otherwise moderate evangelicals.

◆

According to Wagner, the most basic method of spiritual warfare is *ground-level spiritual warfare*, which refers to casting demons out of individuals who may be experiencing a demonic attack. Another term for ground-level spiritual warfare is exorcism, a long-standing practice within the Roman Catholic Church. Evangelicals, many of whom reject Catholic teachings, tend to believe that demons are real spiritual beings who can wreak havoc but can be subjugated through the name of Jesus. Though this form of spiritual warfare is not without controversy—for example, attempting to cast out a demon can brutalize the person who is "possessed," and some exorcists have further stigmatized individuals with mental illness by attempting to cure it through exorcism—what Wagner called ground-level spiritual warfare is widely accepted outside of the NAR and other dominionist circles.

The next tier is *occult-level spiritual warfare*, which attacks Satan's minions who are assailing an area more widespread than an individual person. This tier was seen during the 2008 election season, when a video surfaced of an apostle from Kenya, Thomas Muthee, praying over Sarah Palin at her church as she began her 2005 run for governor of Alaska. In the video, Muthee prayed, "We come against every hindrance of the enemy standing in her way today. In the name of Jesus, *in the name of Jesus*, every form of witchcraft is what we rebuke in the name of Jesus."[7] Witchcraft and the occult are two examples, in this line of thinking, in which demonic powers can operate at levels that influence many people all at once. By rebuking the forces of witchcraft that might be attacking Palin and her campaign, Muthee was drawing directly on this form of spiritual warfare that Wagner was promoting. Occult-level spiritual warfare does not have a meaningful precedent in church history, outside of cult movements and the 1980s hysteria of the Satanic Panic, and is seen almost exclusively in dominionist circles.

According to Wagner, *strategic-level spiritual warfare* is the highest level of spiritual warfare because it attacks the most powerful demons in Satan's army, those who hold authority over massive geographical regions. NAR dominionists, including the apostle Che Ahn and the prophet Cindy Jacobs, engaged in strategic-level spiritual warfare in the build-up to the Capitol Riot and on January 6 itself. Acolytes on the National Mall assisted in this effort by blowing shofars—a practice that Sandford and his followers engaged in before Shiloh fell.

◆

By the time Bush coined the term 10/40 Window in 1990, Wagner had already developed many of his ideas around strategic-level spiritual warfare. "The great Lausanne II Congress on World Evangelization," he began in the introduction to a 1990 book on spiritual warfare, "was in itself a highly visible and prophetically symbolic stepping stone into the decade of the '90s." He went on to clarify by emphasizing the prevalence of spiritual warfare in the congress' teachings: "Remarkably, the three most attended workshop tracks (of 48 offered) were on the Holy Spirit, spiritual warfare, and prayer."[8]

He applied strategic-level spiritual warfare to the 10/40 Window by claiming that a territorial spirit called the Queen of Heaven is causing the darkness and oppression in this part of the world. Hence, the expedition to Mount Everest to dethrone the Queen of Heaven and open the 10/40 Window to rapid evangelization.

A similar concept called *spiritual mapping* also developed in Wagner's circles, especially through the influence of a man named George Otis, Jr. Otis owned a production company called The Sentinel Group, which produced a series of videos called *Transformations* that showcased communities which had been transformed by the kingdom of God. Thomas Muthee, the Kenyan apostle who in 2005 prayed over Sarah Palin, came to the attention of her church because he was featured in a *Transformations* video.

Spiritual mapping is the process by which prayer warriors use maps and on-the-ground research (usually through *prayerwalking*, walking through a geographic area while praying) to determine which demonic powers hold sway over a particular geographic area. When one can identify those powers, strategic-level spiritual warfare can be engaged to dismantle them and make room for the kingdom of God to advance. According to a 1998 article from the mainstream evangelical magazine *Christianity Today*, spiritual mapping was gaining widespread acceptance among evangelicals—more so than among charismatics—in the 1990s. And with Wagner and Bush's influence, strategic-level spiritual warfare and spiritual mapping were becoming part of the Lausanne strategy for world evangelization.

Wagner and Bush, through the organization AD 2000 and Beyond, set the ambitious goal of evangelizing the entire world by the new millennium. And there was a massive influx of missionaries into the 10/40 Window to work on accomplishing exactly that task. But then the entire world watched in horror as two commercial planes crashed into the World Trade Center on September 11, 2001. Everything was about to change.

"Allah is the proper name of a spirit being," Wagner wrote in the aftermath of the worst terror attack in American history. Although "Allah" is the Arabic name for God and is used by both Arab Christians and Muslims, Wagner went on to say, "He is no more God than is Wormwood or Beelzebub or Apollyon or Shiva or Buddha or Baal or Lucifer."[9] This last reference to a "deity" worshipped by people of other faiths is none other than the devil himself. What Wagner was in effect saying is Allah, the Arabic name for God, is actually a high-ranking demon who is worshipped every day by a billion Muslims. In fact, he claimed that Allah's counterpart is the moon goddess Allat, and he elsewhere claimed that the moon goddess is also a host for the Queen of Heaven.

Mainstream evangelical writers, including those who wrote for Billy Graham's magazine *Christianity Today*, pushed back against claims that associated the world's one billion Muslims with demonology. On an evangelistic level, Christians needed to view Muslims with love and compassion in order to engage them with the love of Christ. But on a global level, the years after September 11 brought unprecedented chaos to Christian-Muslim relations. The terror attacks were viewed by many as a "clash of civilizations" between

East and West, Muslim and Christian. Tensions simmered to a boiling point on both sides of this imagined divide, and the influx of evangelical missionaries into the 10/40 Window was leading to sometimes-violent confrontations.

In this "clash of civilizations," Western missionaries often made the simplistic assumption that Muslims needed to know Christ in order to find true peace. These missionaries, especially evangelicals who focused on converting people rather than humanitarian aid, failed to grasp the complexity of the Islamic faith and the cultures associated with it. And firebrands like Wagner were dousing the already-tense situation with gasoline and then handing matches to their followers: the whole Muslim world needed to be exorcised through strategic-level spiritual warfare. In the eyes of many Muslims, Western Christians were engaging in very literal warfare, vis-à-vis President George W. Bush's War on Terror. The American military and heavy-duty weapons flowed alongside an influx of missionaries who sought to Christianize an area that they saw as literally demonized.

At the same time, the NAR was beginning to move out of the cult-like fringes of evangelicalism through the years-long Toronto Blessing, as well as the unparalleled influence of Lou Engle's The Call. NAR institutions, such as the International House of Prayer, began opening ministry training centers that acted as alternatives to traditional seminaries. Students could learn directly from NAR apostles and prophets, who in turn allegedly learned directly from God. These students become empowered to serve as a new vanguard for the End Times: the Manifest Sons of God.

In 1998, the prophet-apostle duo of Bethel Church, Kris Vallotton and Bill Johnson, opened the Bethel School of Supernatural Ministry (BSSM). The school had only a few dozen students the first few years, but it has since exploded to include thousands of students annually, many from countries around the world. Students affectionately refer to BSSM as "Hogwarts for Christians" because they are training for a life of ministry not by studying church history and theologians, but rather by casting out demons and miraculously healing people who are sick or live with disabilities. "Our mandate is simple," Johnson wrote in 2003, the year that America invaded Iraq. "Raise up a generation that can openly display the raw power of God."[10]

Johnson and Vallotton both teach that demons and/or people agreeing with the lies that demons bring to their minds are often at the source of sickness, mental illness, chronic disease, relationship conflict, and disabilities. "It's not complicated," Johnson wrote in 2018. "Loss, death, and destruction are the things left behind when the devil has had influence in a given situation."[11] Death is not as much a part of life as is birth, like the author of the biblical book of Ecclesiastes wrote thousands of years earlier. Rather, sickness, death, and loss are only by-products of demonic activity.

In fact, Vallotton has insisted that medical professionals do not understand the true source of many problems that plague their patients because they do not understand the spiritual realm of angels and demons. "Part of the problem," he wrote in *Spirit Wars*, "is that most health care professionals, whether Christian or secular, view the spirit world as some kind of fairy tale perpetuated by uneducated and ignorant souls."[12]

"What would your city look like if the Kingdom of God were superimposed over every realm of society?"[13] Vallotton asked his readers in 2016. Here, he was alluding to the 7MM, which he interprets as not ruling over people but rather as dismantling demonic forces that occupy culture. In other words, strategic-level spiritual warfare is a means of accomplishing the 7MM. "Speaking of the mountains," he said in a video series meant to clarify Bethel's positions on controversial issues, "it's like, get involved in culture. And I've heard a lot of the mountain-taking. Let's take this mountain, and let's dominate this mountain. But," he clarified, in an effort to show that the 7MM has nothing to do with governance over people, "the context, in the teachings that I've heard and that I've taught has always been, that mountain that the demonic world, the principality mentioned in Ephesians 2, Ephesians 6, and that Daniel dealt with in Daniel 10, that Persian demonic prince, he's ruling that mountain." The 7MM, to Vallotton, has always been about demons, especially strategic-level spiritual warfare. He went on, "And we're like, take him down from that mountain. It's not about, take over those humans. It's, let's dominate that mountain in the sense of, pull that spirit down so people can have this sense of free will."[14]

When Johnson and Vallotton are teaching that demons are the source of so many of the problems that people face, while Wagner is insisting that one billion Muslims around the world pray to and worship a demon named Allah, at a time when much of American evangelicalism believes that the world is engaged in a "clash of civilizations" and the military is engaged in a war in the Muslim world, the result does not take much creative thinking. There is not a far leap from, "Muslims are worshipping a demon," to, "Muslims are demonized, and this prevents them from becoming Christians. Their countries are governed by demonic spirits, which must be cast down through strategic-level spiritual warfare." This politically volatile view spread throughout much of the NAR as it began moving into the mainstream of evangelicalism, a period that concurred with the attacks of 9/11 and the ensuing War on Terror

All the while, British Israelism was humming in the background, having informed new approaches to Christian Zionism. An overwhelming majority of American evangelicals espouse political and military support for the state of Israel, regardless of its use of American-provided weaponry against Palestinian civilians. A core reason is because Christian Zionism is not based on a humanitarian concern—either for the Jewish people or neighboring Arabs—but rather on forms of prophecy belief that claim Israel will be at the center of an End-Times drama. Christian Zionism is nothing new within American evangelicalism; the concept has been thriving in some form or another for over a century. However, there was an important shift in how evangelicals approached Christian Zionism in the aftermath of 9/11, especially with the rise of American militancy in the Middle East, rapid growth of the NAR's influence, and increasing comfort with the idea of spiritual warfare.

Americans have long talked about Israel in ways that are metaphorical. When the earliest Pilgrims crossed over from England to the New World, they saw their "errand in the wilderness" in terms of leaving the bonds of Egypt for the Promised Land—a recreation of the biblical story about the Israelite slaves leaving Egypt for Canaan. Enslaved Africans who toiled on Southern plantations used similar language to describe their quest for freedom and even referred to Harriet Tubman as Moses, a reference to the leader who brought the Israelites out of Egyptian slavery. American civil religion has long drawn comparisons with Israel, and they are exactly that—comparisons. America is *like* Israel because it was chosen by God to be a light to all nations.

British Israelism insists that America is not *like* Israel but rather that America *is* Israel. There is no metaphorical comparison but instead a sameness, a sense that America and Israel are both one. An exception to this association between America and the Jewish people is found in the Serpent Seed theory and its religious offshoot, Identity theology. Yet by and large, in the aftermath of September 11, with the NAR hitting the evangelical mainstream through The Call and readers of *Christianity Today* espousing Wagner's ideas about the 10/40 Window, the British-Israelist foundations of the NAR began to transform expressions of Christian Zionism.

An important verse for Christian Zionists has long been Genesis 12:3, in which God tells the patriarch Abraham, "And I will bless those who bless you, and the one who curses you I will curse. And in you all the families of the earth will be blessed" [NASB]. Christian Zionists have tended to view this verse as a biblical mandate to support Israel, as ultimately Christ himself came from the Hebrew nation in fulfillment of God's promise that "in you all the families of the earth will be blessed." NAR-style Christian Zionism takes this verse further and insists that in order for God to continue blessing America— that is, a version of the prosperity gospel—America must act first by blessing Israel. And a significant component of this "blessing" is militaristic aid that has been used in scorched-earth warfare against civilians. In effect, America is not merely coming to Israel's aid but America is aiding itself by arming Israel. Unlike previous iterations of Christian Zionism (namely dispensationalism), this paradigm does not exist merely because of prophecy belief regarding the End Times but primarily because of a more explicit identification with Israel.

This NAR-style Christian Zionism could be seen in how President Trump approached Israel during his first term (2017–21). One reason why evangelicals so enthusiastically supported his candidacy, despite his complete lack of moral values that they have so long promoted in public policy, was because he positioned himself as a champion of Israel. President Obama (2009–17) had allegedly betrayed America by not expressing enough support for Israel, despite the enormous military aid that his administration had provided; this betrayal threatened God's blessing on America and perhaps even America's continued existence. Trump could undo this betrayal through singular support for Israel, regardless of all political, religious, and cultural complexities in the Middle East. This was one way that he could "Make America Great Again"—an identificational relationship with Israel that saw America's and Israel's interests as one and the same.

John Hagee, founder of Christians United for Israel, wrote about Trump, "He started making very bold statements that he would be the defender of Israel, that he would move the embassy from Tel Aviv to Jerusalem." To show how this allegiance to Israel was God-ordained, he went on, "And that's when he started going up in the polls. I believe that's when God Almighty got involved in this electoral process and appointed him by the very supernatural power of heaven. Because the Bible says the Lord raises up a leader and God puts down a leader." To Christian Zionists such as Hagee, Trump was God's chosen man to lead America, not because of his moral qualities, but precisely because of his lack of them. He was going to carry a big stick and intimidate anyone who crossed his path—and his path included Israel's path. "And everyone is saying there's a supernatural element. I assure you that when Donald Trump started saying good things about Israel, the winds of heaven got behind his political sails and pushed him right to the White House."[15]

Though Israeli settlements in the West Bank have long been condemned by the American government, the Trump administration actively supported them. On December 6, 2017, Trump recognized Jerusalem, not Tel Aviv, as the capital of Israel, a move wildly supported by his Christian Zionist base. And to commemorate seventy years of Israel as a modern state, in May 2018, he moved the US embassy to Jerusalem.

Christian Zionists responded to Trump's election loss against Joe Biden in a vein drawn from British Israelism. After numerous court cases and "Jericho Marches" that attempted to bring the power of God out of heaven and onto his chosen president, Dutch Sheets and other NAR leaders galvanized Christian Zionists to the US Capitol on January 6. There, they blew shofars, some of which had American flags on them, engaging in strategic-level spiritual warfare against the US government.

7

The Seven Mountain Mandate in Africa

"We know Uganda's been under tremendous pressure," Lou Engle shouted into the microphone. "We've felt that same pressure. But I felt like The Call was to come and join with the church in Uganda." Ever since The Call DC in 2000, Engle had become a leading figure in America's culture wars, and he had preached this message many, many times throughout the United States. In November 2008, he had preached it to tens of thousands of evangelicals who had flooded San Diego's Qualcomm Stadium in protest of same-sex marriage and the Proposition 8 ballot initiative. The Call moved from being a one-time event that declared the cultural mandate of the Columbine martyrs into a series of praise and worship rallies that Engle was holding across the country; the event regularly brought together tens of thousands of Christians to worship and pray for righteousness to return to America. At Qualcomm Stadium, Engle had claimed that same-sex marriage "will release a spirit that is more demonic than Islam, a spirit of lawlessness and anarchy and sexual insanity."[1]

On this day, in May of 2010, he was leading The Call in Uganda, a landlocked African nation that was still recovering from the brutal dictatorship of Idi Amin (in power 1971–9), followed by the onset of the AIDS crisis. "In the nations, you are showing courage to take a stand for righteousness."[2] Engle rocked back and forth as he continued with America's dominionist message that he was helping export to Uganda.

Standing beside Engle was David Bahati, a Ugandan politician who had introduced legislation that would impose the death penalty for "aggravated homosexuality," an offense that could be interpreted to mean that someone was accused by a neighbor of engaging in gay sex. Though Engle later attempted to distance himself from the law, on that day, he stood at the apex of a movement that was organized not by Africans but by American culture warriors. These culture warriors had been actively working with African clergy and politicians, including Bahati, to stir up an anti-gay sentiment that would continue gaining popular support and eventually be codified into law.

Evangelicals have long viewed foreign missions as a means of sharing the gospel of Christ with people who live in countries that do not have widespread access to it. Missionaries often engage in church planting by converting individuals to Christianity and then bringing small groups together regularly to pray, worship, and study the Bible. Often, evangelical missionaries accomplish their goals of evangelizing people by engaging in humanitarian work. They may go into severely impoverished areas and distribute critical aid—food, medicine, blankets—or implement development projects—job-training programs, teaching, digging wells, for example.

Dominionist missions—born of the charismatic, Pentecostal tradition rather than other forms of evangelicalism—are different. The goal is not evangelization but rather nation-building.

"Is it possible to transform a community, a city, a country?" Loren Cunningham (1935–2023) wrote in his 2007 manifesto, *The Book That Transforms Nations*. "Jesus must have thought so. He told us to pray that his kingdom would come and that his will would be done on earth as it is in heaven." By the time Cunningham wrote those words, he was winding down a breathtaking international career that had included visits to every single country in the world. In 1960, he had founded Youth with a Mission (YWAM), an organization that engages teenagers and young adults in charismatic missions around the globe. "He told us to disciple all nations and teach them to do all that he has commanded us."[3] By the time Cunningham wrote these words, YWAM was one of the largest missionary organizations in history.

The Gospel of Matthew records Jesus as telling his disciples, shortly before he ascended into heaven, "All authority in heaven and on earth has been given to me. Go, therefore, and make disciples of all the nations" (Matthew 28:18b–19a, NASB). Christians throughout the past two millennia have seen these verses— part of what is known as the "Great Commission"—as Christ telling them to go into different nations to evangelize so that people can become his disciples. Dominionists, particularly within the NAR, interpret these verses differently, as Christ telling his followers to disciple not individuals within nations but to disciple entire nations. If he has all authority—all *dominion*, dominionists might add—then nations themselves are to follow biblical standards. So Cunningham wrote, in a book about the power of the Bible to bring nations into places of wealth and influence, "He told us to disciple all nations." During the 1970s, he and his friend Bill Bright had developed the means to do this by forming the precursor to the Seven Mountain Mandate.

In Cunningham's telling, he was visiting the mountains of Colorado in 1975 when the voice of God told him, "I want to give you some classrooms to disciple, that is to teach the nations."[4] Those classrooms were family, religion, education, celebration/the arts, public communication, economics, and government. This idea of there being different spheres of culture, each of them independent of the other and governed separately, is not unique to Cunningham. He attributed it to Abraham Kuyper (1837–1920), a Dutch theologian and statesman who became prime minister of the Netherlands. Kuyper taught that society is biblically divided into distinct spheres that do not overlap and identified the primary spheres as the family, the church, and the state. The state regulates state matters, the church regulates church matters, and the family regulates family matters; because the family and church do not originate with the state, the state cannot regulate them. This teaching is known as *sphere sovereignty*.

Cunningham adapted the concept of sphere sovereignty for a different purpose than what Kuyper originally intended: to provide a means for his YWAM missionaries to engage in nation-building around the world. "You, too, can be a nation builder by obeying Jesus and applying his Word in any one of the seven spheres that influence society,"[5] he wrote in 2007. To him, the different spheres of culture were not distinct governorates but rather aspects of society that could be influenced and transformed with the gospel. In his telling, shortly after he received the word from God listing out the seven spheres, he had dinner with his friend Bill Bright, the founder of Campus Crusade for Christ. Both men shared with each other a nearly identical list of seven different spheres that they needed to influence with a Christian witness.

Cunningham taught that the key to influencing the seven spheres was tapping into the supernatural power of God—hearing God's voice and walking in the miraculous. This was actually his take on the Keswick theology that had influenced Aimee Semple McPherson a half-century earlier. This strand of evangelical thought urges Christians to seek supernatural encounters with God that lead to the victorious and prosperous "higher life," to let go and let God. In Cunningham's teachings, one can experience this higher life by making Jesus the Lord of one's entire existence; the Lordship of Christ in one's life begins with letting go of attachments to all worldly constraints—material possessions and family, for example. Healing the sick and even raising the dead just by praying over them could become part of the normal—the higher—Christian life if one can let God be Lord of all. Let go and let God.

For Cunningham, the teachings of Keswick and dominionism blended seamlessly in fulfilling the Great Commission, making disciples of all nations. "The kingdom, and I'd like to add the 's', the kingdoms of this world have become the kingdoms of our Lord,"[6] he intentionally misquoted from Revelation 11:15. The text has been translated from Greek as saying both the *kingdom* of this world and the *kingdoms* of this world, depending on which New Testament translation one uses. What is striking is that Cunningham said that he is adding an "s," indicating that his translation said *kingdom*, and he was intentionally misquoting it to make a point about his own theology. "The kingdoms of this world have become the kingdoms of our Lord." And he interpreted this gospel of discipling entire nations to mean that not only would they belong to God but would also belong to Christians. "This is God speaking, God saying to you, I want to give you nations."[7]

As YWAM has grown to become the largest missionary organization in the world, it has adopted the idea of supernatural missions alongside dominionism on a global scale. Cunningham began YWAM by sending out teenagers and young adults with no experience in cross-cultural living, no theological training, and—critically for dominionist movements—no accountability. YWAM remains a very decentralized and deregulated organization, empowering its members to begin new ministries in countries all around the world with very minimal oversight. Accounts of spiritual abuse, cult-like indoctrination, sexual assault, and even using missionary cover to promote far-right insurgencies have proliferated.

By 2016, YWAM was partnering with the International House of Prayer in Kansas City and with Lou Engle's The Call. A YWAM Facebook post about The Call Azusa, held in 2016 to commemorate the Azusa Street Revival, shows Cunningham linking arms with Mike Bickle and Bill Johnson, just behind Lou Engle as he spoke to the crowd. "These are leaders from prayer and worship movements, signs and wonders movements, and the missions movement," the post reads. "God is bringing it together for such a time as this."[8]

YWAM has become entrenched in the NAR and used its global reach to spread dominionist ideas around the world. During the 1980s, YWAM leadership began promoting strategic-level spiritual warfare, especially with the publication of YWAM leader John Dawson's 1989 book *Taking Our Cities for God*. Dawson worked directly with C. Peter Wagner to write and teach about strategic-level spiritual warfare, a practice that has become embedded in the fabric of how YWAM does mission work. And the model of supernatural missions to engage in nation-building has spread among non-YWAM missionaries, especially those who have been influenced by the NAR.

"Heidi, God wants to know, do you want the nation of Mozambique?" the apostle Randy Clark asked at the Toronto Blessing. Heidi Baker and her husband, Rolland, had been serving as missionaries since the early 1980s, first in Hong Kong, Indonesia, and then Mozambique, an island nation off the east coast of Africa. "God is going to give you the nation of Mozambique. You are going to see the dumb speak, the lame walk, the blind see and the dead be raised."[9]

In the century-plus since Pentecostalism's origins, the movement has grown explosively in Africa. The Azusa Street Revival saw the beginning of Pentecostal missionaries heading to Africa, sometimes working alongside of Western imperial powers, sometimes working alongside local peoples who faced colonial rule and oppression. Regardless of the motives and power alignments of Pentecostal missionaries, the message took deep root among Indigenous people groups: God is with you, and God is for you. God's presence can be experienced in everyday life, and God's wonder-working power is for the present as much as it was for the time of Christ.

When the Bakers arrived in Mozambique in 1995, they began an orphan-care ministry for children who had lost their parents in the war-ravaged country. But they were soon so tired and burned out that Heidi said she was ready to take a job at K-Mart. Two years later, they traveled to the Toronto Airport Christian Fellowship to take part in the Pentecostal renewal that was bringing together prophets and apostles to form the NAR. Heidi described the experience by claiming, "The power of God hit me like lightening. I vibrated and screamed." This ecstatic episode lasted "for seven days and seven nights after that. I felt the presence of God so intensely that I was disabled. I was unable to walk, talk, or move." She went on to say of the Toronto Blessing, "many people laughed. ... There was nothing funny about it to me. It was a powerful and holy time."[10] And there, Randy Clark told Heidi and her husband that deaf ears would be opened and blind eyes would see.

"I would literally go out and look for every blind person I could find. Living in one of the poorest nations of the earth, they're pretty easy to find," Heidi claimed. "I must have prayed for 20 blind people, and none of them saw. But I kept praying. I kept remembering those prophetic words that the Holy Spirit poured into my heart," she continued, contending for what she experienced at the Toronto Blessing. "There was such a powerful presence of the Holy Spirit as those words were spoken over me. I just said, 'I'm not giving up. ... One day they're going to see.'"[11]

In 2010, a group of researchers published astonishing findings in the *Southern Medical Journal* that suggested the Bakers' faith-healing practices actually were generating positive results. Candy Gunther Brown, a professor of religion at Indiana University, had led a group to Mozambique, where they attended one of the Bakers' crusades and used medical equipment to measure the hearing and vision of local people. What the study found was a statistically significant improvement in some of the people who had received proximal intercessory prayer. But the study is far from conclusive, as the sample size was too small, with only fourteen auditory subjects and eleven visual subjects. The test itself also faced considerable restraints—ambient noise, time constraints, and no control subjects to measure the placebo effect. Still, promises of faith-healing remain the engine of the NAR, allowing it to attract large numbers of people who would otherwise reject heterodox teachings about modern-day apostles and prophets, the 7MM, or strategic-level spiritual warfare.

The Bakers have not openly promoted the 7MM, yet they are widely connected with NAR ministries, including the apostolic network that Heidi cofounded with Bill Johnson and John Arnott, Revival Alliance. She is a frequent guest speaker at Bethel Church and was regularly featured at IHOP-KC before its collapse. "Do you understand? Agree with God," Heidi told the crowd at an IHOP-KC event in May 2022. "Would you like to agree with him? Would you like to just yield yourself a little, little, little more?"[12] Yield yourself, let go, and agree with God. Let go and let God. But just what should one let go of and let God do? This question opens up the space of where the NAR's heterodox teachings are able to flourish. And parallel to far too many other faith healers in the NAR, the Bakers' ministry is riddled with sexual abuse. Heidi has publicly shared numerous stories of sexual abusers inside of her ministry receiving radical love and forgiveness, rather than accountability for the crimes committed against the children in her care.[13]

Before the Bakers began their work in Mozambique, the German faith healer Reinhard Bonnke (1940–2019) worked closely with Loren Cunningham to engage in "Holy Spirit evangelism in demonstration"[14] across Africa. When he finished preaching to crowds that could number well over a million, the time for healing would begin. People with all kinds of maladies—seizures, paralysis, deafness—would stream to the front to be prayed for by Bonnke and his associates; in faith, the sick would receive divine healing for whatever ailed them. These miracles theoretically provided evidence that what Bonnke proclaimed was not a dead religion but rather the living Christianity that Christ himself taught. "God sent his son so that he would carry away our burdens, fears, diseases, and carry them away on the cross of Calvary. Alleluia!"[15] The problem, as with so many faith healers before and after him, was that the miracles he declared to have happened could not be verified. In fact, when videographers went behind the scenes at one of Bonnke's crusades in 2001, cameras showed people struggling to stand up from their wheelchairs, trying as hard as they could to effect the miracle that Bonnke promised, but falling back down.

At its core, NAR dominionism teaches that when Adam and Eve first sinned in the Garden of Eden, the kingdom of Satan took possession of the earth. Humans became the children of the devil, predisposed to all kinds of evil and experiencing sickness and death, until Christ came with the kingdom of God. Through the influence of his people, Christians, the kingdom of God has been expanding for the past 2000 years as they push back the darkness. Sometimes pushing back the darkness means engaging in faith-healing to bring people's bodies into the wholeness that can be found in the kingdom of God. Promises of faith-healing help pave the way for other methods of expanding the kingdom of God, including the implementation of the 7MM.

But what happens when implementing the 7MM means executing people whose bodies are in need of healing from one of the worst epidemics in human history?

◆

In October 2009, the Ugandan parliamentarian David Bahati introduced legislation that would provide the death penalty for "aggravated homosexuality." The AIDS epidemic had torn through Uganda, beginning in the 1980s; from the mid-1980s until the mid-1990s, an estimated 20 percent of Uganda's general population—all men, women, and children—were infected. Back in the United States, Jerry Falwell had been preaching against LGBTQ+ lifestyles since the 1950s, and he had been warning that the judgment of God would soon fall on America for its toleration of such. When AIDS was first identified among a group of gay men in 1981, he and his fellow anti-gay crusaders immediately labeled the disease as the "gay plague." Western missionaries, as well as Ugandan clergy trained in Western seminaries, helped spread this hyperbolic explanation for what causes AIDS to Uganda. So when Bahati introduced a bill that provided the death penalty for gay sex, he had broad support in Uganda despite a strong international outcry. His constituents remembered the AIDS epidemic. Many believed that it was caused by queer individuals.

Bahati likewise had support from American dominionists, who have suggested that fulfilling the 7MM means potentially executing queer individuals. In the United States, gay rights had been on the ascendancy, including among younger evangelicals; by 2009, gay rights was becoming a winning issue on ballots and in court cases. Mike Johnson, who would become the Speaker of the House two decades later, bemoaned the 2003 *Lawrence v. Texas* Supreme Court decision, which struck down sodomy laws as violations of privacy. While plenty of politically active evangelicals, especially dominionists, still agitated against gay rights, they did so knowing that the battle, at least for now, was lost. Bahati's anti-gay legislation in Uganda provided a means for getting involved in a battle that they could win.

Missionaries do not usually get involved in culture wars, as their ability to stay in their adopted countries depends on staying in the good graces of the government and local people.[16] However, the model of missions encouraged by dominionists like Loren Cunningham promotes nation-building, and plenty of American dominionists got involved in the effort to pass Bahati's legislation. So Lou Engle brought The Call to Uganda and stood on the stage next to Bahati to declare righteousness in Uganda. Missionaries from IHOP-KC, which has long been associated with Engle, supported the bill. And YWAM's involvement went much deeper.

Until 2009, official records listed that a house on C Street in Washington, DC—the infamous "C Street House"—was owned by YWAM. About five members of Congress regularly rented bedrooms there for far below market value, and other members met there for Bible study. The Bible studies were a bit different than what one might find at a Wednesday-night group meeting in an urban church, however; talk focused on world domination, and leaders glorified the likes of Adolf Hitler, Josef Stalin, and Mao Zedong. Able to convince their followers to go to war for them and to even kill their own family members, these authoritarians truly understood Jesus. So claimed Douglas Coe, leader of The Family. YWAM insists that it sold the C Street House to The Fellowship International, a nonprofit associated with The Family, in the late 1980s. However, registration documents still showed YWAM DC as the owner until a 2009 series of congressional sex scandals associated with the C Street House created a national uproar and cast an unsavory light on YWAM.

David Bahati and YWAM may not have been directly connected with each other, but both are intimately involved with The Family. When Bahati introduced the anti-gay legislation, he was the secretary of Uganda's branch of The Family; the journalist Jeff Sharlet, who has spent years covering the activities of The Family, traveled to Uganda to meet with Bahati. There, Bahati told Sharlet, "The [kill the gays] bill is the Fellowship [The Family]."[17] It was the direct product of an American political group under the sway of dominionist teachings connected to Loren Cunningham, whose DC branch of YWAM owned a house where dominionism was spreading among

American politicians. YWAM distanced itself from the C Street scandals by insisting it sold the house. However, YWAM is intentionally decentralized and deregulated to such an extent that national directors often do not know what ministries YWAM groups are engaging in within that country. And YWAM is also connected to The Family; documents from 2000 show The Family flying congressmen to Kona, Hawaii, a small town of less than 10,000 people, but the home of Loren Cunningham and YWAM's University of the Nations.

The seven spheres are much more than what Cunningham initially described as areas of culture in which to apply a Christian witness. They are about discipling entire nations, and sometimes discipling nations means supporting political movements that want to apply capital punishment to queer individuals. Dominionism was tied into the seven spheres long before Lance Wallnau took the concept and turned it into the 7MM. Cunningham insisted that the Great Commission meant that Christians were to disciple entire nations by bringing the seven spheres under the Lordship of Jesus Christ; in turn, God would actually give them nations. When Wallnau took Cunningham's concept of "seven spheres" and turned it into the 7MM, he supercharged what Cunningham was already teaching. "There's never been a nation taken as a result of an evangelism harvest," Wallnau declared. Rather, the point of missions was that "[Christians] are to take over spheres and administrate them for the glory of God." Power and influence, not meeting the needs of the poor and bringing them the gospel of Christ.

"My generation is so sentimental about the poor, they do it backwards. The first century had to remember the poor because they knew they had to go to kings. My generation forgets about kings and they're obsessed with the poor."[18] In teaching about the 7MM, Wallnau completely subverted 2000 years of Christian missions. The goal was no longer to evangelize people; evangelism was a distraction from the real task of taking over the seven spheres, what Wallnau came to call the Seven Mountains. Missions was not about reaching the poor, as Christ himself taught when he said, "The Spirit of the Lord is upon me because he anointed me to bring good news to the poor" (Luke 4:18, NASB). Wallnau's obsession was with kings, people with power and authority that they wielded over their mountains.

In the end, the approach of going to the kings and attempting to change laws so that they reflect dominionist ideals worked. Uganda's parliament passed Bahati's anti-gay bill in 2014, though Prime Minister Yoweri Museveni reduced the harsher punishments before signing it into law. However, in 2023, a new law was passed in Uganda that effectively denies queer individuals their civil rights—they can be imprisoned and even executed for their sexuality—and makes them targets of vigilante violence.

Part Three

America's New Culture Wars

8

Lights, Camera, Dominion!

In September 2003, *People* magazine ran a profile piece on a supersized family living in Northwest Arkansas. In a way, there was nothing unusual about this piece. *People* magazine—as well as the profile's author, Andrea Cooper—regularly ran stories about individuals with unconventional lifestyles. This piece showed a picture of a father and mother leading a whole parade of children—thirteen kids, standing in a line, smiling awkwardly into a camera that would surreptitiously thrust them into the national spotlight.

The boys looked like miniatures of their father, Jim Bob Duggar, with hair neatly trimmed and combed, shirts tucked into pants, a belt conspicuously around each waist. The girls, following the style of their mother Michelle, had long, curled hair and ankle-length skirts. The photo looked like a relic from the 1950s—or for the girls, the 1850s—but it was also surprisingly modern.

Because the Duggar family was about to become America's biggest television sensation.

The channel Discovery Health picked up on the photo and decided to run a documentary, titled *14 Kids and Pregnant Again*, on the supersized family whose ways seemed anathema to contemporary America. All sixteen family members shared a three-bedroom, two-bathroom home, and the parents had a total commitment to debt-free living; this meant not only scorning credit cards but also refusing to take out a car loan or a mortgage.

"If we don't have the money, we don't buy it," Jim Bob told the camera. "That includes our house, or cars, whatever we need. We just buy used and save the difference."[1]

To reduce costs on a larger home for the ever-expanding family, Jim Bob was having the older boys do most of the construction for a 7000-square-foot build. The show did not question whether children who were not yet teenagers had the skills necessary for the sturdy craftsmanship of a new home or whether children should even be doing heavy construction. Instead, the show celebrated the children's diligence and work ethic. Preteen Jessa was in charge of doing laundry for sixteen people, and the girls were constantly helping their mother cook to feed the giant clan. There is little mainstream debate over whether or not children should contribute to the family by doing chores, but the Duggar children were engaging in hard labor—on television.

The home's inner workings relied on what Michelle called the "buddy system," in which each of the older children had a younger child to care for. These older "buddies" did everything from helping their younger buddies with meals and brushing teeth to teaching them how to read and write. *14 Kids and Pregnant Again* seemed to laud this paradigm as a way for older children to develop responsibility while making sure the younger children got enough attention. Yet the euphemism "buddy" downplayed the reality that ten-year-olds were raising their siblings.

The show's reception was electric.

Raising children typically comes with chaos and financial strain. The cost of daycare, managing tantrums, getting kids out to the school bus in the morning, helping them with homework, participating in the Parent Teacher Association—all of these things can quickly lead to unbearable stress and marital difficulties. But *14 Kids and Pregnant Again* gave no indication of emotional outbursts from the Duggar kids or difficulty in keeping up with school. They were all homeschooled, and Michelle had the family so tightly organized that the times when each child would shower every day were listed on a chart. In this way, the Duggars were not necessarily anti-modern as much as they were the answer to the problems associated with modernity. Parents could raise children without facing unmanageable levels of debt or losing their wits when age-appropriate behavior feels out of control. Instead of caving in to the strains of parenthood, parents could experience vibrant marriages and live the way that God intended.

The secret to the Duggars' success was alluded to toward the end of *14 Kids and Pregnant Again*, when the family took an RV for a road trip to a homeschooling conference in Texas. Hitched behind the RV was a trailer, the back of which read, "ATI Bound." ATI stands for Advanced Training Institute, and as one documentary turned into five and then a weekly reality show, the influence of ATI on the Duggar life became increasingly apparent.

When *17 Kids and Counting* first aired in 2008, it was an immediate hit. The children were always clean and immaculately dressed, unless they were charmingly enjoying a mud bath outside. The girls wore skirts that went down at least past their knees, and the boys typically donned polo or button-up shirts with khakis or blue jeans. And as the popularity of the show soared, many Americans—conservative, liberal, and everything in between—turned to the Duggars as the wrong answer to the right question.

Because the Duggars were more than docile girls wearing pioneer dresses and strapping boys with their shirts tucked in. They were the face of a movement that had a generations-long plan for dominion.

In ways that were not readily apparent to their television audience, the Duggars were modeling for America the teachings of Bill Gothard and his Institute of Basic Life Principles, or IBLP. Gothard's organizing concept was authority, and his most central teaching was known as "umbrellas of authority." This was regularly depicted with a visual of three umbrellas, a small one at the bottom labeled "wife." Underneath this umbrella were children, who could be protected from the storms of life by submitting to her authority or, as the visual taught, remaining under her umbrella.

Above the "wife" umbrella was one labeled "husband," as his job was to protect and provide for his family—the wife and children underneath him. If the wife remained under his umbrella, just as the children are to remain under hers, then she will likewise be protected from whatever storms may blow. Above the "husband" umbrella is an even larger one labeled as "Christ," who protects the husband as the husband submits to him. Thus, the whole family is protected by Christ, as long as each member follows the chain of command established by the umbrellas of authority.

The show *17 Kids and Counting* (followed by *18* and then *19 Kids and Counting*) never explicitly mentioned the umbrellas of authority. Yet Michelle regularly directed her face toward Jim Bob's, not looking at him but physically looking up to him, showing her deference to his decision-making. The children were expected to obey their parents unconditionally; the horde of enough kids to fill a public-school classroom was so submissive that, at least on camera, neither parent ever raised his or her voice.

In her book *The Duggars: 20 and Counting*, Michelle explained that the secret to inculcating this level of submission from children was a method known as "blanket training." Blanket training is done on children as young as six months old by placing them on a blanket with a favorite toy just out of reach. When the child reaches for the toy, the mother swats the child's bottom to teach that the focus should only be on obeying the authority, not on curiosity about the world. While this practice has been roundly condemned—in no small part because children have died from blanket training—it created the Duggar family structure that was built around Gothard's umbrellas of authority. In fact, the IBLP endorsed the book that explicates and promotes blanket training, *To Train Up a Child* by Michael and Debi Pearl, who taught parents how to spank their children as severely as possible without children's services getting involved. Though Michelle downplayed the severity of blanket training in *The Duggars: 20 and Counting* by saying that she reprimanded the toddlers with a stern voice, in the back of the book, she endorsed the IBLP, which in turn endorsed *To Train Up a Child*. In no small part because of blanket training, the Duggar children submitted completely to Michelle, who was unconditionally deferential to Jim Bob. Then, this family structure was put on righteous display all across America, especially to parents who were desperate to get their kids to behave.

Gothard's concept of "umbrellas of authority" looks startlingly similar to an offshoot of the Latter Rain known as the Shepherding Movement. As the charismatic revivals of the 1940s through 1970s tended to disavow denominations, a group of men associated with the Latter Rain—Charles

Simpson, Bob Mumford, Don Basham, Derek Prince, and the former assistant to William Branham, Ern Baxter—developed an organizational structure in the 1970s that bypassed denominational hierarchies. This model relied on house churches, small groups of Christians who meet outside of traditional churches, usually inside a member's home.

Instead of "umbrellas," believers in these house churches had "shepherds" who directed their lives for the sake of spiritual growth. Each shepherd would oversee a handful of sheep and was in turn overseen by a more senior shepherd. At the top of this pyramid structure was the "Fort Lauderdale Five": Simpson, Mumford, Bashan, Prince, and Baxter. And at the center of this pyramid was the concept of authority, that a Christian must submit to those above him or her in order to attain God's blessings.

Shepherds did not merely direct the lives of sheep; according to the instructions by the Fort Lauderdale Five, shepherds controlled their sheep. One could not make any decision without the consent of the shepherd, whether that decision be in regard to finances, career choice, dating, or marriage and family life. The prevailing idea was that the shepherd would provide a spiritual covering for the sheep, thereby ensuring God's blessing and protection from any demonic attack. In reality, the system became so authoritarian and abusive that it all but collapsed within a decade. The concept lived on, however, within the NAR—the concept of authority informed the role of apostles and prophets—as well as the IBLP.

In other words, what the Fort Lauderdale Five referred to as "shepherds," Gothard referred to as "umbrellas," and Michelle Duggar referred to as "buddies." The older children in her home were the shepherds to the younger children; she was the shepherd to all of the children, and Jim Bob was the shepherd to her.

Another of Gothard's teachings, that of "rhemas," also has parallels in the Latter Rain and informs the roles of NAR apostles and prophets. Gothard taught that rhemas are inspiration from the Holy Spirit, be it a conviction that one should do something (such as talk to a particular stranger about Christ) or a prompting toward a particular verse in the Bible. Gothard's critics, many of whom worked inside his ministry before defecting, insisted that rhemas were merely his personal opinions, disguised as Bible verses taken out of context or as guidelines given by one that God placed in a position of authority. One such rhema was that females should keep their hair long and curly, something that most of the Duggar girls and their mother adhered to despite a lack of scriptural basis. But this discrepancy mattered little, as to Gothard's followers, the rhemas that he gave were functionally equivalent to the Bible. The revelations that NAR apostles and prophets claim that God gives to them look very similar to Gothard's rhemas.

Another influence, however, brought the IBLP into line with the hardest form of dominionism in America, that of Reconstructionism. In 1963, a white supremacist and Holocaust revisionist named Rousas John Rushdoony published a book called *The Messianic Character of American Education*. He was part of a backlash to a Protestant movement from the late 1800s called the Social Gospel, which called on Christians to express their faith through advocacy for the poor. This advocacy included education for inner-city children, public utilities that could be accessed by everyone, and nutrition assistance for people who struggled to afford food. When Franklin D. Roosevelt became president in 1933, he began institutionalizing many Social Gospel programs in the US government through a massive overhaul known as the New Deal. Public schools had long been a component of American life, but through the New Deal, they proliferated, with one goal being providing children from impoverished families the means for upward mobility.

Rushdoony referred to public schools as "government schools," as they were run by the government and served the government's—not God's—agenda. In *The Messianic Character of American Education*, he insisted that the government was playing God by engaging in "social salvation," that is, using tax-funded resources provided by the state to perform tasks that rightly belonged to the male-headed family. The solution was for children to be educated in church-run Christian schools or at home, with the mother caring for them and her husband, who worked to provide for the family's financial needs.

This goal of abolishing public schools in favor of Christian schools or mothers homeschooling their children is at the center of Rushdoony's answer to the Social Gospel and New Deal, the program that came to be known as Reconstructionism. Reconstructionism seeks to severely limit the scope of the government by abolishing all government services that are not necessary for the protection of private property. All other tasks are to be performed by patriarchal families and local churches. Gender norms are strictly enforced, and the punishment for coming out as queer is death by stoning.

Gothard did not talk openly about Reconstructionism. However, under his IBLP is the Advanced Training Institute—the "ATI" that the Duggars set out for at the end of *14 Kids and Pregnant Again*—which provides homeschool curriculum based on Gothard's teachings about male authority. He urged his followers to have as many children as possible, believing that large families were God's will for Christians to have influence in society. This model segued almost perfectly with Rushdoony's belief that patriarchal families, not public schools and other government-run services, should be at the center of society. In practice, there is significant overlap between organizations run by Rushdoony's disciples and those run by Gothard's.

Despite ties to (what were then) some of evangelicalism's most extremist, fringe movements, Gothard and his IBLP initially became famous for many of the same reasons that the Duggars did. Gothard never married, nor did he have any children, so his success could not have been due to methods that he had tested out and proven in his own personal life. Rather, during the 1950s and 1960s, he recognized that American life was changing rapidly. Dr. Benjamin Spock was urging parents to raise their children without spanking them, and then urging a generation of children who had not been spanked to burn their Vietnam War draft cards. The Supreme Court was not only declaring school segregation to be unconstitutional but also banning prayer and Bible-reading in public-school classrooms. At the same time, the Civil Rights Movement, Women's Rights Movement, and Gay Rights Movement were upending the consensus of the white male at the center of society. America's entire social order was in a state of upheaval and change.

Plenty of people celebrated these changes, including a number of progressive evangelicals. But for the frantic parents of children who no longer respected traditional forms of authority and seemed to be in rebellion against all established social norms, the story was different. Many feared that their children would turn to the drug and hippie culture that seemed to be flourishing, or that they might even come out as gay. Enter Bill Gothard, who had a solution. He had the formula for parents to ensure that their children turned out right.

So the appeal of the Duggars was not that they were weird—as the initial *People* article meant to show—but rather that they were so incredibly ... normal. They represented the 1950s, an idyllic symbol of life before the upheaval of the 1960s. In a world of chaos, they displayed order. Men held doors open for women, women respected men, and children obeyed their parents. To avid viewers of their show, this is what had been missing from American public life, what had caused so many families to unravel and children to come out to their parents as queer. Two generations after the youth of the 1960s had come of age, plenty of Americans wanted a return to life as it supposedly had been, a golden age before they had to worry about their children experimenting with drugs or a queer lifestyle. They wanted normalcy. So they welcomed the Duggars into their living rooms as the ultimate expression of normal.

When the Duggars became the number one television show on TLC, they brought a family-friendly dominionism into living rooms all across America. People who would out-of-hand reject everything about Shepherding, Reconstructionism, and the IBLP sat in rapt attention every week as they watched a family with nineteen children promote those exact dominionist programs.

◆

In the popular imagination, cults are closed groups that erect thick walls between themselves and the rest of society. Admission to these groups can be very difficult, as cult leaders must sift "true believers" from outsiders who are merely curious. Members isolate themselves within communes, where they only interact with other cult members in what quickly turns into an echo chamber that amplifies their own beliefs. Their teachings and practices run counter to those of mainstream religion and can include seemingly bizarre ideas, such as the leader being a messiah who called upon his followers to commit mass suicide (Jim Jones and People's Temple) or that the passing of a comet necessitates mass suicide (Marshall Applewhite and Heaven's Gate).

The reality of cults in America is much more complex. Many religious groups that are considered mainstream actually began as fringe groups that could be considered cults. One example is Seventh-Day Adventism, today a robust movement within America's Protestant landscape but that began in the 1800s as a group known as the Millerites. A man named William Miller made the proclamation in 1831 that Jesus Christ would return between 1843 and 1844. By 1840, Millerism had become a national movement, with true believers selling off their possessions in anticipation of the Second Coming. When 1844 came and went with no eschatological significance, the millennial fervor of Millerism settled down into the religious sect that came to be known as Seventh-Day Adventism. Even Christianity itself began as a sect of Judaism—what can be deemed a cult—before it became the state religion of the Roman Empire in AD 380.

In analyzing cult structure and the movement of cults from the fringe and into the mainstream, what may be more helpful than the oddity of true believers' convictions is the level of obedience that they have to a leader. In other words, their understanding of authority. The extent to which they will follow the teachings of a prophet or apostle, the allegiance they feel they owe to a political messiah, and their efforts to enshrine their beliefs into public law that everyone else must follow. In this regard, the Duggars are a cautionary tale of a cult that has moved to the center of American public life.

What caused the Duggar family to first gain public notice was Jim Bob's political career. He ran for, and won, a seat in the Arkansas State House of Representatives in 1998 and again in 2000. His children, who had a somewhat lax schedule because of homeschooling, regularly sat in the gallery of the House and even mingled with state politicians. One of those was Mike Huckabee, who served as Arkansas governor from 1996 until 2007. Like Representative Duggar, Governor Huckabee had deep connections to the IBLP and worked tirelessly to promote its agenda in state politics, under the guise of conservative family values.

To continue promoting IBLP politics in public life, Jim Bob ran for a seat in the US Senate in 2002. There, campaign pictures of his massive family caught the attention of the media and eventually led to the 2003 profile in *People* magazine. Jim Bob took a decisive defeat in the race, but what came next had a much greater impact on America's cultural politics than any legislation that he could have introduced in the US Senate. Instead of introducing rogue, far-right legislation that promoted dominionist goals, the reality television empire that was built around his family was like a boulder dropped into a lake, with ripples that captured the hearts and minds of the entire country.

The IBLP was never merely a means by which parents could homeschool their children and raise them to be unconditionally obedient. It was always a movement that allied itself with power at every level, from local city councils and mayors to state governors to federal senators and representatives. One of those city council members and mayors was Sarah Palin, who served the city of Wasilla, Alaska, as a council member from 1992 until 1996 and as mayor from 1996 until 2002. Her tenure in city politics was mired in controversy as she pushed far-right agendas that mirror the politics of the NAR church she attended as well as those of the IBLP. When Palin became governor of Alaska in 2006 and then John McCain's vice-presidential candidate in 2008, she had immense appeal among conservative evangelicals who were shifting from the old-guard politics of Jerry Falwell toward the more extremist politics of dominion.

Josh, the oldest Duggar child, immediately went into political activism upon reaching adulthood, initially by working as a conservative consultant. In 2008, when Mike Huckabee ran for the Republican presidential nomination, Josh worked on the campaign. And in 2013, he became the executive director of Family Research Council Action, an anti-gay organization that helped fund the movement in Uganda. And he was far from the only alumnus of the IBLP to get involved in conservative activism. The firebrand Madison Cawthorn, who became America's youngest congressman when he was elected to the US House of Representatives in 2020 at the age of 25, was homeschooled in the IBLP. He held his congressional seat from 2021 until 2023, becoming infamous for promoting Donald Trump, conspiracy theories, and incendiary rhetoric, as well as his numerous sex scandals and bringing firearms to airports.

But *17*, *18*, and *19 Kids and Counting* were not about any of these political connections or far-right ideologies. The show was about family values, a smoothly operating household, and Christian faith. To Jim Bob, the show was a ministry, an evangelistic outreach for guiding those outside of the fold into the way of life that God intended for everyone.

◆

Everything unraveled for the hyperbolically normal family long before *14 Kids and Pregnant Again* introduced the Duggars to stardom. Though there were fourteen kids in the family at the time of the photo in *People* magazine, only thirteen of them were featured. In a pattern that has been repeated over and over again among dominionists, the oldest child, Josh, had molested at least five girls by that time and had been sent to an IBLP facility. There, he was engaging in hard labor meant to purge his soul of the wickedness that had led to his crime—and he was not receiving any psychiatric treatment or legal consequences. A few years later, when US Marshals arrested him for downloading and possessing hard child pornography, the IBLP could not get him out of trouble.

Because none other than Bill Gothard himself had also come under fire and was finally being held accountable for his decades of grooming and molesting underage girls at his IBLP facilities. In 2014, the year before the Duggar scandal broke, Gothard had been placed on leave by the organization that he had founded because the board found the accusations against him to be credible.

In other words, the patriarchal structure of the IBLP and insistence on teaching very young children immediate obedience to those in authority was actually a way of grooming entire generations of evangelical girls and funneling them into the groping arms of Gothard and other men in authority over them. And keeping these girls at home, away from the prying eyes of schoolteachers and other professionals who are required by law to make reports to children's services, meant that children had to suffer in silence, with no one to tell about what was happening to them.

Bob Jones. Mike Bickle. Paul Cain. Madison Cawthorn. Josh Duggar. Bill Gothard. Heidi Baker. The same story of dominionist leaders using their spiritual authority to groom and sexually assault children and young women, or of ministers allowing offenders to access children and refusing to hold anyone accountable, is repeated over and over again among the different sects that make up American dominion.

9

Paleo-Confederates

"The institution of slavery has so blackened the Southern position," wrote the homeschool advocate and anti-government extremist Doug Wilson, "that nothing about the South can be viewed as good or right." He went on to say, about the role of slavery prior to the Civil War, "Slavery is considered to be such a wicked practice that it alone is sufficient to answer the question of which side was right in that unfortunate war."[1]

Wilson disagreed with the mainstream consensus that slavery was the driver of the antebellum Southern economy and the catalyst for the Civil War. "We must know the truth about slavery," he wrote in his 1996 booklet, coauthored with Steve Wilkins, entitled *Southern Slavery As It Was*. "The South has been stigmatized and slandered, and generations have been misled over the true nature of the 'peculiar institution' and as a consequence, they have not understood the true nature of the South in general."[2] That true nature, he argued, was not only altogether good; it was biblical—including much of the owning and selling of human beings that was practiced in the antebellum South.

Wilson's booklet created a firestorm in the small college town of Moscow, Idaho, where he was quietly building a far-right empire. Not at first, as the booklet was hardly taken seriously by anyone with even a passing knowledge of American history; never mind that 20 percent of the booklet was plagiarized from a discredited source. And Wilson had already been in Moscow for upwards of three decades, having completed his undergraduate and master's degrees in classics and philosophy at the University of Idaho at Moscow.

Locals already knew that Wilson's Christ Church, Logos Christian School, New Saint Andrews College (founded in 1994), and Greyfriars Hall (a seminary founded in 1998) did not promote historical Christian teachings and that Wilson had cemented his power by organizing a small group of church members against the board of elders in 1993 and 1994. But even Professor Nick Gier, who had overseen much of Wilson's coursework at the university, did not realize until the fall of 2003 that he was engaging—on a serious, intellectual level—with Neo-Confederacy. That was when flyers advertising *Southern Slavery As It Was* blew through Moscow and surrounding communities.

"Slave life was to them [slaves] a life of plenty, of simple pleasures, of food, clothes, and good medical care,"[3] the flyers quoted from the booklet. Students at the university had the opportunity to meet the authors, one of whom was the local pastor and one of whom was a cofounder of the neo-secessionist organization League of the South. Wilkins served as pastor of the Auburn Avenue Presbyterian Church, based in Monroe, Louisiana, and one of his congregants was Michael Hill, the president of the League of the South.

A citywide uproar ensued among Moscow residents who did not want to see Neo-Confederate ideals being plastered across their small Idaho town. While a number of towns and cities in the South continue to stage Civil War reenactments and boast statues of Confederate leaders, Idaho is on the other side of the country from what was once the Confederacy. What were these ideas doing in a town like Moscow? And why was Doug Wilson promoting them? The ensuing fervor embroiled virtually everyone living in the Washington/Idaho border region known as the Palouse.

Photos showed that at Wilson's K-12 school, portraits of Confederate generals hung in elementary classrooms; reports indicated that the school commemorated the birthday of Robert E. Lee instead of his American rival, President Abraham Lincoln. Wilson acknowledged in 2006 that he had been flying the Confederate battle flag at the school and at church functions. This Neo-Confederate sentiment had been building long before flyers promoting *Southern Slavery As It Was* were distributed in 2003, or even before the booklet's publication in 1996.

In the heat of anti-Confederate, antislavery angst in a hyperlocal region, few could see that the Neo-Confederate ideas being promoted by Wilson and Wilkins were already infiltrating mainstream culture and even America's electoral politics.

◆

Christian nationalism usually begins with the claim that America was founded as a Christian nation. American fundamentalists, almost as a rule, look to the country's founding as a "golden age" of a Christian civilization, overseen by Christian men establishing a Christian government. What one regards as the founding—the first founding of when Pilgrims began landing in what became the British colonies, or the second founding of the Revolutionary era—matters little, as both foundings represent to Christian nationalists the Christian ideal to which America must return. Righteous laws that were based on the Bible, a decentralized, deregulated economy, and a miniscule federal government are central to the political goals of Christian nationalists; in other words, recreating what they see as the golden age of the founding.

Rousas John Rushdoony was different. To him, the golden age was actually the Confederacy (1861–5), which he saw as a Bible-based republic that came to an untimely end when the South lost the Civil War. Not that Rushdoony entirely rejected the idea that the founding was a Christian era, but humanism and secularism had—in his view—displaced the biblical nature of the Constitution; however, this biblical basis for society was preserved in the Confederacy. The war itself was not a struggle over slavery but rather a righteous conflict between the Bible-believing South and the Unitarian, humanistic North. And one thinker who influenced both him and Doug Wilson was Robert Lewis Dabney (1820-98), a preacher, theologian, and Confederate army chaplain who had spent five months of the Civil War as chief of staff for General Stonewall Jackson.

In his 1861 "Cornerstone Speech," Confederate Vice President Alexander Stephens gave the reason for the existence of the Confederacy four years before its collapse at Appomattox: "Our new government is founded upon exactly the opposite idea [of the Union]; its foundations are laid, its cornerstone rests, upon the great truth that the negro is not equal to the white man; that slavery subordination to the superior race is his natural and normal condition."[4] Dabney believed this condition to be not only "natural," as Stephens claimed, but also biblical. Africans were morally inferior to whites, and their predisposition was enslavement.

Scarcely had the treaty been signed at Appomattox Courthouse and the defeated Southern troops begun their slow march home when Dabney began lamenting the loss of a truly Christian society. During the Civil War, the overwhelming majority of white Southern Christians were convinced that God was on their side and that, through divine aid, they would prevail over the North. When they lost the war, not only were their cities devastated and their countryside ravaged, and not only were their slaves now free and seeking civil rights and political office, and not only were Northern troops now occupying their states in what is known as Reconstruction (1865–77). Their entire belief system was threatened with collapse as they had to reckon with the fact that God Almighty had not come to their aid and brought about divine victory.

As Union troops came to occupy the South during the contentious years of Reconstruction, Northern educators came as well and established schools that educated not only white males but also females and the children of freed slaves. Dabney opposed this widespread institution of public schools, not because he did not espouse education (he believed that the best and brightest should be educated at public expense), but because he did not believe that freed slaves should be educated. In his mind, they would soon return to the cotton fields.

Dabney consciously rejected all things that he saw as coming from the North, including any form of learning that did not begin and end with the Bible. He saw the North as humanistic and denying the Trinity, rather than Bible-believing like the South was. And Northern-style education, which was infiltrating the South *en masse* following the Civil War, would certainly bring about moral calamity and a loss of all biblical values. Not only would African American children sit in classrooms with their white peers—this mingling of the races inevitably leading to intermarriage—but the minds of white children would be corrupted with a humanistic, rather than biblical, education.

When Rushdoony began developing the thought that became Reconstructionism, he essentially resurrected Dabney, the long-forgotten theologian and prophet of the Confederacy. Rushdoony imagined a feudal society centered on the white landowning male, not a Catholic feudal society such as Medieval Europe but rather the Protestant one of the Confederacy.

And this sentiment has been echoed at New Saint Andrews College, one of the schools founded by Doug Wilson, where a student told a reporter, "We want to be Medieval Protestants."[5]

To Rushdoony, the appeal of the Confederacy went beyond support for white supremacism and subjugation of Africans. The Confederacy was designed to have a weak central government, with power concentrated more at local levels and especially within male-oriented, patriarchal families. This order, to Rushdoony, reflected the God-given social order that he saw as rooted in the Bible. Like Rushdoony, Dabney had singularly rejected all calls for women's rights, including women's suffrage; women's participation in public life would, Dabney and later Rushdoony believed, upend the biblical order for society. "The fact of law introduces a fundamental and basic inequality in society," Rushdoony wrote in 1973. "The abolition of law will not eliminate inequality, because then the very fact of sheer survival will create an elite and establish fundamental inequality."[6] In other words, the feudal model of the Southern plantation—a wealthy white landowner with his submissive wife and obedient children at the center of a miniature fiefdom worked by slaves and not interfered upon by a strong federal government—was God's way.

Rushdoony's solution to the problems of Northern humanism being preached in what he termed "government schools" was the proliferation of Christian schools and, later, the submissive mother homeschooling her children in a patriarchal family. In like manner, Wilson's ministry also has a homeschool component, with classical curriculum and guides for parents on the "why" of homeschooling. Rushdoony and Wilson both found inspiration in the Dutch Calvinist statesman and theologian Abraham Kuyper and his concept of sphere sovereignty. "Each God-created government has authority within its assigned sphere," Wilson preached during the Covid pandemic. "And this is commonly referred to as sphere sovereignty."[7]

While there are many criticisms of sphere sovereignty—including that the state *must* get involved in family life to protect children who are experiencing abuse and neglect—it does suggest a separation of church and state, as both must exist entirely independently of each other. Kuyper believed that Christians should engage in the public sphere, including government and politics, but his vision of what this engagement looked like was pluralistic. Christians might have primacy within the church, but in other spheres, they had to engage with people who might profess other models of Christianity, other faiths, or even no faith at all. Though Rushdoony relied on a version of Kuyper's sphere sovereignty, he altogether rejected the idea that Christians should cooperate with people of different religious persuasions in public life. In Rushdoony's view, only Christians should engage in public life at all.

Americans, including American Calvinists, largely rejected Kuyper's ideas during his lifetime. But in 1898, he delivered the Stone Lectures at Princeton Seminary and gave the famous line, "There is not a square inch in the whole domain of our human existence over which Christ, who is Sovereign over all, does not cry, Mine!"[8] In more recent years, this line has been used by dominionist evangelicals—especially Wilson—to promote their theocratic ambitions. "We were asked how you would summarize what's going on in Moscow," Wilson said when asked about his thoughts on the quote from Kuyper's Stone Lectures. "What are you guys trying to do? What's this all about?" The booklets that sanitized slavery, the embrace of Dabney and Rushdoony, the rejection of women's rights, the insistence that parents keep their children out of government schools. "We want to embrace a vision of all of Christ for all of life."[9]

Here, there is an almost imperceptible sleight of hand: that *Christ* has dominion over all—what Kuyper and plenty of other Protestants have long asserted—turning into *Christians* have dominion over all. The change seems subtle, but worked out on a practical level, means the difference between historical forms of Christian thought, including the teachings of Calvin and Kuyper, and the present-day dominionist movement that is grounded in a longing for the Confederacy.

◆

"Give me liberty or give me death!" are words enshrined in America's national conscience, spoken at the Second Virginia Convention in 1775. Patrick Henry (1736–99), the orator who spoke those words, was a Virginia statesman who ardently defended slavery in the country's founding documents—the

Constitution and its Bill of Rights. Though Northern representatives wanted to phase out the slave trade and end the practice altogether, Henry helped ensure that Southern, slave-friendly positions found their way into the Constitution. One of those principles was a weak central government, as a strong government could outlaw slavery or enact laws that would necessarily lead to its demise. As such, Henry was an Anti-Federalist who made efforts to scuttle the Constitution before it could be ratified. Less than a century later, his championing of a weak central government found its expression in the Confederate States of America.

Founded in 2000, Patrick Henry College (PHC) has been the gold standard for homeschooled students who want a classical Christian education that provides access to the halls of power in Washington, DC. Michael Farris founded and presided over PHC after building a career defending the rights of parents to homeschool their children. In 1983, as the homeschool movement was accelerating among conservative Christian families, Farris cofounded the Home School Legal Defense Association (HSLDA) to provide resources and legal aid for homeschool families. The core belief of HSLDA comes straight from Rushdoony—that the government has no right to regulate the education of children.

PHC embodies the ethos of its statesman namesake along with its Reconstructionist-oriented founder, Farris. According to the 2024–5 college catalog, Farris founded the school to answer the concerns of homeschool parents about colleges that were not only Christian but that also taught "fidelity to the spirit of the American founding."[10] And there can be no question about which version of the founding Farris is referring to, given that he named the school after the Anti-Federalist Patrick Henry. When the school first opened in 2000, the only degree that it offered was in government. Students could take part in apprenticeships in Washington, DC, and, upon graduation, begin working in politics.

The school has been remarkably successful at achieving its vision of placing homeschool graduates in positions of power in or near America's capital. Many of those students came from Gothard's IBLP, including Madison Cawthorn (who attended PHC but did not graduate), as well as Wilson's homeschool program. Prelaw students regularly score in the 98th percentile on the Law

School Admission Test and go on to Supreme Court clerkships, congressional seats, and even cabinet positions. The homeschool curricula of IBLP may have been farcical, but students who moved from IBLP and similar homeschool programs to PHC can go directly into government work. And in 2021, Doug Wilson's accrediting body, Association of Classical Christian Schools, awarded Farris with its Boniface Award "in light of his continual sacrifices and tireless efforts to stand for freedom and religious liberty."[11]

Not that all homeschooling is necessarily connected to Rushdoony, Wilson, and/or Farris. Homeschooling families have their own whys, and invariably, each "why" has to do with what parents believe is best for the children. However, Rushdoony pioneered a theological rationale for homeschooling as part of a Christian civilization, as well as homeschooling's legal defenses *as a reaction against public schools*. And with the rise of PHC, homeschooling itself became a weapon against the federal government, aiming to replace secular values with biblical ones, and the idea of biblical government serving as a stand-in for the Confederacy.

In fact, Wilson describes himself as a Paleo-Confederate, meaning he does not "surrender the principles that were involved in the fight." He makes a distinction between his views and Neo-Confederacy, as Neo-Confederates "are still fighting the war";[12] Wilson recognizes that the Civil War is over yet insists that the South was waging a righteous battle against Northern—humanistic, anti-Christian—aggression.

Perhaps there should be little cause for national concern about a far-right, pro-Confederacy empire in a small town in Idaho… as long as that empire *stays* in its small town. But in 2013, the prestigious evangelical magazine *Christianity Today* named Doug Wilson's book *Evangellyfish* its fiction book of the year. In spite of, or perhaps because of, his beliefs that align with a romanticized view of the Confederacy, Wilson is almost imperceptibly influential in mainstream evangelical circles. And given the influence of PHC in national politics, Wilson's fingerprints are now on virtually all aspects of the American government.

◆

What Dabney could not have foreseen was how the Confederacy became increasingly sacralized in the two generations after the war. A mythology known as the Lost Cause emerged out of the Confederacy's wrecked belief that God would divinely preserve its biblical way of life; the Lost Cause imbued Confederate heroes, from the teenage boys who died in battle to the generals who led the charge, and the Confederacy itself with religious significance. At the heart of the Lost Cause is the very idea that Wilson promoted in *Southern Slavery As It Was*, that slave owners were benevolent and paternalistic, not cruel and ruthless, and the war was fought over something other than slavery. Like British Israelism, the Lost Cause has been overwhelmingly rejected by mainstream historians. Yet it lives on, not only among pro-Confederate white separatists, such as those of League of the South, but also among evangelicals who have been radicalized by Wilson.

Some ministers of the Lost Cause, including Dabney, insisted that God allowed the South to lose because it was under divine judgment; the North was not under God's judgment because it had abandoned God entirely, and he had allowed them to go their own way. Others claimed that the South had been through a baptism of blood and, though defeated, had emerged sanctified and holy before God. Despite different explanations that the Lost Cause gave for the South's defeat, the mythology gave rise to the reign of white terror that was admired by Charles Fox Parham: the Ku Klux Klan.

Several of the Klan's founding members were ministers, and the church's relationship with the Klan was often one of accommodating and even of sanctifying it. In fact, the Klan saw itself as a Christian institution with the mission of protecting white Christian Southerners from African-American barbarity. The myth of the Lost Cause wove those "Christian" beliefs of white supremacy into a biblical narrative in which Southerners were the people of God who bravely fought a War of Northern Aggression to retain their Christian heritage.

The Lost Cause rewrote history in a way that vindicated the defeated, "Christian" South. The mythology that emerged insisted that—despite ample evidence to the contrary—the Civil War was about states' rights, not slavery. In this view, the Northern abolitionist efforts to dismantle slavery infringed on the Southern states' constitutional right to perpetuate the practice. Because the federal government, especially the newly elected Abraham Lincoln, sympathized with the North, the rights of the Southern states were being trampled on, and they therefore had the right to secede and create the Confederate States of America. Today, many white supremacist heirs of the Lost Cause have a similar attitude to the federal government and focus their efforts on states' rights.

Unironically, Wilson's New Saint Andrews College in Moscow is a mere 90 miles from the headquarters of Aryan Nations in Hayden Lake, Idaho. Like several branches of the Ku Klux Klan, Aryan Nations promotes Identity theology—the British Israelism and Serpent Seed of Wesley Swift and William Branham, combined with an extremist anti-government stance that can perhaps only be compared to Rushdoony and his Reconstructionism.

This anti-government white separatism played out before a national audience in August of 1992 in a remote outpost in Idaho known as Ruby Ridge. A white separatist named Randy Weaver had moved to the mountains with his family and built a cabin, where they believed they could survive what they believed was an impending apocalypse. This apocalypse was the culmination of biblical prophecy about the wrath of God, based on their British-Israelist beliefs and reading of the best-selling prophecy book *The Late Great Planet Earth*.

As far removed as the Weavers were from civilization, some of their closest neighbors were other white separatists. In fact, they socialized at the Aryan Nations headquarters at Hayden Lake. While the Weavers chose not to join the group, many of their beliefs dovetailed with Identity. One of those beliefs is that the government that currently exists is illegitimate, and its wickedness will be revealed when Christ returns and destroys it. Identity followers cope with this paradigm of an illegitimate government by arming themselves heavily to protect themselves from government intrusion. Many, many Identity families, including the Weavers, homeschool their children.

While this Identity mainstay of stockpiling weapons to use against the government often sounds like paranoia, for Randy Weaver and his family, it was prescient. He was charged with felony firearms violations when he told an undercover federal agent at Aryan Nations headquarters that he could provide sawed-off shotguns, which are illegal. When Weaver did not appear for his court date, a standoff began between him and the federal government—a move that fit into the prophetic schema and white separatism that he espoused. In this view of prophecy, as well as the reality of what unfolded, the government was out to get him, and he had to arm himself to protect his family.

What came next was an eleven-day siege, with federal marshals and the FBI surrounding his property. Marshals shot and killed Weaver's dog and then his fourteen-year-old son, Sammy. Next, they shot and killed his wife, Vicki, while she was inside the cabin holding their ten-month-old daughter. The standoff finally ended when a neighbor, Bo Gritz, convinced Weaver that his friend, Kevin Harris, who had been on the mountain with them and had been wounded in the melee, needed to get medical attention.

The Ruby Ridge siege is significant for many things. It is considered the birth of the modern militia movement. It was an enactment of Identity theology, what it looks like in action, and shows how the prophecy-laden beliefs of white separatists can be unwittingly fulfilled by a federal government that does not understand prophecy belief or Identity.

To Doug Wilson, at least some of the significance of Ruby Ridge is that it was part of the long march toward what he saw as the government-sponsored election fraud that placed Joe Biden in the Oval Office. "Waco. Ruby Ridge," he wrote in a blog post three decades after the event. "Abruptly changing election rules on the eve of elections. 2000 mules ... Objecting to tyranny defined as whiteness." Then, to top off a long list of what he saw as government abuses and fraud, "And the current resident [President Biden] denouncing his political opponents as enemies of democracy in front of a crimson set with a couple of Marines standing there like they were still defending a free country or something, and the president looking for all the world like a cartoon fascist leader in a fever dream."[13]

What Wilson omitted from his long list of infractions that he insists the federal government has made against his Lost Cause pseudo-reality is the Oklahoma City Bombing on April 19, 1995. The bomber was also connected to Identity theology, and in attacking a government building and killing 167 people—including 19 children, most of whom were attending daycare in the building—he was enacting his own understanding of biblical prophecy. The government had to be annihilated in an End-Times race war that would herald the Second Coming of Christ. This is Identity. And it is intimately connected to the worldview that Wilson promotes, not among a few far-right disciples in Idaho, but within mainstream evangelicalism and, by way of PHC, in American government.

Not that Wilson espouses the prophecy beliefs that drove the Weavers and the Oklahoma City bomber. His theology claims that the church will be victorious as it reforms society into what he sees as Christian norms. Identity teaches the destruction of much of society in a race war that will culminate in the Battle of Armageddon. Though theoretically distinct, Wilson's movement may functionally have more in common with Identity than with historical forms of Christian thought.

◆

In other words, one cannot truly grasp the depth and breadth of dominionism in American life without grappling with its roots in the Confederacy and its contemporary expression in Neo-Confederate groups. Much of today's dominionist movement is nothing more than the dry bones of the Confederacy coming back to life; dominionism is the embodiment of the Lost Cause. January 6 did not happen because of voting irregularities that favored Joe Biden over Donald Trump. It happened because of a romanticized view of the Confederacy that is deeply ingrained, not only among white-separatist militias, but within the dominionist teachings that have gone mainstream within American evangelicalism.

Understanding this paradigm helps us realize that the presence of Confederate battle flags alongside Appeal to Heaven flags at the Capitol Riot was not an accident but rather a historical necessity. Once the disparate groups of Reconstructionism, Identity, and the NAR rediscovered their common heritage in the Confederacy and the Ku Klux Klan and joined forces to create a viable movement, *they were going to attack the US government.* This is a fundamental reality of dominionist teachings.

10

From Homeschool to the Secular Academy

"[Fisher Ames] noted that the Bible was the principal source of sound morals in America and therefore must never be separated from the classroom,"[1] David Barton wrote in a booklet about separation of church and state. Ames (1758–1808), a minor figure in America's founding period, served in the Massachusetts convention that ratified the Constitution and then was elected to the first US Congress. In Barton's estimation, however, Ames was a giant, a Christian exemplar for a politically faithful method of running America's public schools.

Barton earned a bachelor's degree in religious education from Oral Roberts University, the eponymous school founded by one of the leaders of the Latter-Rain revival. Despite having no formal credentials as a historian, in 2005, Barton was listed in *Time* magazine as one of the twenty-five most influential evangelicals in America, owing to his tireless work in portraying Christian nationalism as the only correct understanding of American history. He has advised countless politicians, written *amicus* court briefs in cases that have gone to the Supreme Court, and even served as an expert advisor for educational standards and textbook material used in public schools.

"The 51-year-old Texan's thesis," according to the *Time* article, is "that the U.S. was a self-consciously religious nation from the time of the Founders until the 1963 Supreme Court school-prayer ban (which Barton calls a 'rejection of divine law')."[2] At the center of his teachings, the cornerstone on which all of his lectures on American history and the Christian faith rest, is the assertion that the Founders never intended for there to be a separation of church and state, at least not as courts understand the concept today; any separation was to be one-way, in which the government cannot influence the church, but the church has every right and obligation to be heard in government.

Even when the article was written in 2005, long before the Covid-19-era upheavals on school boards and public libraries, before he helped usher through a new public-school curriculum in Texas that overtly teaches Christian nationalism, Barton was a force to be reckoned with. "Many historians dismiss his thinking," the article noted, "but Barton's advocacy organization, WallBuilders, and his relentless stream of publications, court amicus briefs and books like *The Myth of Separation*, have made him a hero to millions—including some powerful politicians."[3] Those politicians have included school-board members and city mayors, up through state congressmen and even then-US House majority leader Tom DeLay. When Mike Johnson became the Speaker of the House in 2024, Barton called him a long-time friend and ally. And Barton himself served as vice-chair of the Texas Republican Party from 1997 until 2006.

"Clearly, the use of the Bible in public school classrooms did not violate Fisher Ames' view of the First Amendment—and he was one of the Framers most responsible for the wording of the Amendment,"[4] Barton continued in his booklet. Elsewhere, he has showed a correlation between the removal of prayer and Bible-reading from America's public schools with decreased SAT and ACT scores, as well as increased conduct problems with students. He makes necessary criticisms of falling standards—although critics have insisted that the correlation he makes between prayer and Bible-reading and those falling standards is not actually causation—and has spent decades striving to apply a Christian witness to those problems. In the process, though, he has brought the dominionist program out of the confines of homeschool circles and squarely into America's public schools.

Barton insists that he is not a dominionist. However, his goal in all of his work has been to bring Christianity back to the center of American public life and dismantle the wall of separation between church and state, as has long been understood by courts and legislators. *This is precisely the goal of dominionism*: to give Christian leaders power in the political realm and the ability to use that power to enact a theocratic agenda in American government. And Barton has focused much of his work on bringing his brand of Christian nationalism into public-school curricula, thereby building a movement by educating children all across the country into his understanding of American religion, history, and values.

◆

"Most people do not realize that there was a paid chaplain in Congress even before the Revolutionary War ended." This quote could have been lifted from one of Barton's hundreds of speeches that he has been delivering every year for decades. However, it comes from a source text that profoundly shaped the Christian nationalism of the Religious Right in the 1980s. "Also we find that prior to the founding of the national congress all the early provincial congresses in all thirteen colonies always opened with prayer," Francis Schaeffer (1912–84) continued in his 1981 book *A Christian Manifesto*.[5] Just the title of Schaeffer's final book can account for much of Barton's thinking on American history, as the concept of a Christian manifesto stands to contradict the *Communist Manifesto* (1848), *Humanist Manifesto* (1933), and *Humanist Manifesto II* (1973). Against these secular histories and worldviews, Christians should—must—look to something greater. This was Schaeffer's parting message to an American evangelicalism that he had spent three decades shaping.

Schaeffer had perhaps the most peculiar career of any of the movers and shakers of evangelicalism's Christian nationalism in the twentieth century. Born into a working-class family, he converted to Christianity as a teenager and then attended Westminster Seminary during the 1930s. Westminster Seminary had broken off from Princeton Seminary during the Fundamentalist-Modernist Controversy of the 1920s, a time when churches and entire denominations split over debates about science, history, and the Bible. Schaeffer remained a staunch fundamentalist throughout his life; he castigated scientific theories that he saw as contradicting a literal reading of the Bible, claiming that evolution diminishes the value of humans as created in the image of God. He also decried modernist approaches to the Bible that sought to understand the Christian scriptures as an ancient text, comparable to other literary works of the ancient world. To him, the threat of theological modernism—the foil of America's fundamentalist movement—stood in opposition to everything the Bible teaches about God, humans, sin, and redemption.

Yet Schaeffer was not to remain on the front lines of American fundamentalism's war with theological modernism. In 1948, he and his family moved to Switzerland, with the goal of spreading the fundamentalist movement among Europeans whose belief systems and entire way of life had been shattered by two world wars. There, he encountered disaffected youth who—in Schaeffer's estimation—suffered from an existential despair. The secular philosophies that they had studied in their universities before dropping out left them believing that there was nothing beyond this present, material existence—no God, no spiritual life, no hope.

Schaeffer saw these philosophies as the source of the modernist theology that he had long been warning people about. So he did what possibly no American fundamentalist before him had done: he had conversations with the university dropouts who came to his L'Abri retreat center and showed them how their belief systems, their worldviews, stood in opposition to the truth of Christianity. Communism, for example, begins with the presupposition that there is no God, and its entirely materialistic worldview leaves its devotees grasping for the meaning of their own existence. He had extensive conversations about Georg Hegel, Immanuel Kant, and Soren Kierkegaard. Taking these conversations as a cue, he began publishing books for an American audience back home, beginning with *The God Who Is There* and *Escape from Reason* in 1968. He may have never read the actual writings of the philosophers that he critiqued, but his own writings prompted conservative evangelicals to engage with secular culture rather than withdraw from it. And he cared deeply about the youth he encountered who experienced meaninglessness and despair.

Schaeffer popularized a phrase for how one should understand theological modernism, with all of the philosophical systems that fed it: secular humanism. He saw secular humanism as a religion unto itself, albeit a nontheistic religion that denies the existence of God and places humans at the center of reason. For conservative evangelicals of the Religious Right from the 1980s and beyond, secular humanism became the bogeyman of Christian culture and the enemy that had to be defeated. And secular humanism was everywhere: public schools, meetings of Congress, the Beatles, even churches that had adopted theological modernism. America was in a war for its very survival, and the two combatants were conservative Christians, holding down the bastions of America's godly heritage, and the secular humanists who wanted to tear down everything that has made America great.

As Schaeffer's star rose among American fundamentalists and evangelicals during the 1960s and 1970s, he was studying the writings of none other than Rousas John Rushdoony. Not to disprove Rushdoony, but to understand the foundations of America's Christian heritage and how Christians can win their country back for God. In fact, both Schaeffer and Rushdoony had taken their cues from the same professor of theology, Cornelius Van Til (1895–1987). Van Til taught *presuppositional apologetics*, which claims that all belief systems are built on a set of metaphysical presuppositions. He claimed that only Christian presuppositions are rational, and non-Christians who begin with different presuppositions cannot be consistently rational. Van Til's disciples, Schaeffer and Rushdoony, saw little to appreciate in modernist, non-Christian culture—secular humanism—but Rushdoony in particular found much to wage war against. For his part, Schaeffer was enthralled by the art and beauty of premodern Europe—the Sistine Chapel, gothic architecture, the paintings in the Louvre. To him, these relics were all that was left of a pre-Christian Europe that had been overtaken by secular humanism.

"Nowhere have the divergent results of the two total concepts of reality, the Judeo-Christian and the humanist world view, been more open to observation than in government and law,"[6] Schaeffer wrote in *A Christian Manifesto*, a book whose content was inspired by a devotee of Rushdoony named John Whitehead. Not that Schaeffer espoused any form of Neo-Confederacy, and he was willing to disagree with aspects of Rushdoony's thought. Yet on the whole, his teachings about America's Judeo-Christian heritage may have been formed by Rushdoony more than anyone else. "The Founding Fathers of the United States (in varying degrees) understood very well the relationship between one's world view and government,"[7] he went on. "This linkage of Christian thinking and the concepts of government were not incidental but fundamental."[8]

Schaeffer's work was not an evidentiary history of America's religious heritage, done by careful scholarship of evangelical historians such as Mark Noll,

David Bebbington, Randall Balmer, and John Fea. This was *presuppositional history*, which begins with the assumption that the Christian worldview is the only rational one, evidence and context be damned. And this presuppositional history is exactly what David Barton has been promoting—to public school districts, state- and national-level lawmakers, churches, magazines, anywhere that he can get a hearing.

"The courts also consider Secular Humanism to be a religion, equivalent under the law to Christianity," Barton wrote in his 1993 booklet *America's Godly Heritage*. "What is the primary tenet of the religion of Secular Humanism? It is the conviction that life revolves around man rather than God—it is a man-centered philosophy that excludes God."[9] He went on to lament, in a manner preceded by Schaeffer, that various nontheistic groups now have religious protections. The courts not only afford them free speech but also offer tax exemptions; if even nontheistic groups are afforded this religious protection, then Christian freedoms are actually placed at risk. "Now, however, the constitutional protections for the genuinely religious have been expanded to include *every* individual, even the non- and anti-religious, thereby eradicating true religious protections."[10] In other words, if everyone is religious, then no one is religious, and truly religious Christians lose their constitutional protections.

With Barton, as with Schaeffer before him, the real issue of concern is what courts mean by the separation of church and state. If the courts accept paganism and Wicca as religions, but religious displays are not allowed in public schools, then why is there no outcry when teachers decorate their classrooms with witches and goblins? The same argument applies to the religion of secular humanism. If religion cannot be taught in public schools, but secular humanism is a religion *and is the foundation of public-school curricula*, then why is no one crying foul? "Today's 'separation of church and state' only means that Biblical principles must be kept out of public, not the principles, beliefs, or practices of other religions (or even so-called religions)."[11]

Schaeffer may have been one of the original developers of what became the Seven Mountain Mandate, working alongside Bill Bright and Loren Cunningham in the 1970s. This cannot be proven from primary sources, and Schaeffer may have never himself been a true dominionist. However, the contemporary lore about the 7MM includes him in those early conversations. Further, his work was influenced greatly by the most extreme dominionist of all, Rushdoony, and it continues to inspire dominionist leaders today—including Barton.

◆

Barton regularly depicts the cosmic struggle between secular humanism and Christianity in mundane terms: Democrats versus Republicans. The GOP has been the party of choice for America's Christian nationalists ever since the Religious Right burst into public life in the late 1970s and early 1980s. As thought leaders like Jerry Falwell and Tim LaHaye shaped nationalist discourse among evangelicals, they demonized the Democratic Party, literally. Women's Liberation, the Civil Rights Movement, and the Gay Rights Movement were all satanically inspired, as were the welfare programs that Democrats tended to champion and Republicans tended to malign. Barton served as the vice-chair of the Texas Republican Party from 1997 until 2006, indicating his affinity for it. And the way that he has portrayed American history consistently casts Republicans in the role of God-fearing Americans who value their country's Christian heritage, against liberal, secular Democrats who want to tear down everything that has made America great.

"Why is it so many Blacks were the victims of the Klan?" Barton asked his audience in a 2008 video about the Civil Rights Movement. "It's real simple," he went on. "If you were Black in America, you were Republican back then."[12] Elsewhere, he claimed, "Had it not been for Republicans, the Civil Rights Act of '64 and the Voting Rights Act of '65 would not have passed." When the Civil War ended in 1865, the majority of Republicans lived in the North, which was much more supportive of abolishing slavery than the Southern states that had comprised the Confederacy. Southerners were overwhelmingly Democrats—fearful of a strong central government, adamant about states' rights, and very much opposed to racial integration. Freed slaves, who gained the right to vote with the passage of the Fifteenth Amendment, almost universally voted Republican, even when they lived in the Democratic-controlled South.

"In 14 years, we passed 23 civil-rights laws," Barton said, referring to America's Republican-led Congress years between 1861 and 1875. "We didn't do it again until 1964. Why? Because in 1876, Democrats regained partial control of Congress."[13] He did not seem to be giving a historical account of Klan violence and the struggle for civil rights as much as giving a rationale for voting Republican. He conveniently omitted—or perhaps was unaware of—the "great switch" between the Republican and Democratic parties that occurred with the passage of the Civil Rights Act of 1964 and Voting Rights Act of 1965. He did not mention that the Civil Rights Act was signed into law by the Democratic president Lyndon B. Johnson the summer before the 1964 election. White Southerners who felt betrayed flocked to the Republican candidate Barry Goldwater, supporting his campaign promise to repeal the Civil Rights Act. The two parties effectively switched platforms, with the Democrats becoming the party of civil rights and the Republicans prioritizing big business, states' rights, and a weakened federal government.

Barton's portrayal of American history as a perpetual struggle between God-fearing Republicans and God-hating Democrats makes his historical analysis so asinine that no mainstream historian has taken it seriously. But it has fallen on welcome ears. Millions of conservative evangelicals, who have been on the receiving end of this kind of partisan rhetoric since the 1970s, eagerly anticipate scholarship that casts American politics in terms of a cosmic war between good and evil. Among this audience, Barton has a voice so profound that he is a *New York Times* best-selling author.

Building on Schaeffer, Barton teaches that the struggle between Republicans and Democrats is intertwined with separation of church and state, going back to Thomas Jefferson (1743–1826). "The 'Republican [Jeffersonian] Revival' of 1800–1801 is one of the most neglected significant episodes in American intellectual and political development," Barton's book *The Jefferson Lies* quoted from Alan Heimert, the late Harvard expert on American religious history. "There were many preachers—many more than historians allow—who avidly and vocally supported the Republican party, and did so in the conviction that Republicanism embodied the first principles of evangelical Christianity."[14] Barton's use of Heimert's analysis does not seem to be showing the difference between Jefferson's Republicans and today's Republican Party, which did not form until nearly three decades after Jefferson's death and eventually switched platforms with the Democratic Party. Rather, Barton was establishing continuity between Jeffersonian Republicans and today's GOP; Republicans have always been the party of Jefferson and the choice of evangelicals.

Though separation of church and state in America can be traced back to the Puritans of the seventeenth century, the phrase entered political parlance through an anecdote from Jefferson's presidency (1801–9). The Baptist Association of Danbury, Connecticut, wrote a letter to Jefferson upon his election, urging him to see religious freedom as an inalienable right rather than a government-sanctioned privilege; he responded with a letter that used the phrase "a wall of separation between church and state" to show his support. Barton, however, flipped the concept on its head. "Significantly, the entire history of the separation doctrine centered on preventing the State from taking control of the Church," Barton wrote in *The Jefferson Lies*. "Throughout history, it had been the state that had seized and controlled the church, not the opposite."[15] The state could not interfere with the goings-on of the church, Barton argues consistently, but nothing stops the church from seizing control of the state. This understanding opened the door for Barton's crusade to promote Christianity in public schools and ultimately has led prophets and apostles to call for the church to take control of the state.

When Thomas Nelson published *The Jefferson Lies* in 2012, it hit the *New York Times* bestseller list. However, there were so many misrepresentations and factual inaccuracies that the publisher soon pulled the book, even though it was selling enough copies to earn Thomas Nelson a handsome profit. If such a scenario befell mainstream historians with actual credentials, the level of embarrassment could turn into a career-ending scandal. But Barton's base refused to desert him, and that base still includes the Republican Party in his home state of Texas. And there, he has spent decades on the committee for the Texas Education Agency that approves social studies textbooks. Once approved, students across the state use these textbooks in public-school classrooms. His job there is expert reviewer.

Though much of the United States adopted the standards of Common Core beginning in 2010, Texas has not. Instead, the state relies on its own set of standards, the Texas Essential Knowledge and Skills (TEKS). TEKS informs textbook publishers what must be included in order for a textbook to be adopted. When a new set of TEKS was proposed in 2009, Barton was an expert reviewer for social studies—despite not even having a bachelor's degree in history, economics, or government. He wrote in his review of the 2009 TEKS, "Written documents were the norm for every [American] colony founded by Bible-minded Christians. After all, this was the Scriptural model: God had given Moses a fixed written law to govern that nation—a pattern that recurred throughout the Scriptures."[16] Granted, early America was overwhelmingly Christian, but Barton's presuppositional approach to history suggests that *only* biblical laws should govern America. And based on his suggestion, the textbooks that the Texas Education Agency adopted in 2014 include the biblical figure Moses as an influential figure in American history.

"The most notorious and widespread of the Southern vigilante groups was the Ku Klux Klan (KKK)," reads one section of a US history book the TEA approved for high schoolers. "The Klan's goals were to destroy the Republican party, to throw out the Reconstruction governments, to aid the planter class, and to prevent African Americans from exercising their political rights."[17] If the ordering on this list indicates importance, as is grammatically correct, then the textbook is claiming that the most significant goal of the Klan was the destruction of the Republican Party. Of everything that could have been said about the first iteration of the Klan—how it was comprised primarily of Confederate soldiers, how members frequently lynched freed slaves, how Nathan Bedford Forrest turned it into the "Invisible Empire" that effectively created a shadow government in the South—the textbook almost mirrors Barton's assertion that the Klan's goal was to destroy the Republican Party. The textbook does not mention him as one of the experts who contributed to the book, but his name is all over the TEKS, and he is an influential voice among the committee members who approved the textbook.

This idea of the Klan engaging in political rather than racial violence has long been an important component of the Lost Cause. In Texas textbooks, the Lost Cause is not presented as a political ideology but as a historical fact. When Barton mixes his historical neglect of American religious culture with an insistence that the Ku Klux Klan was not racially motivated to commit acts of violence against freed slaves, he recreates the Lost Cause for a new generation of conservative evangelicals. Elsewhere, he has promoted the Lost Cause more explicitly, such as when he pointed to a Confederate book called *Christ in the Camp* as evidence for America's Christian heritage. He seemed unaware that the kind of Christianity presented in *Christ in the Camp* is exactly what morphed into the Lost Cause once the Civil War ended.

Because Texas constitutes such a large share of business for textbook publishers, the content that is ultimately approved by Texas ends up in textbooks that the publishers produce for other states, as well. In other words, the content in these books is shaping what kids all over the country learn—including the Lost Cause. Within a decade of Texas introducing textbooks that sanitized the Ku Klux Klan, the Barton-guided TEA would approve a new curriculum for public schools that explicitly teaches Christian nationalism to children as young as five.

◆

The reality is that people are more than their worldviews. They are sons, daughters, mothers, fathers, aunts, uncles, and cousins. They are shaped by their environment and by their genetics. Their brains and personalities form in response to love as well as trauma, with a dose of inherited traits mixed in. Relationships and experiences, financial well-being or the lack thereof, level of education and other opportunities, these things all go into shaping a person. No one—not Jefferson, not Rushdoony, not Schaeffer, not even David Barton—is a one-dimensional character who can be reduced to a political party or an assent to Christianity or secular humanism. People do not vote for Democratic candidates because they are God-hating liberals, and they do not vote for Republican candidates because they are locked in a cosmic battle between good and evil. Citizens vote on what they believe is their personal interest, based on the messaging that candidates and the parties writ large put forth.

Similarly, history is much more complex than a struggle between competing worldviews. The rise and fall of nations, the advent and decline of slavery, the progression and regression of civil rights, wars, and revolutions—these metanarratives are bigger than conservative versus progressive politics.

Reducing them to such, as Barton has managed to do in many of America's public-school textbooks, creates a self-fulfilling prophecy: this approach teaches generations of children that their participation as American citizens is us versus them. Christians against progressives, Republicans against Democrats, America lovers versus America destroyers, God versus anti-God, me versus my neighbor. And that is the opposite of what Jesus Christ taught when he told his disciples, "Love your enemies, and pray for those who persecute you" (Matthew 5:44, NASB).

Part Four

Post-Democratic America

11

Tea Party Dominionists

On May 15, 2007, staffers at Liberty University walked into the office of the school's founder and chancellor, Jerry Falwell, Sr. They found the 73-year-old veteran of evangelical political activism unconscious on the floor. Two hours later, an announcement was made to his community at Liberty University and Thomas Road Baptist Church that he had suddenly passed away of a heart attack.

News outlets jumped on the story and the obvious question behind it: *What would happen to America's Religious Right, now that the pastor who had organized evangelicals into a conservative voting bloc had died?* In fact, the question had already been looming for years. George W. Bush had declared during the 2000 presidential debate that his favorite philosopher was Jesus and marked himself as America's evangelical president. At times, his actions regarding the September 11 attacks and ensuing conflict in the Middle East seemed to be driven by prophecy belief more than geopolitical realities. By the end of his second term, the man whom evangelicals had elected as one of their own had become radioactive, his political messianism threatening to poison the careers of elected leaders who aligned with him.

Furthermore, by the time of Falwell's death, millennials were coming of age and entering the voting booth. They were facing different social problems than their Baby Boomer parents and thereby less inclined to vote as Falwell would have wanted. Instead of pushing back against the Civil Rights Movement and the hippie sixties, evangelical millennials had gone to school with children of other races and played with them at recess. Many placed racial justice as a political priority, rather than the rejection of civil gains, as promoted by Falwell and his Moral Majority. Evangelical millennials had also been profoundly shaken by the Columbine shooting, which was a formative event for kids who suddenly went to school knowing that they could be killed by gun violence while studying in the library. They also recognized that an environmental catastrophe was looming, and political action was needed to curb the fossil fuel emissions driving climate change. And with their peers fighting in Iraq and Afghanistan, many—though certainly not all—evangelical millennials prioritized peace in the Middle East over a one-dimensional Christian Zionism.

In other words, the Religious Right, at least as Falwell had organized it, no longer existed. When he died, not much changed.

Or rather, everything changed because dominionism had been on the ascendancy ever since Lou Engle organized The Call DC as a response to Columbine. Falwell's death brought the Religious Right into a new era that would be led by dominionists. What they needed was a political leader who could give them a national voice and bring the patchwork of the NAR, Reconstructionism, and Neo-Confederacy into one cohesive movement. They were about to get such a leader, who would become the public face of an insurgency known as the Tea Party. Far from being a grassroots movement, the Tea Party was a coming together of different strands of dominionist thought, turning a patchwork of ideologies into a political movement that would soon take over the Republican Party.

"It was the Alaska State Fair, August 2008," Sarah Palin wrote in the opening lines to her memoir. "With the gray Talkeetna Mountains in the distance and the first light covering of snow about to descend on Pioneer Peak, I breathed in an autumn bouquet that combined everything small-town America with rugged splashes of the Last Frontier."[1] Against this backdrop of majestic mountains and the picturesque Americana of Alaska's Mat-Su Valley, Palin received a phone call from John McCain, the Republican nominee for president. He asked her if she wanted to help him make history.

She did.

So on September 3, 2008, the governor of Alaska stood on the stage at the Republican National Convention to accept the nomination for vice president of the United States. No one had heard of her, but she was surrounded by establishment Republicans: Rudy Giuliani, President George W. Bush (who attended virtually due to a hurricane), Mitt Romney, Mitch McConnell, Bill Frist. There was also a number of up-and-coming politicians who were not "establishment"—had not attended Ivy League schools and/or been groomed for politics by people who already had access to power. Mike Huckabee, the Southern Baptist minister-turned-governor-turned-Republican primary candidate who was a close friend of Jim Bob Duggar. Sam Brownback, then a US Senator from Kansas with close ties to Lou Engle, the International House of Prayer in Kansas City, and The Family.

And Palin, who had worked as a sports broadcaster before becoming mayor of the small town of Wasilla and then governor of the state of Alaska. "I've learned quickly these last few days that, if you're not a member in good standing of the Washington elite, then some in the media consider a candidate unqualified for that reason alone,"[2] she said in a spunky acceptance speech. Drawing on her small-town roots and growing up in what was then very much a frontier town, Palin recognized something that the establishment Republicans present at the convention did not see: Americans were tired of the *status quo*. High taxes, high gas prices, big government spreading its tentacles everywhere.

So she declared at the Republican National Convention, "Politics isn't just a game of clashing parties and competing interests. The right reason is to challenge the status quo, to serve the common good, and to leave this nation better than we found it."[3] She had gotten into the small-town politics of Wasilla as a mom who wanted her children to grow up in a community where they could thrive. "So I signed up for the PTA because I wanted to make my kids' public education even better," she quipped. "And when I ran for city council, I didn't need focus groups and voter profiles because I knew those voters, and I knew their families, too."[4]

But during her tenure on the Wasilla City Council and then in the mayor's office, there were warning signs of what would soon explode in American public life as her star soared within the national Republican Party. In an eerie foreshadowing of debates about book bans and attacks on librarians, she tried to force the Wasilla Public Library to remove books that she found objectionable. When the library refused, she slashed its budget so severely that it nearly had to close. She also forced all heads of city departments—fire, police, public works—to hand in resignation letters and then forbade any city employee from speaking with the media unless she gave consent.

After her stint in city politics ended in 2002, Palin made a name for herself doing exactly what Donald Trump promised to do during his 2016 campaign: she cleared the swamp. Governor Frank Murkowski (father of Senator Lisa Murkowski) appointed her as one of three commissioners on the Alaska Oil and Gas Conservation Commission in 2003. Her job was to oversee the management of the state's oil production and how those oil dollars were used. This was no small task, given that ever since the construction of the Alaska pipeline in the 1970s, the state's economy has been entirely dependent on oil revenue. In the swamp of Alaska's state politics, numerous scandals have erupted because of how much control oil companies have over politicians; much of their electioneering and voting habits are based on managing the state's oil reserves and petrodollars, and a significant portion of campaign funds also comes from the oil companies that work in Alaska. The commissioner job was perfect for an up-and-coming politician who was already savvy about navigating the complexities of oil politics and negotiating petrodollars.

Palin soon realized that her fellow commissioner, Randy Ruedrich, had been making backroom deals between the oil companies and the Alaska Republican Party. Ruedrich was its chairman, and in order to expose the corruption occurring in Juneau and within her own party, Palin was going to have to take on the entire political establishment. So she did. She exposed evidence of how Ruedrich was soliciting bribes from oil companies to fund the state's GOP and then resigned. Palin became a hero to Alaskans for rooting out corruption within her own party and was soon elected governor.

And when John McCain faced off against Barack Obama, the first African American on a major party ticket, he needed a woman to run alongside him. Palin seemed to be a perfect match. She was immensely popular in her state but unheard of on a national level, making her an unknown with political star power.

Her rise in politics came at an opportune time, and not only because the Religious Right needed someone to replace Falwell. In the late 1990s, banks had begun a subprime-lending spree by offering mortgages to customers who had poor credit, few assets, and no reliable way of paying off the mortgage. These mortgages had relatively low initial payments that increased over time—almost always far beyond the ability of the borrower to make monthly payments. Housing prices soared as people who would otherwise not have been able to buy a home flooded the market, albeit with a mortgage that the banks knew would not be repaid. An economic bubble formed that was going to pop. And by the time it did, in 2007 and 2008, America's financial markets were saturated with subprime mortgages as one home after another after another went into foreclosure. When Palin took the stage at the RNC, home values were plummeting, banks were collapsing, and gas prices were at historic highs.

At the forefront of the election cycle was how the government would handle what was coming to be known as the Great Recession. Palin did not address this situation, however, possibly because the state of Alaska was not in a recession. It was in an economic boom, fueled by high gas prices that meant the oil flowing from the North Slope and into the state's coffers was worth more than ever. Palin worked in the governor's mansion not to handle a spate of foreclosures but rather to administer a surplus of cash. And her management of the surplus made her more popular than ever: every qualified Alaskan got a check for $3000, in addition to their annual Permanent Fund Dividend payment of $3000. While families in the rest of the country were losing their homes, Alaskan families with four people received checks for $24,000; families of five got $30,000. She could handle a surplus of oil money; she did not have a plan for a financial crisis that was seeing hundreds of thousands of foreclosures, surges in homelessness, and a collapse of financial markets.

Still, her sunny optimism carried the day as she connected with everyday people whose small businesses were being crushed by high taxes and international competition. When "Joe the Plumber" reached out to Democratic nominee Barack Obama about how his proposed tax plan would impact the plumber's business, he became a hero to the McCain-Palin ticket. "Joe the Plumber" was a stand-in for middle-class Americans who felt that they were being ignored while politicians focused on collapsing banks and low-income Americans facing foreclosure.

Palin did not ignore Joe the Plumber. He looked like the Alaskans that she had grown up with and represented in city and state government, small business owners who had forged their way despite government programs that seemed to work against them. As she campaigned, tens of thousands of "Joe the Plumbers" flooded her events, eager to know that they would not be left behind.

When Barack Obama won the election, middle-class voters felt more alienated and estranged from their government than ever. When he started his term in 2009 by pushing through a bailout plan for banks facing collapse and homeowners facing foreclosure, funded by their tax dollars, they were enraged. And the next year, when his plan for healthcare reform became the taxpayer-funded Affordable Care Act, they were ready for an insurrection.

And they had a spokesperson: Sarah Palin.

She had long attended a Pentecostal church, Wasilla Assemblies of God (later renamed Summit Worship Center), that embraced NAR theology. And ever since her beginnings in city government, she had been part of a prayer group called Intercessors of Alaska, later renamed Windwalkers. Mary Glazier, the founder of the prayer group, had partnered with none other than C. Peter Wagner to build prayer networks throughout the state and develop a strategy for spiritual warfare. Through her connections with Intercessors of Alaska, Palin had been rubbing shoulders with NAR prophets and apostles since long before McCain tapped her. One of those apostles was Thomas Muthee, the Kenyan witch hunter who, while she was running for governor, had prayed over her to bind the forces of witchcraft.

"Esther removed corruption from the Persian government and Haman fell,"[5] the Lou Engle had written to Palin right before her debate with the Democratic vice-presidential candidate, Joe Biden. Referring to the biblical queen who saved the Jewish people from genocide, Engle continued, "She didn't have experience, she had grace and favor. Sarah, don't hide your identity tonight. There will be questions given to you that you don't know, and I have been weeping over you. I believe the Lord would have you be real." Engle told her that her lack of experience, compared with Biden's three decades, mattered little, because she had been placed here by God at exactly the right moment.

Recognizing what Palin knew, that Americans were tired of the *status quo*, he went on. "I believe America is not looking for more knowledge, they are looking for more character and more truth, and that is who I am. I refuse the politics of neutrality. I will stand for the family, I will stand on foundations of truth and this nation will be better for it."

Engle was not content to be on the sidelines, cheering Palin on as she barnstormed the country with her populist message. Instead, he wanted to fill the metaphorical role of Esther's uncle, Mordecai, who had discovered the corrupt governmental plot to exterminate the Jewish people. "Sarah, I could be wrong, but I've been praying for five years for an Esther, with dreams of being a Mordecai to that Esther. I believe you're the one." To Engle and other proponents of the nascent 7MM, which in 2008 was far from widespread among evangelicals, Palin was an apostle to the government. This vision of placing one of the NAR's own in the White House did not go away just because McCain and Palin lost the election to Obama and Biden. She would continue sweeping the world of electoral politics, just not running as a candidate herself.

On February 26, 2009, President Obama unveiled his first budget as president of the United States. The budget provided for increased federal spending to boost the production of clean energy, moving the country away from reliance on fossil fuels. It also included programs to boost education and healthcare. This effort would help revive an economy strained by the Great Recession, but at a tremendous cost: an unprecedented $1.75 trillion deficit. The next day, protests erupted in cities across the United States as enraged middle-class taxpayers demanded fiscal responsibility. To these protestors, the new president was forcing them to bail out irresponsible homebuyers while saddling their children with a national debt that could not be repaid. The Tea Party was born. Or so the story goes. In reality, the insurgency had been in the works for years, engineered by dominionist thought leaders whose ideas about government and economics support the same goals as the oil leaders who have long been funding them.

One of those thought leaders was David Barton and his WallBuilders organization. By 2011, he was consulting with Tea Party presidential candidates and speaking at the Tea Party Caucus in Washington, DC. "So the Bible is real clear on what we would call the capital gains tax," he told his audience in a video. "If I work really hard, and I exchange my blood, sweat, tears, and time for money, I get a paycheck for that. That money is my property, and government is supposed to protect property, not take property."[6] This message of biblical taxation has fallen on welcome ears in Texas' oil industry. The oil billionaire Farris Wilks has donated more than $3 million to WallBuilders; along with his brother Dan, he has also given $3 million to PragerU, whose videos reflect much of Barton's ideology. In 2015, the Wilks brothers gave $15 million to a super PAC—connected to Barton—supporting the Tea Party senator Ted Cruz. Mike Huckabee famously quipped that every American should be forced at gunpoint to listen to Barton's lectures, and the Fox News host Glenn Beck gave him a platform on national television; the quack with absolutely no credentials became the *de facto* historian of the Tea Party. In turn, public-school textbooks in Texas deny and/or minimize the reality of human-caused climate change while championing conservative and/or libertarian theories.

Another of the Tea Party's thought leaders was a libertarian economist named Gary North (1942–2022), who happened to be the son-in-law of Rushdoony. He served as an associate scholar with the Mises Institute, named for the economist Ludwig von Mises (1881–1973), who promoted libertarian, *laissez-faire* economics. Founded in 1982 at Auburn University, the Mises Institute was engaging with unmistakably Neo-Confederate ideas by the 1990s and even hosted a 1995 conference on secession—symbolically held in Charleston, South Carolina, where the Civil War began. At least one scholar associated with the Mises Institute, Donald Livingston, has argued for the right of secession; articles on the Mises Institute's website have promoted a "national breakup"[7] between Red and Blue states as recently as 2022. And to the economic thinkers at the Mises Institute, the Tea Party insurgency did not go nearly far enough. While Palin and the Tea Party opposed the Wall-Street bailouts, North and other Mises economists opposed the entire system of fiat money that the federal government guarantees; North, in particular, saw fiat money as a form of fascism.

As the banking crisis of 2008 unfolded, he recognized that a groundswell of people was not merely dissatisfied but livid with the way that the federal government was handling the situation. Instead of bailouts, North promoted a solution that had long been on the margins of economic thought in America: ending the Federal Reserve altogether, in favor of relying on the gold standard. This would mean that the government no longer guarantees the currency that it issues, so the value of the dollar is determined by how much gold supports it—not the full faith and credit of the US government via the Federal Reserve. This monetary concept had long been supported by America's libertarian senator, Ron Paul, who, by 2008, had been working with North for four decades. The Tea Party followed many of Senator Paul's cues, though the public face of the insurgency gave the impression that it was less extreme. The Tea Party presented itself as against the bank bailouts, for example, when its thought leaders who helped guide the movement were against the Federal Reserve and fiat currency altogether.

North's ideas dominated Tea Party discourse about economics, in no small part because of the extent to which Barton relied on him. Both North and Barton have derived their ideas from a Reconstructionist version of sphere sovereignty, the idea that distinct spheres of society should govern themselves; when they mentioned the federal or civil government and its economic policy, they meant something small and with extremely limited authority. In fact, much of the Tea Party's idea of limited government has its origins in Rushdoony, whose thought holds broad appeal in the NAR (whose version of sphere sovereignty informs the 7MM) as well as among Neo-Confederates.

Perhaps no thinker has filled the role of promoting libertarianism among evangelicals more than Rushdoony. He was greatly influenced by the libertarian economists Friedrich Hayek (1899–1992), the author of the seminal text *The Road to Serfdom* (published 1944), and his predecessor, Ludwig von Mises. Rushdoony loathed the concept of a strong central government, believing that it was playing the role of God by educating children in public schools and taking on additional responsibilities that belong to the family and the church. Hayek and von Mises had already proposed economic models in which the government was not involved at all.

Though Rushdoony's concept of Reconstructionism may look like the implementation of an authoritarian state that executes children for rebelling against authority, Reconstructionism embraces libertarian ideas. Hayek especially had critiqued the government for interventionist programs that curtailed individual liberty; Rushdoony believed that Hayek had not gone far enough. He imagined an America governed by a corrupted understanding of Kuyper's sphere sovereignty: the patriarchal family led by a father who provided for the family's finances and the children's home-based education; local churches that administered justice by hewing to Old Testament law; and a civil government whose only job was to protect private property. In other words, he aimed to resurrect seventeenth-century Puritans, with a civil government that looked a lot like the Confederacy. To him and his followers, this was not autocracy; this was Christian libertarianism, a life free from governmental control, a society in which individuals could flourish according to their own merits.

◆

Palin may have never understood concepts such as sphere sovereignty, fiat money, or government tax policy (Alaska has no state income tax and actually sends its residents a check every year for oil dividends), but she did help popularize them. She returned to the governor's mansion in Juneau after losing the election, but by mid-summer, she had resigned her position to stump for conservative fiscal reform and soon became the public face of the Tea Party insurgency.

"The way forward lies in energy independence," she wrote in her memoir after losing the election and resigning her governorship. "It will make us a more peaceful and more prosperous nation." Alaskans, she insisted, understood the prosperity that oil dollars can bring when they are generated domestically, from America's own oil fields. After all, the state's economy is entirely dependent on oil dollars, and qualified Alaskans receive a payment every year to represent their share of ownership in the state's Permanent Fund.

Her familiarity with petrodollars and oil politics placed her in good company. Rushdoony died in 2001, well before the Tea Party burst onto the scene in 2009. But his apparatus of homeschool networks and the dissemination of his ideas through leaders such as Bill Gothard and Michael Farris had deep roots in the movement that became the Tea Party, going back at least to the

1990s. Farris's homeschool advocacy group, the Home School Legal Defense Association, was part of a political lobby called Get Government Off Our Backs, whose goal was the deregulation of the private sector—including the education of children and the functioning of private markets. This lobby was funded in no small part by Koch Industries, the world's largest privately held oil company, a decade and a half before the Tea Party protests erupted in 2009. And the biggest funders of the Tea Party were none other than the oil tycoons Charles and David Koch.

By the end of 2009, Palin was scheduled to serve as the keynote speaker for the very first Tea Party Conference. There she extolled what observers considered to be a grassroots movement, saying, "The soul of this movement is the people—everyday Americans who grow our food and run our small businesses, teach our kids, and fight our wars." She went on to praise this hardworking, common-sense people, "They're folks in small towns and cities across this great nation who saw what was happening. And they saw and were concerned, and they got involved." They did what she had done a decade and a half previously: they joined PTAs and ran for local office. They joined protests and contacted their elected representatives.

And soon, they would upend the establishment of the Republican Party. Tea Party insurgents like Ted Cruz would be elected to national office, supported by the likes of Barton, North, and Cruz's father, Rafael, a conservative provocateur and leader within the NAR.

◆

As the next presidential election cycle got underway in 2012, an eighteen-year-old community college dropout named Charlie Kirk founded Turning Point USA to promote libertarian politics on college campuses. Not only had Kirk come of age when the libertarian Tea Party was on the ascendency, but his father worked for the architectural firm that designed Trump Tower in Manhattan. Upon dropping out of college, Kirk began an unlikely career by touring college campuses to speak about libertarian values to young voters, many of whom would be voting in their first election. Within a decade, he had established 1400 branches of Turning Point USA at college campuses across the country. Like Campus Crusade for Christ, Turning Point USA did not necessarily focus on Christian colleges or even those with a conservative bent. Rather, Kirk aimed to bring his insurgent viewpoints to *all* colleges—conservative, liberal, faith-based, and secular. And on these campuses, chapters of Turning Point USA organized college students to vote and worked with school administrations to bring in Tea Party speakers. While many millennials had been turning away from conservative politics, Kirk began reversing this trend by creating conservative hot spots on college campuses and delivering the young-adult vote to Tea Party insurgents.

Not that Kirk was a Christian nationalist, at least not at first. As recently as 2018, he was insisting that politics should be secular and that separation of church and state must be honored. Still, his American jingoism and secular version of libertarianism segued almost perfectly with the Rushdoony-style libertarianism of the dominionists who had come together under the Tea Party. And the charismatic young man was incredibly successful speaking on the college circuit, bringing millions of dollars into Turning Point USA every year by the time Trump was the GOP presidential candidate.

When Trump was working to clinch the Republican nomination, the Tea Party had already moved into the mainstream of Republican politics. In other words, the patchwork of dominionists who came together under the Tea Party took over the GOP nearly two election cycles before Donald Trump was elected in 2016. He was going to be the Republican nominee, given his embrace of fossil fuels, support of libertarian economics, and apostle-like insistence that Christians should have power.

And with the soaring influence of dominionism—through faith healers like Bill Johnson and Kris Vallotton, through worship music like what was being played in evangelical churches, through ministry-training institutions like the International House of Prayer University and Bethel School of Supernatural Ministry, through political-not-political prayer rallies like The Call and The Response, through family-friendly shows like *18 Kids and Counting*, through public-school curriculum like what Barton endorsed in Texas, through college activism by Charlie Kirk and Turning Point USA—the overwhelming majority of white evangelicals were going to vote for him.

Because he was going to give them dominion.

12

The Trump Prophecies

Before Paula White blessed the rioting crowd on January 6, before she led the prayer at Trump's 2017 inauguration, before she became his spiritual advisor in the early 2000s, she and her then-husband, Randy White, were serving as the co-pastors of Without Walls International Church in Florida. The church was not affiliated with any denomination, so there was no oversight body that could determine whether her prosperity-style sermons, which urged congregants to donate entire paychecks so that they could receive material benefits from God, were in keeping with an accepted understanding of the Bible and Christian theology. Instead, the church functioned as a business that the couple ran. This business sold Jesus; Randy White said that businesspeople need to "believe in their product" before asserting, "My product is Jesus."[1]

With her Oscar de la Renta dresses, Gucci heels, immaculate manicures, and exquisite hair highlights, White was the picture of femininity. Yet she defied evangelical gender roles by refusing to confine her ministry outreach to women and preached—many evangelical churches do not allow women to preach—to hundreds of thousands of men. In late 2001, she signed a deal with Black Entertainment Television (BET), where she developed a persona as a televangelist who could tackle tough life issues, as if Oprah was leading her shows with the prosperity gospel. The December 2004 edition of *Ebony*, a magazine that celebrates African American life, said of her show *Paula White Today*, "You know you're onto something new and significant when the most popular preacher on the Black Entertainment Television is a white woman."[2]

Without any theological training, she stood as the singular head of a vast evangelical empire worth tens of millions of dollars, and she was accountable to virtually no one. Even when the US Senate opened a 2007 investigation into her misuse of church funds to pay for a lavish lifestyle, she made the church's internal affairs so opaque that she was ultimately not held accountable. By the 2010s, she had grafted herself into the NAR as she had come into the orbits of the prophets and apostles who wanted to see the 7MM fulfilled in American politics. And she would ultimately connect them with her most prestigious follower when he ran for president of the United States, turning the 7MM and a conspiracy-tinted worldview into national politics.

◆

White caught the attention of T.D. Jakes, the African American megachurch pastor in Dallas, as well as the resident of Mar-a-Lago, who regularly listened to her inspirational, prosperity-laced sermons. She became Trump's pastor and a close enough confidant that, when he considered a presidential run for the 2012 election, he consulted with her. In White's telling, she believed that the time was not yet right. Four years later, however, it was, and he had her full support by the time he came down the golden escalator.

While plenty of old-guard leaders of the Religious Right put their politicking behind more evangelical nominees—Ted Cruz, Marco Rubio, Jeb Bush—rising dominionist leaders such as White and Lance Wallnau saw Trump as their apostle to take over the mountain of government. White had little to no credibility at the evangelical flagship magazine *Christianity Today*; Russell Moore, who became *Christianity Today's* editor-in-chief in 2022, referred to her as a "charlatan." But she already had a strong presence at what was then the little brother of *Christianity Today*, a magazine circulated for Pentecostals and charismatics called *Charisma*.

In July of 2015, a NAR prophet named Jeremiah Johnson wrote a piece for *Charisma* that predicted Trump would become the next president. "Just as I raised up Cyrus to fulfill My purposes and plans," the article read, referring to the Old Testament king of Persia who allowed the exiled Jews to return to their homeland and rebuild the temple in Jerusalem, "so have I raised up Trump to fulfill my purposes and plans prior to the 2016 election." Johnson not only compared Trump to an Old Testament king who may have followed the Zoroastrian faith but even said that Trump would be God's trumpet to

America. "You must listen to the trumpet very closely for he will sound the alarm and many will be blessed because of his compassion and mercy." Though few evangelicals supported the Trump candidacy at this point and many were being turned off by his bluster, Johnson urged his readers to look beyond the gruff, even narcissistic exterior. "Though many see the outward pride and arrogance, I have given him the tender heart of a father that wants to lend a helping hand to the poor and the needy, to the foreigner and the stranger."[3]

The article was soon deleted, and Johnson said that he became a laughingstock for foretelling that Trump would be elected president. After all, the announcement that Trump intended to run was, at least in the summer of 2015, seen as a national joke. But Lance Wallnau, the NAR leader who turned the Seven Spheres into the 7MM, picked up on the theme of Trump as a modern-day Cyrus and turbo-charged it. Shortly after the *Charisma* article, Wallnau wrote in his blog, "Don't ask 'WHO IS THE MOST CHRISTIAN CANDIDATE?,'" [emphasis in original] indicating that he had no desire to see someone with historical Christian values, such as humility and compassion, occupy the Oval Office. "Instead ask, 'WHO IS THE ONE ANOINTED FOR THE TASK?'" [emphasis in original] He went on to connect Trump to Cyrus by pointing out that in Isaiah 45, "God declared through the prophet Isaiah that a foreign man, a non Jew [*sic*] named 'Cyrus' would be the anointed shepherd of his people and rebuild Jerusalem."[4] The upcoming election would be for the forty-fifth president, and according to Wallnau, the Cyrus prophecy of Isaiah 45 applied to the forty-fifth president. The coincidence of the number 45 was prophetic; Donald Trump had to be God's man for the job.

The idea of Trump having the Cyrus anointing—that God had called Trump the way he had called the ancient Persian king—spread like wildfire through NAR and other dominionist circles until it hit mainstream evangelicalism. By the spring of 2016, Trump was the evangelical choice, not because of his Christian values but because of his lack thereof. Instead of humility, he had machismo and bravado. Instead of compassion, he had violent insults for anyone who stood against him. These were the qualities that had allowed him to ascend the mountains of business via his real estate empire and entertainment via his reality shows, *The Apprentice* and *The Celebrity Apprentice*. And these were the qualities that would allow him to take over the mountain of government.

When one apostle after another—Paula White, Bill Johnson, Brian Simmons, Che Ahn, Kenneth Copeland, Bill Hamon, Rick Joyner, Doug Stringer, Lou Engle—endorsed Donald Trump for the presidency, they were doing more than suggesting that he was a worthy politician. They were extending their model of church governance into civil politics and claiming that Trump was to be the leader, in effect, the *apostle* to America's government. "He genuinely wanted to hear—what does God have to say?" White said of a 2011 meeting between Trump and about thirty evangelical leaders. "To really make America great is real to him, that's not a slogan, [it's] genuinely so."[5] Not that Trump is the first president who has tried to hear from God, or at least claim as much. Yet the apostles who have surrounded Trump boast of their having *unique* access to God and to blessings that are only available to those who submit to them. And this idea of God blessing his apostles extended to Trump, who could supernaturally bless all who submitted to him.

Like the apostles who endorsed him, Trump could govern over the territory that God had given to him without accountability, as he answered to God alone. And because America had been given to Trump by God, no one had the right to take it away.

◆

Once Trump was elected, a new kind of prophecy emerged: Q drops. These prophecies—postings that an anonymous figure made on internet message boards—did not come from the Bible or a modern-day prophet, and they were not overtly religious. However, they gave "true believers" a sense that they can rest easily knowing that the future is taken care of. Trump, these Q drops insisted in a manner akin to the 7MM, is in control.

"Hillary Clinton will be arrested between 7:45 AM–8:30 AM EST on Monday—the morning of October 30, 2017,"[6] read the first Q drop, posted on October 28, 2017. This text made a bold prediction about the goings-on of America's upper echelons of power, where NAR leaders saw not a president but an apostle with a mandate from God. But the text was never meant to be taken seriously. This first Q drop was posted on the message site 4Chan, an internet board that trafficked mostly in memes and internet subculture—hardly a site for a sitting US president or high-ranking military leader to post classified intelligence. And there is little chance that NAR leaders saw the first Q drop when it appeared. But a movement grew around the postings from the mysterious figure known as "Q," and a consensus emerged that the political prophecies that Q made came from the Oval Office.

The movement around Q posts became known as QAnon as it absorbed antisemitic conspiracy theories. The earliest Q drops were posted on 4Chan's /pol/ message board, a particularly antisemitic part of the website and a fertile ground for disseminating conspiracy theories: that a demonic plan is underfoot to make whites a minority in America and that Jews are behind the scenes, pulling the strings of power (a conspiracy theory known as Zionist-occupied government, or ZOG). And some of the earliest responses to Q drops and posts about them were violently antisemitic. "TRUMP IS GOING TO NIGHT OF LONG KNIVES THE JEWS,"[7] read one early post from a Q superfan (or possibly Q himself, posting from a secondary account), referring to when Adolf Hitler ordered the SS to murder hundreds of his perceived opponents in 1934. This post indicated that Trump would purge the Jewish elites who supposedly run the Washington government. Other early posts and responses connected to the Q drops praised Hitler and glorified the Holocaust, and the avatars for these posters featured swastikas and other antisemitic symbols.

Within a month, Q had stopped posting on 4Chan and had moved to the swampland of 8Chan, a site replete with child pornography and white supremacism. The movement's most ardent followers remained antisemitic white supremacists; however, as it spread onto Reddit message boards, YouTube, and other social media sites, it picked up Trump supporters who were not necessarily antisemites but who thrived on conspiracy theories. Divorced from the antisemitic sewage that had given birth to the movement, these followers began imbibing elements of antisemitic conspiracy theories, including the medieval canard of blood libel.

During the Middle Ages, Christian communities that lived in proximity to Jewish communities made false accusations that Jewish leaders were kidnapping Christian children to harvest their blood and use it in Passover rituals. This widespread conspiracy theory became known as blood libel and resulted in many, many Jewish communities being violently attacked. QAnon breathed new life into blood libel with the central claim of the movement: Hollywood and Democratic elites are part of a cabal of Satan-worshipping pedophiles that is kidnapping children. The Frazzledrip component of QAnon claims that there is a video of Hillary Clinton and her long-time aide, Huma Abedin, murdering a young girl so that they could drink her blood. Not only was this claim completely unhinged from any kind of evidence, but it hearkened back to the blood-libel claim that Jews are kidnapping Christian children to drink their blood.

The central belief about Democratic elites running a child sex-trafficking ring also stems from the ZOG conspiracy theory. ZOG claims that a Jewish cabal is pulling the strings of power; to dominionists of the Tea Party and then Donald Trump, the deep state is a swamp that is replete with corrupt, elite insiders. Many of Q's earliest supporters identified with ZOG, while those who came in once the movement erupted into mainstream social media followed Trump's rhetoric about the deep state. ZOG and the deep state had much overlap, with the deep-state conspiracy serving as a softer version of ZOG that did not explicitly call out the corrupt power brokers as Jewish. In this way, QAnon was able to serve as a ramp for philo-semites—notably white conservative evangelicals, including NAR leaders—to engage with violently antisemitic rhetoric. Apart from white supremacists, conservative white evangelicals were the demographic most likely to subscribe to QAnon, in part or in whole. A Public Religion Research Institute survey from 2022 found that, while about 18 percent of Americans believed the QAnon conspiracy theory in its entirety, that number jumps to 27 percent of white evangelicals.

As the movement surged into the mainstream, Q continued posting prophecies about Trump. The most significant of these prophecies was "the storm," an event in which he would publicly arrest the members of this shadowy cabal that has been kidnapping and trafficking children. Wallnau was one NAR leader who adopted this language of "the storm" and blended it with a demonology that insists spiritual warfare is being played out in the realm of American politics. "The Storm is Here,"[8] he titled one of his mass emails a week before the 2020 election. While Wallnau may not have been referring specifically to QAnon's prophesied storm, he used rhetoric that would have easily appealed to QAnon followers who also subscribed to his teachings. "The nation is dealing with an 'invisible enemy,'" he wrote in the body of the email.

"If we do nothing to stop this demonic turbulence, it will not simply go away, it will actually increase and intensify." He went on to add, in a manner that foreshadowed his role in the upcoming January 6 riot, "We must learn to deal with the organizational structures looking to exploit the turbulence and the spirits working behind them."[9] He was there at the Capitol Ellipse that day, stoking the crowds that he had helped bring to Washington, DC.

◆

A few leaders of Turning Point USA also adopted the language of QAnon and sometimes shared QAnon content on social media. The young man's star had soared since founding the organization when he was eighteen years old. At the Republican National Convention in 2016, the 23-year-old Kirk was the youngest speaker—ever. During the first Trump presidency, Kirk began working with Candace Owens (born 1989), an African American political commentator and far-right culture warrior. Together, they became the faces of young conservatism for a generation of voters who felt disaffected with both the Republican and Democratic parties. Kirk was tall, handsome, well-spoken, dignified; Owens was elegant and poised. She became the urban engagement specialist for Turning Point USA in 2017 and then the communications director.

And she went much, much further than many of the latecomers to QAnon by using the conspiracy theory's tropes to talk directly about Jewish people. Josef Stalin and Vladimir Lenin "were literally a part of the Jewish cabal," she said in a podcast episode in which she interviewed Tristan Tate. The Jewish psychoanalyst Sigmund Freud was "a homosexual pedophile, just like all of the elites. What was the Weimar Republic that you're speaking about? Why are we being lied to about World War II?"[10] According to the interview between Owens and Tate, "we are being lied to about World War II" because the real genocide was not the Holocaust but rather the attempt to exterminate the Anglo-Saxon race in Germany.[11]

In 2018, Owens began a public friendship with the African American rapper Kanye West, who had made a much-publicized comment about people choosing to be slaves. "When you hear about slavery for 400 years ... for 400 years? That sounds like a choice,"[12] he told the entertainment outlet TMZ. The duo later appeared together for Paris Fashion Week wearing shirts that said, "White Lives Matter."

Not that West's rhetoric caused NAR leaders to distance themselves from him. He had recently converted to evangelical Christianity, perhaps into the NAR itself. Jeremiah Johnson, the Trump prophet, soon took to prophesying about West. "Just as the Lord raised up Donald Trump to be a wrecking ball to this nation, so God has raised [West] up as another wrecking ball for such a time as this," he wrote in 2020. "Trump has wrecked the political landscape in America, but [West] shall wreck the religious one."[13]

As Turning Point soared during the Trump campaign and his first presidency, Kirk began partnering with Jerry Falwell, Jr., the son of the prime organizer of the Religious Right, to open the Falkirk Center at Liberty University. Falkirk, a portmanteau of Falwell and Kirk, is also a Scottish city known for its associations with William Wallace, the medieval freedom fighter who has long been a revered figure for America's far right. The Falkirk Center became the home for Turning Point USA in 2019.

As Turning Point was moving into the intellectual center of the Religious Right, Owens and West were bringing blatantly antisemitic rhetoric right into Turning Point. Owens said in 2019 that "if Hitler just wanted to make Germany great and have things run well, okay fine."[14] Though she did not make this comment through Turning Point, she was a high-ranking representative of the organization, and Turning Point did not distance itself from her rhetoric.

"I just think that's what they're about, is making money,"[15] West said on Fox News in response to Trump's Jewish son-in-law, Jared Kushner, organizing the 2020 Abraham Accords. His comment played into a medieval antisemitic trope that suggests Jewish people run the world's finances and are at the center of a global conspiracy to rule the world. This trope formed the basis for *The Protocols of the Elders of Zion*, which inspired both the antisemitic fervor that culminated in the Holocaust and the formation of some components of Identity theology.

This antisemitism matters not only because many dominionists have been Holocaust revisionists, but also because the white-supremacist Identity theology is fiercely antisemitic. In fact, West has claimed that Black people are actually the Jewish people, showing a possible alignment with a movement known as the Black Hebrew Israelites (BHI). BHI is a mirror to British Israelism; instead of claiming that white people are the true Jewish people, BHI claims that Africans and African-descended people are. And though not nearly as violent as Identity, some BHI groups are fiercely antisemitic and insist that the modern Jewish people are imposters. West infamously posted on Twitter in the fall of 2022 that he wants to "go death con 3 on JEWISH PEOPLE."[16]

◆

Along the way, Turning Point's extremism became too much for the intellectual center of the Religious Right. Soon after Trump lost the 2020 election and then led an insurrection on the US government, Falwell fell to a series of scandals that included sex, financial fraud, and institutional malpractice. In 2021, Liberty University declined to renew its contract with Kirk, and he relocated Turning Point USA to Phoenix, Arizona. There, he has partnered extensively with Dream City Church, a megachurch whose longtime pastor, Tommy Barnett, was raised in the Latter Rain. In fact, while Barnett was growing up, his family hosted several of the revivalists; he said in his memoir that he was greatly impressed with William Branham, the faith healer who was ordained into ministry by the National Imperial Wizard of the Ku Klux Klan and later spread Serpent Seed theory.

In Barnett's memoir *What If*, he described a seminal moment in his younger years: "Decades ago when I was an evangelist, I drove past Angelus Temple, the historic and magnificent church built in Los Angeles in 1928 by Aimee Semple McPherson." He did not mention the dubious results of her faith-healing ministry, her longtime association with the Klan, or the role that the church played in the development of Identity theology. Instead, he referred to his deep longing to be part of Angelus Temple when he went on, "I sensed a strong impression from the Lord: 'Someday you're going to be the pastor of that church.'"[17]

And in 2001, Barnett and his son, Matthew, became the pastors of none other than Angelus Temple. Their partnership with Turning Point USA represents the dominionist movement, bringing conservative evangelicalism all the way from the Moral Majority of Falwell and his Liberty University to the hub of faith-healing and birthplace of Identity theology. Turning Point had become a centerpiece of not only far-right politics but of conservative evangelicalism itself, and now it was based at Dream City Church, the church that partnered directly with Angelus Temple.

Not that either of the Barnetts or even Kirk has endorsed antisemitism, the Klan, or Identity theology. They do not. But at an event that Turning Point USA hosted at Dream City Church in June 2024, Donald Trump appeared on stage with the notorious sheriff Joe Arpaio. And Arpaio had previously declared in a televised interview that it was "an honor, it means you're doing something," to be compared to the Ku Klux Klan.

Many of the ideas represented by leaders of Turning Point USA—and looking even further, by David Barton and Rushdoony—are not new. They are old, at least as old as the Confederacy and the Lost Cause. They have also historically been on the fringes of American public life, bursting into the mainstream occasionally. What has happened with the rise of dominionism, its takeover of conservative evangelicalism, the Republican Party, and ultimately the White House, is that these ideas have become entirely mainstream. These events show that the path of dominionism may have been forged by Christian Zionists, but given the movement's deep alliances with racist extremists, the signposts on this path read: Holocaust revisionism, white supremacism, and antisemitism.

13

The Battle over Public Schools

"Even to suggest making the Bible a schoolbook today, you can't do that. Well, that's only today," David Barton told a packed-out audience in 2012. "If you don't know, it was not until 1963 that we said we can't use the Bible in schools. For 320 years, we did."[1] He was at one of America's largest megachurches, Gateway Church, in the wealthy enclave of Southlake, Texas. An Assemblies of God pastor named Robert Morris had founded Gateway Church in 2000 with a small group that met at a nearby Hilton Hotel. The church grew explosively, so much that in 2010, it opened its iconic 64-acre campus in Southlake. The campus features a full-size bookstore, a coffee shop, and a 4000-seat auditorium; the children's wing has indoor play areas that attracted hundreds of young families each week. Gateway Church was a cheerful, happy place, full of enthusiastic worshippers who entered its services ready to lift their hands in praise of God.

Within a decade of opening the Southlake campus, Gateway Church had launched a dozen campuses across the Dallas-Fort Worth Metroplex, including two prison ministries that functioned as campuses. The church also opened its own campus of the Pentecostal school The King's University, which offers fully accredited undergraduate, master's, and doctorate degrees. At its height, Gateway Church had 100,000 attendees across all of its campuses every single week, and the worship music that its band produced was sung in churches around the world. Some of the most famous musicians and pastors from churches affiliated with the NAR traveled regularly to Gateway Church to host conferences; leaders from Hillsong and Bethel Church have been regulars.

So have been more mainstream figures, including the stars of the television show *Duck Dynasty*, the inspirational speaker Nick Vujicic, the politician Rick Santorum, and the evangelical superstar Michael W. Smith. And of course David Barton, whose WallBuilders organization was based on the other side of the metroplex, in the town of Aledo. The world-class worship leader Kari Jobe, who in 2024 performed her original songs in Carnegie Hall, began her career leading worship at Gateway Church. And when Trump became president, Morris served on his evangelical advisory board.

"Starting back in 1647, the first public-school law in America passed so we'd have the Bible in schools," Barton continued. He spoke rapidly, using his customary "Gish Gallup" method of moving through arguments so quickly that listeners cannot stop to think about the speciousness of his claims. "We believed you couldn't have a comprehensive education without the Bible, because how could you understand fine arts? How could you understand English grammar and language and all these other things if you didn't know the Bible?" Barton spoke these words in 2012, eight years before pandemic-era school closures led to a dominionist insurgency on America's school boards. Twelve years before Morris became yet another dominionist leader who would fall to a sex scandal when a survivor came forward with a credible story of him molesting her from the time she was twelve until she was seventeen.

What few could imagine was that the overwhelmingly Republican city of Southlake was already becoming a red-hot district in America's reinvigorated culture wars. David Barton, Gateway Church, and the Southlake's school district would become ground zero in the fight to take over the mountain of education.

◆

"You need to get to know the Evangelicals," Ralph Reed told Donald Trump in 2011. The star of *The Celebrity Apprentice* was toying with the idea of a run for the Republican nomination in 2012, and he was making the rounds of political operatives from different interest groups. To many Washington insiders of the 2010s, Reed was the face of the Religious Right. He had formed the Faith and Freedom Coalition in 2009 along the lines of the Tea Party insurgency, with the goal of drawing in more evangelical voters. "They're half of all Republican primary voters," he explained to Trump, "and there's no path to the Republican nomination without them."[2] Reed was not referring to charismatics, like Paula White and other NAR leaders, who were already beginning to see Trump as one of their own. Rather, he was thinking of A-listers in the world of evangelical politics—James Dobson, Tony Perkins, James Robison, to name only a few. The unconventional would-be politician had won Reed over with his talk of opposing abortion and supporting Israel, but there was more to Trump than the way he toed the party line. He was, as Reed described him, "a whale in a bathtub."[3] Brash, uncompromising, and willing to give power to evangelicals in return for help getting him into the White House.

Unlike Jerry Falwell and his Moral Majority in the 1980s, Reed had a winning political message. Falwell had agitated as a crusader for moral reform and built up a national groundswell of conservative evangelical voters. Yet by the time he disbanded the Moral Majority in 1988, analysts concluded that it had accomplished no meaningful policy changes; in fact, the Reagan Revolution would have occurred without the Moral Majority. Pat Robertson, a Pentecostal televangelist and close ally of Falwell, had run for the Republican nomination in 1988. When his campaign fizzled out, he put his remaining campaign funds and resources into developing the Christian Coalition, an organization that would pick up where the Moral Majority had left off.

Reed took over the leadership of the Christian Coalition in the early 1990s and led with an entirely different approach than Falwell and even Robertson had. Instead of rhetoric around moral reform, he used the language of "rights" to insist that, without implementing the policy goals that Falwell had introduced a decade earlier, the rights of Christians would be at risk. And instead of a national groundswell that had its eyes on the White House and Congress, Reed built a grassroots army that had a much smaller—and, as time would tell, much more meaningful—target: local school boards. He declared in 1996, "I would rather have a thousand school board members than one president and no school board members."[4]

Though Christian Coalition was a national organization, its foot soldiers took over school boards by building political coalitions inside their local churches. The Johnson Amendment has long prevented churches from engaging in politicking at risk of losing their tax-exempt status, but school boards are supposed to be nonpartisan races that are primarily concerned with the well-being of children in the community. So local churches distributed voter guides that presented *all* school board incumbents—including conservative Republicans—as big-spending liberals who needed to be replaced.

By 1993, the strategy was showing clear signs of success. One school board in the Los Angeles area passed a measure that introduced teaching creationism into the school curriculum. A school board in Florida disbanded the Head Start program that serves low-income preschoolers, on the grounds that young children should be at home with their mothers. In Pennsylvania, classes stopped for a month because a dispute between teachers and the Christian-Coalition-led school board devolved into a strike. Sex education curriculum was replaced with an abstinence-only approach while school boards across the country came to encourage the villainization of queer children and teachers.

Christian Coalition had faced a series of scandals, beginning in the late 1990s, but Reed brushed these off and eventually rebranded his movement as the Faith and Freedom Coalition. By the time Trump called him in 2011, he had become a kingmaker of the Republican Party. He invited Trump to attend the annual Faith and Freedom Coalition policy conference, where a lineup of presidential hopefuls would present their cases for evangelical support. By the time the conference rolled around in June, Trump had decided to sign on for another season of *The Celebrity Apprentice* instead of running for president. Still, he had his introduction to the world of political evangelicalism in 2011, when he came on stage to the lyrics, "Money, money, money, money,"[5] at a conference organized by the man whose strategy had long been to take over school boards.

◆

When Trump assumed office in 2017, he nodded toward Reed with the selection of Betsy DeVos as his secretary of education. DeVos, the daughter of billionaire Edgar Prince, had grown up in the affluent community of Holland, Michigan, and attended private Christian schools before marrying the Amway scion Dick DeVos. "Having grown up in families in the business world, we both believe that competition and choices make everyone better," Betsy told a philanthropic group known as The Gathering. "And that ultimately, if the system that prevails in the United States today had more competition, if there were other choices for other people to make freely, that all of the schools would become better as a result and that excellence would be sought in every setting."

The Gathering began in Arlington, Virginia, in 1985 as a means of bringing together mega-donors from the Religious Right: the DeVos family, the Green family of Hobby Lobby, the Cathy family of Chick-fil-A, and the Coors family that earned its fortune in beer and helped found the far-right think tank The Heritage Foundation. Through The Gathering, these megadonors came alongside and helped fund groups such as the Family Research Council, Faith and Freedom Coalition, Alliance Defending Freedom, and Campus Crusade for Christ to implement policy goals. The Gathering was first organized by The Family, the dominionist political organization that sponsors the National Prayer Breakfast. And at the 2001 meeting in which Betsy and Dick DeVos shared about the importance of private Christian education, one of the featured speakers was none other than the YWAM founder and originator of much of today's dominionism, Loren Cunningham.

"So we're very strong proponents of fundamentally changing the way we approach education," Betsy continued, after emphasizing how many private-school scholarships she and her husband had funded for children whose parents could not afford private school. "And we understand it's going to be a long process to get there. But every child is special and unique, and every child deserves a chance to have a good education." To the DeVoses, this good education was not being offered in public schools, but capitalism presented a solution: use tax-funded vouchers to pay for students to attend private schools, as the increased competition between public and private schools will force the public schools to improve. "And the fact that we could decide where each of our four children went without a second thought about it, we remind ourselves of that often because there are hundreds of thousands, millions of children in this country that are forced to go every day to a school that's not meeting their needs. And it's not right."[6]

While Abraham Kuyper was developing his concept of sphere sovereignty, the role of education in forming and sustaining society was central. He advocated in the Netherlands that Protestant children be educated in Protestant schools.

This did not come from racial tension or religious supremacy but rather from his belief that religion formed its own sphere that should sovereignly govern itself. He was not being exclusive in suggesting that Protestant students attend Protestant schools and even that the government should use public money to finance religious-based education. He believed that children of *all* faiths should get to go to publicly funded schools that reflect their own religious traditions. Dutch immigrants to Betsy DeVos's hometown of Holland, Michigan, founded Holland Christian Schools on a version of this principle: Christian children, and particularly the children of Calvinist parents, should attend Christian schools. Not that Holland Christian Schools was publicly funded. The American government is markedly different from that of the Netherlands, and public schools are required to serve the needs of *all* children, regardless of religion, disability, gender identity, or nationality.

Yet Kuyper's concept of sphere sovereignty has consistently been distorted by his acolytes in the United States. Loren Cunningham used sphere sovereignty to develop the concept of Seven Spheres, which ultimately became the Seven Mountain Mandate. Rousas John Rushdoony used sphere sovereignty to lay out a blueprint for implementing biblical law in America and creating a society that looks a lot like the Confederacy that he idealized. Gary North used sphere sovereignty to promote a severely limited approach to American government that would abolish the Federal Reserve. Doug Wilson used sphere sovereignty to claim that the church should dominate civic life. In the education system that shaped Betsy DeVos, sphere sovereignty provided a means for Christian students to grow up attending Christian schools; as an adult, she came to believe that the government should fund this venture, but only for Christian schools. Kuyper's model called for faith-based schools to achieve certain academic standards. DeVos, on the other hand, wants school vouchers to serve the purpose of educating children in the pseudoscience of creationism and the pseudohistory of Christian nationalism.

◆

In addition to The Gathering, the effort to reshape America's education system has been heavily funded by a secretive organization known as Ziklag. Based in Southlake, Texas, and with leadership input by Lance Wallnau, the goal of

Ziklag is to bring together families with upwards of $25 million in wealth and a history of funding the Religious Right's culture wars. Ziklag has different chairs who oversee individual mountains of the Seven Mountain Mandate and work toward overtaking their respective mountains. Peter Bohlinger, a real estate investor who oversees the mountain of education, aims to not only take over that mountain but also to use hot-button issues in education—parental rights, trans students in school bathrooms and school sports, and critical race theory—to sway elections for the mountain of government. "Our goal is not to just throw stones," he said in a Ziklag meeting. "Our goal is to take down the education system as we know it today."[7] These educational issues that Ziklag highlighted became critical in swaying Trump-weary conservatives to vote for him in 2024. But before that, these wedges divided the town of Southlake around what became hyperpartisan races for the local school board.

There, a number of parents in the diversifying community had wanted the school district to address what they saw as racial and homophobic tensions that were leading to bullying and harassment of their children. Students had been leveling slurs against their peers, and when the targets of this harassment attempted to get administration to address the problem, they all too often found that their complaints fell on deaf ears. The bullying and harassment reached new heights under the first Trump administration, as students repeated the things that they heard the president say about people of color and queer individuals. Given that Southlake is ground zero for the 7MM—home to Lance Wallnau Ministries and Ziklag—there should be little surprise that toward the end of Trump's first term, things got ugly.

In response to stories of discrimination that students had faced, the school board and local community created a cultural competency plan to educate students, teachers, and other faculty members about inclusion. The backlash was swift and severe, with politically connected leaders of the wealthy community coming together under a well-funded political action committee called Southlake Families PAC. Disparaging the effort to make the school district more inclusive for minority students, Southlake Families PAC labeled the cultural competency plan as an effort to indoctrinate children with Marxism and critical race theory. The organization soon set its sights on doing more than dismantling the effort to help children who had experienced bullying because of their race, sexuality, or gender identity. Southlake Families PAC was going to take over the school board and implement sweeping reforms.

At the top of the PAC's 2021 slate of candidates for school board were Hannah Smith, an attorney for religious liberty who had clerked for two Supreme Court justices, and Cameron Bryan, a director of the Federal Aviation Administration. Bryan attended yet another dominionist institution centered in Southlake: Gateway Church. Shortly before the election, Pastor Robert Morris kicked the already-divisive race into a new level of partisanship by casting it in terms of spiritual warfare. During the Sunday morning services, he showed his congregations names of the candidates that the church approved of (but did not officially endorse, due to laws prohibiting politicking in churches) on its jumbotron screens. He then told his massive congregations, "Many of you see what Satan has been trying to do, even in our school systems."[8] When Morris spoke of Satan, he was not being metaphorical, merely using "Satan" as a stand-in for things that he does not like. The bookshop at Gateway Church has been stacked with books by NAR prophets and apostles, and many of the books there are about spiritual warfare. To Morris, Satan is more than the personification of evil; he is locked against God and America's Christians in a struggle for the souls of humanity.

Gateway Church and Wallnau both have a long-standing partnership with yet another local dominionist institution that is itself an artifact of the Latter Rain, Christ for the Nations Institute (CFNI), the Dallas school founded by Gordon Lindsay and later directed by Dutch Sheets. Kari Jobe attended CFNI and has led worship there numerous times since graduating. Her father, Mark Jobe, has been part of Gateway Church since Morris founded it in the spring of 2000, eventually becoming the executive pastor; he speaks at CFNI occasionally.[9] CFNI is an unaccredited school, but Gateway's The King's University provided a way for students to take courses at CFNI and receive full credit. Students can enroll simultaneously in both schools, with The King's University counting courses taken at CFNI for credit toward an accredited degree.

This setup allows teachings based on Lindsay's British Israelism and other idiosyncrasies—including his belief in UFOs—to filter into the megachurch that cast Southlake's school board races in terms of spiritual warfare. Lindsay's son, Dennis Lindsay, has written books with titles such as *The Zodiac: God's Master Plan Revealed in the Stars*, *Lucifer's Illusions: Pyramids, Crystals, and the New Age Mirage*, and *Giants, Fallen Angels, and the Return of the Nephilim* ("Nephilim" refers to mysterious humanoid beings referenced in Genesis 6:1–4). Dennis became the vice president of CFNI in 1973 and became president in 1985, the same year that he enrolled in the School of Leadership at the YWAM base in Kona, Hawaii. Dennis' son, Golan, became the COO of CFNI in 2014, vice president in 2020, and then replaced his father as president in 2025. Today, CFNI students not only take courses on worship leadership and creation science but also on messages in the stars, mystical origins of megalithic structures, faith-healing, and, fittingly for how Morris framed the school board race, demonic deliverance. And even though CFNI is an incredibly fringe institution, it is endorsed by some of the leading prophets and apostles of the NAR, including Bill Johnson and Heidi Baker, as well as the late televangelist Pat Robertson, and Dodie Osteen, the mother of the world-famous prosperity preacher Joel Osteen.

Not that Cam Bryan or Robert Morris necessarily believes in UFO conspiracy theories or that astrology is a legitimate means of understanding God's creation. Perhaps they do not. Yet through the influence of the Lindsay family and CFNI, Gateway Church and Southlake's other dominionist institutions—Lance Wallnau Ministries and Ziklag—are part of a larger ecosystem that promotes pseudoscientific, fringe ideas and conspiracy theories—even allowing for classes that teach these things as historical and spiritual truth to be accredited. And what Gateway Church does explicitly align with is the pseudohistorical, Christian-nationalist teachings of David Barton. In other words, Gateway Church acts as a bridge between Latter-Rain extremism and the broader world of evangelicalism, which since the early 2010s has shifted heavily toward dominionism.

Bryan and his running mate, Hannah Smith, easily won the May 2021 election, taking over two-thirds of the vote in what should have been a provincial matter of local schools, not what became a far-right *cause célèbre*. Not only would leaders of Southlake Families PAC get court orders to prevent administrators from addressing complaints of bias and discrimination, but they would even have the vice president of the school board arrested for texting other school board trustees about the cultural competency plan—allegedly a violation of Texas' open-meeting laws. And once in power, the Southlake Families PAC-dominated school board would force teachers to either remove books that were not neutral about race or otherwise provide another book that presented an alternative viewpoint. This policy effectively meant that children's books on slavery and the Holocaust had to either be removed from classrooms or supplemented with books that denied these historical atrocities had occurred. Teachers who did not align with the PAC's objectives or who spoke out faced swift reprimands from the school board and even termination.

"Education, we got to get on the school boards," Wallnau said in 2021. "We did it in Southlake, Texas right now. A thousand people went in and flooded, took over the school boards." And then, to show that this model was to be repeated over and over again, "You know who it was? Christians did it. The media doesn't know it because we never said it was a church initiative. We called it a community initiative."[10]

The royal *we*. Wallnau was at the center of dismantling his town's schools. And this was part of a much bigger program to upend public education all over the country. Because what happened in Southlake was not a spontaneous parents' revolt that just happened to get ugly. It was organized by well-funded political operatives who were based in that community and were looking for a way to take over the Seven Mountains. And behind those operatives were the billionaire oil scions who had long been working with David Barton to make Christian nationalism the accepted version of Texan, and American, history.

Soon, with the Southlake playbook, similar outbreaks of hyperpartisan politics would disrupt local school board races, with meetings around the country even breaking into threats and outright violence. And Ralph Reed's vision of taking over America's school boards and David Barton's goal of bringing the Bible back into public-school classrooms would soon become more than Christian-nationalist fantasies. In Texas, they would become realities.

◆

Southlake was also home to a discount cell phone carrier called Eos Mobile. Eos was unlike other discount providers in that it marketed itself as upholding conservative values. In 2016, Eos rebranded itself as Patriot Mobile and began aligning with dominionist leaders, including Lance Wallnau and Rafael Cruz, a local NAR leader and the father of US Senator Ted Cruz. Patriot Mobile promised to donate a portion of all net revenue toward like-minded causes, and two of its favorite causes were Turning Point USA and Christian nationalists running in local school-board races.

Barton confirmed the importance of taking over local school districts at a Patriot Mobile event in the spring of 2023. The Supreme Court had recently decided in *Kennedy v. Bremerton* that a district could not refuse to renew the contract of Coach Kennedy because he insisted on praying in the middle of the field after each game. This decision overturned the precedent known as the "Lemon test," which evaluated religious content taught at schools in light of the Establishment Clause. Coach Kennedy's case, Barton told his audience at a Patriot Mobile gathering, "gave us an offensive-minded strategy." He was going to mobilize his followers to violate previous norms around separation of church and state in America's public schools so that the Supreme Court could continue to overturn decades of precedent. "We now have tools in our arsenal we haven't had in a long time." He went on to add, "We can put the Ten Commandments up. We already have it at a lot of capitols, but now start putting it up outside city halls." Then he nodded toward Patriot Mobile's efforts to bring Christian nationalism into Texas public schools: "We've got a bill in Texas this year that says we're going to post the Ten Commandments in every classroom in the state of Texas."[11] He then called on his followers to flood the courts with cases that would bring Christian nationalism into America's public schools.

The next year, the Texas Education Agency approved a new curriculum for use in public schools all across the state. It explicitly teaches Christian nationalism to children as young as five, with kindergarteners having lessons on why the Sermon on the Mount is the foundation for Western civilization and making art based on the seven-day creation narrative in the Bible's book of Genesis. And in 2025, the Texas legislature sent Governor Greg Abbott a bill it had passed that would fulfill the dream of Betsy DeVos: one billion dollars in taxpayer funds toward school vouchers, which families could use to send their children to private Christian schools.

And with what happened in the Southlake school district being repeated all over the country, with groups like Moms for Liberty dividing school boards and entire communities, the most reasonable thing to expect is that the Christian-nationalist curriculum and implementation of school vouchers in Texas will soon become the model nationwide.

14

Let Us Worship

"I'll never forget when I was 16 years old, 17 years old, and I was on the mall in Washington, DC," Sean Feucht told his audience in 2022. "We were with almost half a million people, and I remember praying."[1] That day as a teenager, he was at The Call DC, the massive rally that Lou Engle organized on the Washington Mall in the aftermath of the Columbine shooting. In 1999 and 2000, the myth proliferated that evangelical Christians were so powerless that they were being targeted by gunmen in America's public schools. By the time Feucht spoke these words, however, Donald Trump had given evangelicals—at least those who subscribed to dominionism, which comprised over 80 percent of the white evangelical vote—real power. And the fire that Engle's rally lit inside of the teenage Feucht that day stayed with him as he launched a career as a charismatic worship leader.

When Feucht was in college at Oral Roberts University, he started a worship ministry that he named The Burn, later renamed Burn 24-7. The idea was to light furnaces of worship at churches, coffee shops, anywhere that would have him, and spend 12, 24, 48, even 100 hours in nonstop worship. "The way [God] releases, reveals, and implements His kingdom is through worship," Feucht wrote in his first memoir. "That is what the incense was for in the Temple. It represented the revelation of the knowledge of Jesus Christ spreading like lightning across the earth!"[2] To Feucht, worship is the way that the kingdom of God advances from heaven to earth. He did not partner with any churches—like so many other dominionists, keeping himself away from accountability—until he became a member of Bethel Church and its music team.

While at Bethel, Feucht caught a bug for politics. Actually, he had caught the bug at The Call DC but decided to act on it while working with Bethel Music. "All the prayers I had prayed as a teenager standing on the National Mall in DC came rushing back to me," he said of his decision to run for the US House of Representatives in the 2020 election cycle. "I remember repeating a prayer with the other 400,000 gathered believers that God would raise up leaders in America who would stand for justice and righteousness." He then asked himself, "Was I willing to personally become a fulfillment of those prayers?"[3] He was.

Feucht was a long-haired worship leader with a heavy-rocker vibe, and he knew that as both a political outsider and a conservative, he was a long shot in the liberal landscape of California. But his campaign was run by an upstart manager, Aamon Moss, who had recently helped an outsider win the governorship of Oklahoma. Feucht and Moss came up with an acronym to describe their approach to politics: BID. Burn. It. Down. "We did not want to run this race to blend in, play politics, or go with the flow," Feucht wrote. "We wanted to Burn It Down."[4]

In the midst of his campaign, December 2019, he used his social media to engage with the Wake Up Olive movement that was occurring at his home base of Bethel Church. "And do this, understanding the present time," he posted on Instagram from Romans 13:11, "The hour has already come for you to WAKE UP from your slumber, because our salvation is nearer now than when we first believed." Beneath the verse he wrote, with the hashtag #WakeUpOlive, "Been preaching this verse around the world all year long. Believing for a radical physical manifestation TODAY now more than ever for my friends and community."[5] Miracles were what he contended for, a miracle in the body of two-year-old Olive and a miracle in the political arena with his long-shot campaign. Dominion, really. That Christ's dominion would be manifested as the kingdom of God pushed back the forces of darkness with resurrection power for Olive and a political victory for himself.

And during the primary season, he got the opportunity, along with other worship leaders, including Kari Jobe, to go to the White House to lead worship with President Trump and Vice President Pence. All of the political operatives that he met there were rooting for him.

He figured that God was in this venture; Feucht could not fail.

He failed. The primaries on Super Tuesday in March of 2020 were not even close. But the Covid pandemic was freshly sweeping the world, and Feucht would soon find a new outlet to combine his passion for worship with dominionist politics.

"We're not here for blue or red," he told his audience on October 25, 2020. "We're here for purple, for royalty. We're here for the King of kings and the Lord of lords."[6] Much of contemporary Christian music since the 2010s has leaned heavily into imagery of Jesus as king. And there is something deeply biblical about Jesus as King of the Jews and Jesus, the Lamb of God, seated at the right hand of the Father. This apocalyptic imagery from the books of Matthew and Revelation was composed at a time when the Jewish sect that came to be known as Christians was very much a minority—and not only a minority but a persecuted one at that. Many Christians were killed during the first century, including all but two of Jesus's twelve disciples, Judas Iscariot (who hung himself after his betrayal) and John, who wrote the book of Revelation while exiled for his faith.

This imagery of Jesus as King above the king—Caesar—persecuting these early Christians would have been greatly encouraging for those who knew that any day, they might be called upon to die for their faith.

But what happens when that same imagery of Jesus as a conquering king fuels worship music not for people in a persecuted minority but rather evangelicals whose apostles and prophets have front-door access to the White House?

What happens is Sean Feucht and his "Let Us Worship" tour.

◆

"But thou art holy," Reg Layzell felt God impart to him on a cold morning in 1946, "O thou that inhabitest the praises of Israel" (Psalm 22:3, KJV). Layzell had been preaching a weeklong revival in the small Canadian town of Abbotsford, British Columbia, but the services had not been going well. More broadly, Pentecostal leaders—Gordon Lindsay, William Branham, Ern Baxter, to name a few—saw their once-vibrant, Spirit-filled movement as experiencing a state of malaise. Layzell would help reverse that trend when he interpreted the aforementioned verse, Psalm 22:3, to mean that the church's praise ought to fill the space with the very presence of God. If God inhabits praise, then a true offering of praise should bring God's presence to dwell among the people gathered.

That revelation came to Layzell on a Wednesday morning, the fourth day in the weeklong revival. Something about this new mindset shifted the service that evening; during the very first song, congregants began speaking in tongues. The rest of the revival came as a time of renewal and reinvigoration for the small congregation, as well as for Layzell. Less than two years later, he was in Vancouver, British Columbia, with a group of Foursquare ministers, including George Hawtin, who had traveled from the Sharon Orphanage and Bible School in North Battleford, Saskatchewan. They had come to attend a revival led by William Branham.

When the Latter-Rain revival broke out at the Sharon Orphanage and Bible School in February 1948, Hawtin enthusiastically informed Layzell, who traveled to North Battleford for a camp meeting that summer. Shortly after the camp meeting, Layzell accepted a call to pastor Glad Tidings Temple in Vancouver, a church that would become a centerpiece of Latter-Rain teachings and Layzell's new theology of praise as a means of experiencing God's presence. Three months into his pastorate, Hawtin and a group of nine ministers from Sharon led three weeks of twice-daily services at Glad Tidings. During the musical part of the service, congregants engaged in spontaneous singing that involved glossolalia and harmonization. The result, rather than a cacophony, was seen as a heavenly choir, as if heaven itself had broken into the church—exactly as Layzell interpreted Psalm 22:3. God was inhabiting the church's praise.

As the Latter-Rain revival sent shockwaves throughout Pentecostalism and then subsided, Layzell continued teaching on praise. Praise was more than a means of experiencing God's presence; it was an expression of love, as bride for her bridegroom, church longing for Christ. This theology of worship was never far from the Latter Rain, especially as it found new expression through Mike Bickle's work in Kansas City. One of his earliest books was called *The Pleasures of Loving God*, and several of the songs written by his musicians at

IHOP-KC were based on the erotic love poem Song of Solomon. Feucht may have drawn inspiration from Bickle's idea of 24/7 nonstop prayer as he took his Burn 24-7 movement to cities all across America and countries all over the world. They both used similar language of prayer and worship, as incense rising to God, and claimed that prayer and worship are what would usher in the kingdom of God. Bickle believed that his Forerunners would herald the Second Coming of Christ, and Feucht wrote that worship is how God meets with God's people and advances God's kingdom.

But just as much as a means of engaging with God as a lover, Layzell taught that praise was a weapon against the forces of darkness. "Worship is our weapon," Feucht told his audience in 2022. "It says in 2 Corinthians 10, the weapons we fight with are not the weapons of the world. On the contrary, they have divine power to demolish strongholds."[7]

Feucht had gone on numerous mission trips from the time he was a preteen. With Burn 24-7, he traveled all over the world to lead worship in some of the most dangerous locations for Christians—Iraq, North Korea, Afghanistan, to name just a few. These experiences of gathering with Christians who knew that they could be killed for their faith led him to develop a concept of what Christian persecution is, as well as a resolve to show what he called "brazen faith" in the midst of it.

So when the Covid pandemic led to global shutdowns in the spring of 2020, he thought that he knew what he was dealing with. California Governor Gavin Newsom implemented strict lockdowns to help slow the spread of the virus, and one thing these lockdowns meant was that church services had to transition from in-person to online. Feucht figured that this move was fine for the first couple of months. After all, he had just lost a primary election that he was so certain God would cause him to win. This defeat had led him into a state of depression as he questioned everything about God and faith. Taking a break and staying home with his wife and four children came like a reprieve.

Then came the murder of George Floyd in May of 2020, and lockdowns meant nothing as cities across the country erupted into rioting and sometimes violence. Instead of staying home, people took to the street to protest police brutality and racist policies that have led to countless deaths of African Americans. *Where was the church?* Feucht wondered. As the country descended into the chaos of racial unrest during the Covid summer of 2020, while churches were unable to hold in-person services, he reached the boiling point.

In July, Governor Newsom issued an order saying churches that had begun meeting again could not sing. To Feucht, this order meant that Christians could no longer worship. He had smuggled Bibles into difficult-to-access countries, and now an American government was preventing Christians from worshipping together—at least worshipping as Feucht understood it. "So when we break the law overseas because foreign governments condemn Christian worship and evangelization, what are we to do when the laws of our own nation forbid the same practices?" he wrote in his second memoir, published in 2022.

> Then, as tighter and tighter restrictions closed in around us in California, I started getting texts from connections I had made in those dangerous places overseas, asking me things like, "What's going on with your government? I thought you had religious freedom, and they're saying that you can't gather, you can't preach without a mask, and now that you can't sing?

And then the ultimate question, a challenge really: *"What are you going to do, brother?"*[8]

What he was going to do is use the greatest weapon that God had given to the church to tear down the strongholds that were gripping the country.

He was going to worship.

A few days after Governor Newsom's order, Feucht gathered a crowd at San Francisco's Golden Gate Bridge. He saw prophetic significance in the location, as "one of the gates in Jerusalem that leads to the Temple Mount is called the Golden Gate, and it was through this that Jesus entered Jerusalem."[9] Through the worship that he would lead on July 9, 2020, he would open up the "Golden Gate" to the West for Christ. Hundreds of people came. In Feucht's telling, police officers who patrol the bridge for suicide jumpers thanked him. This event marked the first event in his "Let Us Worship" tour, a cross-country series of massive worship rallies that defied Covid lockdowns and called on the church to wage spiritual warfare against a government that was trying to silence it.

With his guitar, he had what America needed at this critical hour. "Bold worship is like fervent prayer," he wrote of the tour's impact. "It is like the army marching tirelessly … It shouts and declares God's faithfulness in the face of enemy fortifications. It forces the walls of the enemy to absorb the roar of victory before the victory becomes a reality."[10]

But then the question becomes,

Who is the enemy?

◆

Feucht had attended a YWAM Discipleship Training School in Kona, Hawaii, with his parents when he was in middle school. By the time he launched "Let Us Worship," he had a longtime friendship with a senior leader of YWAM, Andy Byrd. Byrd's great-grandmother had attended Angelus Temple, and his great-uncle was personally discipled by none other than William Branham. With their influence, Byrd grew up steeped in Manifest Sons of God theology, what is also referred to as Joel's Army. Feucht, in a 2010 book that he cowrote with Byrd, succinctly summarized the significance of Manifest Sons of God when he wrote of his experience at The Call DC, "To walk out on the Mall that day and behold the masses hungry for God caused me to truly believe in this end-time army God is raising up in my generation!"[11] He went directly on to connect that "end-time army" with the prophecies of Joel. In a perfect blending of this centerpiece of Latter-Rain theology with the teachings of Reg Layzell, Feucht insisted that the weapon of this army would be worship.

And he was its leader.

So he and his team traveled to places where they could engage in spiritual warfare through worship: Skid Row, just blocks away from Angelus Temple; Portland, Oregon, and Seattle, Washington, where protests against police brutality had turned riotous; Minneapolis, the site of George Floyd's murder. "It's amazing how worshiping Jesus could be controversial in 2020,"[12] he said at a "Let Us Worship" gathering in Kenosha, Wisconsin, where protestors had rallied against the police shooting of the 29-year-old African American Jacob

Blake. There, a seventeen-year-old counter-protestor named Kyle Rittenhouse had armed himself with an AK-47, allegedly to protect the peace, and shot and killed two people. "We need to petition heaven," Feucht continued. "We need to remind America that the government is upon his shoulders."

In his writings and speaking, Feucht has seemed genuinely confused that his worship tour could be considered controversial. Yet his opponents in hotspots of racial unrest saw him as taking attention away from the reality of police brutality and drawing it to himself. After all, Feucht and the Bethel ecosystem that he comes from are fiercely opposed to Black Lives Matter. Not that he and the leadership of Bethel Church do not believe that Black lives really do matter. But they oppose the organization and see it as part of a demonic scheme to bring America to its knees. In fact, as America was undergoing this summer of racial reckoning, a group of prophets and apostles came onto the stage at a Bethel worship service to enact a scene from *Lord of the Rings*. Bill Johnson, Che Ahn, and several others grasped a wizard staff that resembles Gandalf's and chanted to the demon of racism—just like the wizard did in the movie to the demon Balrog—"Thou shalt not pass!"[13]

This milquetoast approach to racism, which treats it as if it is a demon to be exorcised through worship services and enactments of movies, is not accidental. Not only have Bethel's apostle-prophet duo, Bill Johnson and Kris Vallotton, repeatedly praised Branham and even publicly prayed that his "mantle" would fall on them, but Manifest Sons of God is baked into everything they teach. The supposed ability of their school's students and graduates to work miracles, worship as a means of bringing the presence of God into the church's midst, and the effort to place aspiring politicians such as Feucht into America's halls of power are all enactments of Manifest Sons of God.

It almost looks as if "Let Us Worship" was an effort to raise up Joel's Army.

Many opponents—and supporters as well—saw Feucht's worship tour as a Covid-era political protest that was closely aligned with the Trump reelection campaign. Feucht often appeared at protests wearing red, white, and blue and led the crowd in patriotic songs, such as "America the Beautiful" and "God Bless America." To be clear, these songs are not controversial in and of themselves and are sung in churches all over the country, especially around July 4. The challenge is how his theology of worship and endorsement of Manifest

Sons of God collide with historical norms around American patriotism and even democracy itself. The result is a violent form of Christian nationalism that demonizes not only the Black Lives Matter movement but anyone who disagrees with his understanding of America and of Christianity itself.

Including American Christians. Because Feucht could not comprehend why some Christians would not agree with what he was doing and would not vote for Trump.

But then again, Manifest Sons of God is the foundation for Serpent Seed theory. Feucht had to raise up an army of End-Time worshippers so that they could stamp out the forces of evil—including in the election.

◆

Feucht's 2020 tour ended at the place where his passion for American politics blended with worship began: the National Mall in Washington, DC. The rally was held on October 25, 2020, one week before Trump's reelection campaign would clash with Joe Biden's bid for the presidency. There, Feucht and his followers would engage in spiritual warfare against liberals who, he claimed, sought to oust Trump and ultimately outlaw Christianity altogether.

"This is not political," he shouted as the rally started, the US Capitol that would soon be attacked in the background and Appeal to Heaven flags waving in the crowd. "This is biblical!" That afternoon and into the evening, Feucht shared the stage with Lou Engle as both marveled at the fulfillment of the dreams he had unleashed twenty years earlier. Revival was coming to America, starting with the political sphere: as the service unfolded, Amy Coney Barrett's nomination to the Supreme Court came one step closer to confirmation, with the Senate moving to end debate and vote for her to take the oath. Engle had spent decades crusading against abortion, and Feucht had followed in his footsteps; they knew that she would be the justice to overturn *Roe v. Wade*. To Feucht and Engle, Barrett's confirmation was a small hurdle to overcome as Joel's Army moved to take dominion over American politics.

"He is a sign and a wonder of the new generation," Feucht said of Senator Josh Hawley, who would infamously raise a white power fist on January 6 and vocally promote dominionist ideals ever since. "He's on fire for Jesus. He's a revivalist filled with the Spirit of God. He's taking a stand for the things we all need to be taking a stand for." Feucht meant much more than abortion here; though he is adamantly pro-life, his vision for the army of Christians that he is raising up for the End Times goes much, much further than abortion. He wants this army to have dominion over all seven mountains.

"Tomorrow night, a vote on the floor of the United States Senate to confirm a justice who is not ashamed to confess that Jesus Christ is Lord!" The crowd erupted in cheers as Senator Hawley gave this update on the program for obtaining dominion not only over the White House but also over the Supreme Court. Not that Justice Barrett is a dominionist; far from it. However, her political views have been aligned enough with dominionists—including the highest dominionist in the land, Donald Trump—to give them the clout on the Supreme Court to push through an agenda built on the 7MM.

◆

There is little left to the imagination as to what unfolded over the next few months. Trump lost the election. A mob, carrying Appeal to Heaven flags and Confederate battle flags, blew shofars as they stormed the Capitol. With Amy Coney Barrett's vote, the Supreme Court overturned *Roe v. Wade*. And for the next four years, NAR prophets and apostles—alongside Feucht and Turning Point USA—continued mobilizing Joel's Army in favor of the man that they believed had truly won the election.

Four years after his rally on the National Mall, Feucht was back, ready to bring revival to a new election. And as he took to the stage, US Capitol in the background, surrounded by banners saying "One Nation Under God," facing an audience waving Appeal to Heaven flags and blowing shofars, he said these words:

We are the army of God.[14]

15

January 6

The murder of George Floyd and the ensuing protests of 2020 did not present the first time that the Trump campaign had to come up against racial unrest. On June 17, 2015, a group of African-American evangelicals gathered for a weekly prayer meeting at the Mother Emmanuel African Methodist Episcopal Church in Charleston, South Carolina. Their topic for the evening was the parable of the sower, a teaching from Mark 4. A 21-year-old Neo-Confederate, whose religious beliefs leaned heavily towards Identity theology, joined them. He read the Bible and prayed with them before opening fire and killing nine.

Reverend Clementa Pinckney
Cynthia Hurd
Tywanza Sanders
Myra Thompson
Reverand Sharonda Coleman-Singleton
Reverend Daniel Simmons, Sr.
Ethel Lance
Reverend DePayne Middleton-Doctor
Susie Jackson

The day before, on June 16, Donald Trump had descended the golden escalator and announced his candidacy for President of the United States. As his campaign began, America was entering a period of reckoning with the racist heritage of the Confederacy and especially the Confederate monuments that dot the South. Nikki Haley, who would become Trump's ambassador to the

United Nations, was then governor of South Carolina and found herself at the center of this racial reckoning. South Carolina was the first state to secede in 1860, and Fort Sumter, the site of the first Civil War battle, sits just outside of Charleston. A Confederate battle flag flew at the South Carolina statehouse until 2015; it only came down because of the Mother Emmanuel massacre. Soon, state governments and anti-Confederate protestors were taking down Confederate monuments, as Charlie Kirk and Turning Point USA joined the Trump campaign and protested the removals. Though Trump said that he supported Haley's decision to remove the Confederate battle flag, Kirk was enraged by what he saw as an effort to erase American history.

As Trump's campaign gained momentum, his growing base of supporters found common cause regarding Confederate monuments: the government had no right to remove them. His style of politics appealed to white supremacists, including Richard Spencer, the well-groomed, well-educated face of what he coined the "alt right." Spencer's alt-right movement celebrated the Trump presidency, with Spencer shouting, "Hail Trump! Hail our people! Hail victory!"[1] and giving a Sieg Heil salute shortly after the 2016 election. His alt right had been promoting a narrative of white genocide, filled with the same conspiracy theories that fueled the Neo-Confederate who attacked Mother Emmanuel. And he saw Trump as a savior figure who would restore white America to greatness. Less than a year after his Sieg Heil, he helped organize an infamous gathering of white supremacists in Charlottesville, Virginia.

The city had plans to remove a monument to Confederate General Robert E. Lee. White nationalists responded by converging on Charlottesville in a protest known as the Unite the Right rally; skinheads marched with tiki torches through the University of Virginia campus, chanting, "Jews will not replace us!"

Trump refused to denounce the rally, instead insisting that there were "very fine people" on both sides. He also Tweeted, "Robert E Lee, Stonewall Jackson—who's next, Washington, Jefferson? So foolish!" and "Sad to see the history and culture of our great country being ripped apart with the removal of our beautiful statues and monuments."[2]

Spencer ultimately became disillusioned with Trump, not because he was failing to empower the alt right—he was succeeding—but because he was not racist enough. Many of his followers in the alt right, however, knew a hero when they saw one. They joined with NAR leaders in Washington, DC, in the aftermath of the 2020 election, as prophecy and spiritual warfare blended with calls for militias and even civil war. The narrative of January 6 brought different strands of dominionism that share a common heritage – Neo-Confederacy, British Israelism, and the Ku Klux Klan – together to support the same goal: keep Donald Trump in power.

◆

"I declare Psalm 89, verse 21," Paula White had pronounced a few weeks before Floyd's murder, from the White House Rose Garden. "Let your hand establish President Trump, and let your arm strengthen him. I declare Psalm 98:1, that your right hand and your holy arm would give him victory."[3] After four years of access to the White House as they worked towards dominion on the mountain of government, the prophets and apostles were not ready to sour on Trump. With Feucht leading the way, they were aiming for another victory.

"I want to say without question, Trump is going to win the election,"[4] the televangelist and former presidential candidate Pat Robertson told his audience on his flagship show, *The 700 Club*. The 2020 election was just two weeks away, and prophets and apostles were ramping up their effort to get evangelicals to vote for Trump. Though Robertson himself has never been considered an apostle or prophet, he had spent decades developing a strong media presence among Pentecostals and was decidedly in favor of Trump. His statement on *The 700 Club* was part of a string of prophecies made about the upcoming election.

"I do believe Donald Trump will be re-elected," said Jeremiah Johnson, the prophet whose 2015 *Charisma* article predicting the first Trump presidency turned into a sensation. "We're going to continue to see civil unrest. I do believe that there's going to be an increase of rioting and looting. But I just simply believe that Trump is waiting to be re-elected for him to deal decisively and swiftly with some of the madness we're seeing on the streets."[5] Yet a massive crisis of faith ensued when the election was called for Joe Biden. Trump had lost. Decidedly, unequivocally lost. What should dominionists do when they have hitched not only their political ideals but their faith in the God of the universe to the whims of a president who ultimately was subject to an election? An election that he could, and actually did, lose?

Johnson refused to recant his prophecy and instead doubled down on it, saying on Robertson's show *CBN News*, "Either a lying spirit"—a demon—"has filled the mouths of numerous trusted prophetic voices in America, or Donald J. Trump really has won the presidency. And we are witnessing a diabolical and evil plan unfold to steal the election."[6] In other words, the numerous prophecies themselves were the evidence that Trump had truly won the 2020 election.

Not alleged voting discrepancies.

Not problems with mail-in ballots.

Not a secret government plot, in a government led by the man who lost the election and had supposedly been clearing the swamp.

Not a left-wing effort by Antifa.

Those justifications for the "stolen election" theory came later. Ultimately, the evidence of Trump's victory was the prophetic pronouncements from the NAR.

One prophet, Bethel Church's Kris Vallotton, apologized for his false prophecy shortly after the election was called for Biden. He seemed to be in agreement with the official results… until dissension set in with his apostle, Bill Johnson, vehemently denying the election results. "I'm 100% confident it was done by fraud," Johnson said of Biden's election. "I don't have any question. It's as obvious as the nose on my face." He offered no evidence, but then cast the election results in terms of demons and spiritual warfare. "We need to pray for the Lord to expose, expel, and break. Expose what happened, expel—cast it out—and break it so it doesn't return."[7] Whatever demonic force had led to the election being called for Biden had to be cast out of America.

"I'm fighting, not just for my president," Johnson's wife, Beni, publicly said. "I'm fighting for the freedom of our country. Listen," she went on, certain that her prophetic giftings had not failed, "I'm a feeler; I'm a seer. I can see what's gonna happen in the future, and let me tell you, if this man, which if—and that's a big if—he gets in, we're going to see so much destruction. You talk about disunity."[8]

Vallotton soon removed the video from Instagram, where he apologized for the false prophecy. "After doing a lot more research, I decided to wait until the official vote count is complete, as it appears that there is a significant amount of discrepancy in the process,"[9] he shared to his followers in what appears to be a turn towards election denial. He did not provide any evidence as to what the "significant amount of discrepancy" was, but he also did not need to. Election denial was reaching a fever pitch, especially within NAR churches and among leaders of the far right. The apostle Rick Joyner was already calling on militias to prepare for civil war.

Today's NAR apostles and prophets are not British Israelists, but they are heirs to British-Israelist ideas, including the belief that biblical history is still unfolding. And it is unfolding not only in Israel but also in America. The Bible tells a story of the ancient Israelites going to enter the Promised Land but encountering the fortified city of Jericho. The ensuing battle was their first military engagement, and it was not a typical means of warfare. In fact, when read along with the theology of leaders like C. Peter Wagner, the story comes across as spiritual warfare—or at least a way to justify spiritual warfare as the NAR promoted it.

For six days, the people marched around the fortified city, its impregnable walls defying them to enter and conquer. The priests would blow shofars as they marched in front of the Ark of the Covenant, the sacred box that provided a resting place for the presence of God. On the seventh day, the Israelites marched around seven times and then shouted at the top of their voices as the priests blew their shofars. The walls of Jericho fell down, and the people were able to conquer.

Apostles and prophets decided to do the same thing as they waged spiritual warfare against the impregnable walls of what they saw as a corrupt election process. They participated in a movement called Jericho March, a network of Trump supporters who would enact the biblical march around Jericho in their state capitols and ultimately in Washington, DC. Jericho March was not an exclusively NAR activity; one of its founders, Arina Grossu, is Catholic. But during her time serving in the White House during Trump's first term, she undoubtedly would have come into contact with Paula White and Trump's retinue of prophets and apostles. Their participation was crucial to turning Jericho March into a national program that, they believed, would cause states to certify their election results in favor of Trump, not Biden.

The largest Jericho March, held in DC on December 12, 2020, was hosted by the conservative pundit Eric Metaxas and featured Michael Flynn. Trump did a flyover of the event in Air Force One. The white supremacist Stewart Rhodes, the founder of Oath Keepers, was part of this Jericho March. He gave a speech that called on Trump to use the Insurrection Act, an 1807 law that allows the president to call on the National Guard to suppress rebellion against the government. "Show the world who the traitors are," he demanded. "If he does not do it now"—if Trump does not use the Insurrection Act—"we're going to have to do it ourselves later in a much more desperate, much more bloody war."[10]

Rhodes' speech was not seen as extremist, at least not extremist in the sense that he had gone too far, and this was not what the NAR leaders were actually calling for. In fact, Three-Percenter flags waved in the crowd, indicating the presence of the anti-government militia group. Followers of QAnon were also there, waving giant cardboard cutouts of the letter "Q." The poised, well-spoken Metaxas came back on stage after Rhodes finished speaking and said, "God bless you! This guy's keeping it real." Metaxas is not necessarily part of the NAR, but his work has certainly been embraced by the prophets and apostles, and he was hosting a NAR-organized event.

Nearby, something close to a riot was already raging as members of the Proud Boys, Oath Keepers, and Three Percenters expressed their fury that Biden might actually take the White House. The NAR leaders and other dominionists did not attempt to distance themselves from this white-supremacist violence. Instead, they continued to do what they had been doing ever since Trump first announced his candidacy the day before the Mother Emmanuel massacre:

They partnered with it.

◆

"How many of you know this is the most important week in America's history?" the apostle Che Ahn asked a crowd gathered in Freedom Plaza on

January 5, 2021. From his megachurch in Pasadena, California, Ahn oversees an apostolic network of churches that is larger than most denominations. During the Covid pandemic, Ahn had fought for what he saw as "religious freedom" by appealing to the Supreme Court to keep his church open against California's intense lockdowns. And he won, against the state of California. Now, he was in Washington, DC, stoking the fury that would soon erupt. "And I believe that this week, we're going to throw Jezebel out. Jehu's going to rise up, and we're going to rule and reign through President Trump and under the Lordship of Jesus Christ!"

Many of Ahn's listeners on January 5 would be at the Capitol Ellipse the next day, though Ahn himself would sleep through the entire riot. Still, he riled up a crowd that carried "Don't Tread on Me" flags and was prepared to fight the government itself to keep Trump in power. "Because I'm telling you, the consequences will be severe if Biden and Harris become president."[11] He went on, "We have to be the head and not the tail, and so we are here to change history! I believe we're going to shift this nation, this election that's been stolen from Donald Trump and from the United States of America." He then called on his listeners to show up the next day and protest the "egregious fraud" that had led to the election being called for Biden. "We're going to take a stand until justice prevails, because the foundation of God's throne is justice and righteousness. And we're going to see President Trump be our president for the next four years." He then cast out the demonic spirit of Jezebel, which he believed sat over the American political system and had led to the fraudulent election of Biden.

Charlie Kirk had sent busloads of people to Washington, DC, for what he called the "March to Save America" on January 6. He even approved $60,000 in speaking fees to have President Trump and Kimberly Guilfoyle, the girlfriend of Kirk's much-publicized friend Don Jr., come to the rally and incite the crowd. Kirk himself did not attend the rally, however, perhaps because he already knew that the people attending were prepared to engage in violence against the government.

◆

"The blood of Jesus, the blood of Jesus."

The crowds began to gather in front of the Capitol before dawn, spurred by NAR leaders and Neo-Confederates who parroted Donald Trump's claim that he had rightfully won the election.

"We cover the Capitol with the blood of Jesus." Shofars blew as worshipers engaged in spiritual warfare. "The blood of Jesus over you. There's power in the blood of Jesus." They prophesied and declared, "Warring angels surround this place because this battle is a spiritual battle."[12] They spoke in tongues as they used their authority, their dominion, that Christ has given them through his death and resurrection. Dominion over an election that their champion had decisively lost.

"No weapon formed against me shall prosper."[13] Though the worshipers were already surrounded by law enforcement and the crowd's temperature was rising, from seething anger to boiling rage, many of the people gathered had come for a worship service. And for victory. Because worship was the weapon they would use to tear down the stronghold of a stolen election.

This gathering, one of many in front of the Capitol, could have almost been a Let Us Worship rally. Indeed, Feucht and Engle had created the model for evangelicals to engage in spiritual warfare in Washington, DC. And before them had come a long line of dominionists who had paved the way by developing the theologies and the movement around British Israelism, faith-healing, Manifest Sons of God, and the Seven Mountain Mandate: Frank Sandford, Charles Fox Parham, John Alexander Dowie, Gordon Lindsay, Aimee Semple McPherson, Wesley Swift, William Branham, Reg Layzell, Paul Cain, Rousas John Rushdoony, Gary North, Bill Gothard, Loren Cunningham, Bill Bright, C. Peter Wagner, Mike Bickle, David Barton, Doug Wilson.

And with them, the Charleston shooter, the Charlottesville rioters, the Oklahoma City bomber, the Aryan Nations that radicalized the Weaver family at Ruby Ridge.

So they sang. They prayed. They prophesied. They waged spiritual warfare against territorial spirits. They declared their dominion. "Justice, justice, justice."[14] The prophet Cindy Jacobs thanked God for what was happening that day and called down the powers of heaven to prevent the event from becoming violent, even as it already was.

They stood in a crowd that included Confederate battle flags alongside large wooden crosses and banners that declared, "Jesus Saves!" In the world of dominionism, there is no irony between these two symbols, the Confederacy and the cross of Jesus Christ. The two are closely bound together, the Confederacy a representation of the idealized American Christian nation that dominionists of many stripes hope to recreate. Whether or not they realize this part of their theological heritage, longing for the Confederacy is just as baked into the dominionist movement as is the white supremacism and antisemitism that consumed William Branham.

So NAR dominionists and Neo-Confederates alike listened to Paula White declare from the Capitol Ellipse, "God, you said you honor your word and your name above all things. So as we hold you, in covenant with you, today, let justice be done." She went on, with bold declarations that came from the dominion she claimed to have in Christ, "As his pastor, I put a hedge of protection around [Trump]. I secure his purpose. I secure his destiny. I secure his life, God, and I thank you that he will walk in a holy boldness and a wisdom, God, and that you will go before him."[15]

They listened to Trump, who told them to "fight like hell." And they obeyed his orders, marching to the Capitol building and breaking the windows to force their way inside. Not everyone who had gathered that morning for a worship service and spiritual warfare entered the Capitol. But NAR leaders had spent months using rhetoric from QAnon to ramp up support of Trump in the weeks and months leading up to the election. They had fanned the flames around the stolen election and worked with Turning Point USA to organize the rally that culminated in the storming of the Capitol. They had openly partnered with white supremacists who imagined militia violence should Biden take office.

"Praise the name of Jesus!" shouted one man once he had entered the Capitol. "Glory to God! God bless America!"[16]

"Father God, thank you," prayed another insurrectionist, who stood in a group that included at least one Oath Keeper. "Thank you for letting us stand up for our country and what we believe in. Guide us so we may do your will."[17]

The QAnon shaman, who became the mascot of the Capitol Riot for his fur cap with horns, prayed, "Thank you for filling this chamber with patriots that love you and that love Christ." He thanked God that they had the opportunity to rid the government of "the communists, the globalists, and the traitors," and "for allowing the United States of America to be reborn." And he closed by saying, "We love you, and we thank you. In Christ's holy name we pray."[18]

Meanwhile, members of Congress had donned gas masks and fled for their lives as rioters called to hang Mike Pence for refusing to break protocol in certifying the election of Joe Biden.

And to cap off a presidency that began with the unrest around Confederate statues, on January 6, 2021, a Confederate battle flag flew inside the United States Capitol for the very first time.

◆

The Capitol Riot was too much for even some of Trump's staunchest supporters. Vallotton soon reposted the video where he apologized for getting the election prophecy wrong. Betsy DeVos resigned her position as Secretary of Education. Mike Pence took over presidential duties as the president sequestered himself at Mar-a-Lago for the remainder of his term. His approval rating plummeted, including among the conservative evangelicals who had not only given him power but had supported him in contesting the election.

But the story was not over. Because that Sunday, the sermons at NAR churches downplayed or even justified the riot. "We condemn violence of any form and shape," Che Ahn told his church the Sunday after the insurrection that he had helped incite. "Having said that," he continued, "unfortunately some Trump followers got caught up in the excitement of the event. And they weren't mature. And they went in the Capitol."[19] He went on to thank God for President Trump, with the audience clapping loudly in response.

"Some politicians are pressing hard to get President Trump completely discredited and out of the way, as quickly and as permanently as they can," Dutch Sheets told his followers less than a week after the riot. "The media is spinning lies and operating completely in tandem with them, manipulating the minds of millions of Americans."[20] He would spend the next four years traveling the country, as he had done following the election of 2000 and his prophetic release in Washington, DC, that he believed had led to the contest finally being called for George W. Bush. With other NAR prophets and apostles, along with dominionists in Congress such as Marjorie Taylor Greene, he would spend the next four years speaking to packed-out stadiums, insisting that Trump had won in 2020 and was the rightful president.

And four years later, the same people who had dropped their support of Donald Trump when they saw footage of the Capitol Riot on their television screens re-elected him.

16

The Election of Mike Johnson

James Dobson received his doctorate in psychology in 1967, six years before the American Psychological Association (APA) formally delisted homosexuality as a clinical diagnosis. In protest, he resigned his APA membership and went on to form what would become a politically connected evangelical stronghold, Focus on the Family. Through magazines, radio broadcasts, and church conferences, Focus on the Family offered friendly and engaging advice to parents, based especially on Dobson's 1970 classic, *Dare to Discipline*. A generation of children had already grown up under the guidance of Dr. Benjamin Spock, who urged parents not to use corporal punishment; Dobson had seen enough of the results during his early years practicing psychology in California: rebellion, drug use, the sexual revolution, hippie culture, and a shocking rise in youth who embraced LGBTQ+ lifestyles. His solution was to admonish parents to spank their children and assert their God-ordained authority.

Dobson believed that his advice would prevent children from becoming gay, a mission that drove much of his career as conservative evangelicalism's psychological guru. But he was more than a friendly radio personality; his anti-gay activism was a political lightning rod. In 1994, he partnered with Seven-Spheres developer Bill Bright, radio personality and financial guru Larry Burkett, former federal prosecutor Alan Sears, and the megachurch pastor and televangelist D. James Kennedy to found the Alliance Defense Fund, later renamed the Alliance Defending Freedom (ADF). The ADF would serve as an evangelical counter to the American Civil Liberties Union and take on cases that could be rebranded over the struggle for religious freedom. Many of its cases explicitly targeted LGBTQ+ people and/or fought to reassert traditional gender roles, with men leading patriarchal families and women serving their husbands and raising children.

In 2000, ADF created the Blackstone Legal Fellowship to train evangelical law students in idiosyncratic understandings of constitutional law and, using Francis Schaeffer's phrase, "Christian worldview." Graduates of the program then receive job placement opportunities that include government offices and prestigious law firms that represent ADF cases to the Supreme Court. John Eastman, who served on the Blackstone faculty and also worked as Trump's campaign manager in 2020, was part of the retinue that attempted to overturn the election results. Prior to becoming a justice of the US Supreme Court, Amy Coney Barrett spoke for Blackstone events five times and described the fellowship in glowing terms. When her confirmation provided the pivotal conservative majority to the Supreme Court, ADF moved forward with the case that would mark a coup for the Religious Right: *Dobbs v. Jackson Women's Health Organization*, the case that overturned *Roe v. Wade*.

Before that, ADF served as the incubator for a new lawyer who, after quietly being elected to the US House of Representatives, would spearhead the effort to overturn the 2020 election results and then become Speaker of the House.

"Probably all of my biggest heroes are in the room tonight." In 2019, four years before becoming elected as House Speaker, Mike Johnson gave the keynote address at a highly secretive group of right-wing operatives known as the Council for National Policy (CNP). "I grew up in the movement … I owe you all so much."[1] He became an attorney for ADF in 2002. The following year, he argued that Texas should retain its sodomy laws that criminalized intimate contact between consenting adults of the same sex. He consistently portrayed LGBTQ+ individuals as sexual groomers and, in 2022, introduced national legislation that, if passed, would criminalize people who spoke with children under the age of ten about *anything* sexual—including gender dysphoria and gender identity—other than affirming one's biological gender from birth. Johnson's bill placed discussions of LGBTQ+ issues on the same level as showing pornography to children.

"I literally was the bag boy for Mat Staver," he went on to his CNP audience, referring to the lawyer who founded the anti-LGBTQ+ Liberty Counsel. In 2017, Liberty Counsel represented Scott Lively, an anti-LGBTQ+ activist who has promoted the pseudohistorical view that the Nazi regime functioned as a gay club. Though gay people in Nazi-occupied Europe were much more likely to be killed than to do the killing and had to wear a pink triangle on their prison-camp uniforms, Lively has insisted that toleration and acceptance of queer people is part of the step toward Nazism. His advocacy has largely fallen on deaf ears in the United States—though David Barton has repeated the claim that the Holocaust was caused by gay people—but his work in Uganda was critical to passage of the anti-LGBTQ+ legislation that provided the death penalty. When the group Sexual Minorities Uganda sued Lively for crimes against humanity, Liberty Counsel presented Lively's advocacy as "nothing more than preaching Biblical truth regarding marriage and sexuality"[2] and managed to get the case dismissed on jurisdictional grounds.

"And Tony Perkins, I was his bag boy."[3] While still in law school in the 1990s, future House Speaker Mike Johnson was mentored by Tony Perkins, who led the Family Research Council (the same organization that hired Josh Duggar) and worked extensively with ADF. Perkins founded the Louisiana Family Forum in 1998 to push back against what he saw as the gay agenda to dismantle American society. In 2004, he spoke at a Louisiana meeting of the white-supremacist Council of Conservative Citizens, and prior to that, in 1996, he paid David Duke, the former Grand Wizard of the Ku Klux Klan, $82,500 for his mailing list. This indiscretion indicated that Perkins, a close ally of the ADF and mentor of the future House Speaker, was targeting the same audience as America's most infamous domestic-terrorism group. Johnson and Perkins had a long-standing relationship that went up to Johnson crediting his longtime mentor with urging him to run for the House speakership.

At the time of Johnson's 2019 CNP address, Congress was in the process of impeaching President Trump for abuse of power and obstruction of Congress. "Scripture tells us very clearly that our people perish for lack of knowledge," he said before describing the proceedings as a symptom of a greater national problem. "Don't take for granted that anyone knows anything anymore. Our people perish for lack of knowledge." Unsurprisingly, a year after Johnson delivered this speech, he was at the forefront of the congressional attempt to overturn the results of the 2020 election. A few weeks after Biden was declared the winner, Johnson was part of a lawsuit that sought to have the election results in four battleground states thrown out due to alleged irregularities in voter counts. The lawsuit came from the state of Texas, and Johnson collected signatures for a legal brief supporting the lawsuit. The Supreme Court rejected it, but Johnson and his fellow election deniers were not finished.

"You know the allegations about these voting machines, some of them being rigged with this software by Dominion, there's a lot of merit to that,"[4] Johnson said, despite a complete dearth of evidence supporting the conspiracy theories that flew around the 2020 election. By January 6, however, Johnson had changed his tune so that he sounded more sophisticated—and less conspiracy-prone—when he called on Congress to not certify electoral votes that would officially deliver Biden the presidency. Even after a deadly attack on the US Capitol, Johnson refused to vote for the certification of Biden's win.

"We have become a nation of biblical and historical and constitutional illiterates," he told his CNP audience. He explained how he and his wife, Kelly, usually spent their Sunday evenings speaking at churches, sharing about what they see as the biblical foundation for America's government; in his telling, hundreds of congregants will sit in rapt attention for hours, until he tells them that he has to leave. "Nobody knows this stuff anymore." Perhaps the reason why is because this particular approach to America's historical and civil roots is not very historical. It is fairly recent, having developed through the work of Rushdoony and gaining widespread attraction with the work of Johnson's friend and political ally, David Barton.

◆

Barton and his colleagues at WallBuilders did not explicitly endorse the effort to overturn the 2020 election, but they could not contain their excitement when Johnson unexpectedly became Speaker of the House in 2023. "We've known this guys for years," Barton's son, Tim, said on the WallBuilders podcast shortly after Johnson's election. "He's been a friend for years." Cohost Rick Green even commented that, in Johnson's acceptance speech, he "sounded just like he was a WallBuilders speaker."[5] There was a reason why Johnson's speech reflected what Barton and his organization have been promoting: Johnson has been connected to WallBuilders for decades and subscribes to the Christian nationalism that Barton teaches. Unsurprisingly, he uses a Barton-like understanding of sphere sovereignty as the foundation for his conservatism.

Ken Ham, the founder of Answers in Genesis, is also a longtime friend of Johnson. Answers in Genesis is a pseudoscientific organization that, like WallBuilders, is extremely popular among conservative evangelicals. Against modern scientific theories, it presents "evidence" that the earth was created less than 10,000 years ago and experienced a cataclysmic flood—recorded in the Genesis account as a deluge that only Noah and his family survived—which produced what mainstream scientists refer to as the fossil record. The Creation Museum, which received a surge of popularity when the Duggars visited it on their show, functions as a pilgrimage site for conservative evangelicals who see the creation narrative as literal scientific truth. Johnson litigated for the Ark Encounter, an exhibit connected to the Creation Museum, when the state of Kentucky attempted to deny it tourism tax credits due to the Ark Encounter's effort to indoctrinate people into a particular religious view.

Not surprisingly, Answers in Genesis is part of a decades-long effort to bring the teaching of creationism into public schools. Yet the views promoted by Ken Ham and his colleagues go much deeper. Ham is convinced that social breakdown—school shootings, child poverty, high divorce rates, to name only a few symptoms—is the result of people not having an appropriate understanding of the Bible. If Americans understand the literal truth of Genesis as a historical and scientific account, then these social evils will naturally end. Johnson has expressed no opposition to using creationism, rather than well-researched public programs with proven records of addressing issues such as poverty and violence, as a solution for social problems. When he told Fox News host Sean Hannity that, in order to understand his views, one just needed to "pick up a Bible off your shelf and read it,"[6] he insinuated that he does agree with Ham.

"If anybody tries to convince you that your biblical beliefs or your religious viewpoint needs to be separated from public affairs, you should politely remind them to review their history,"[7] Johnson said on his podcast series, *Truth Be Told*, just over a month before his election as House Speaker. "And importantly, you should not back down." This quote belies the fact that millions of Americans who do not adhere to dominionist ideals bring their faith into the public sphere every day. They think about their roles as stewards of God's creation when voting for politicians who want to help wean America off of its addiction to fossil fuels. They think about the dignity of all human beings when they support local initiatives that protect the rights of LGBTQ+ individuals. They hope to expose their children to viewpoints other than their own when sending them to public schools. And because their faith compels them to seek better futures for the children in their communities, they serve on PTAs and attend school board meetings. They volunteer their time and resources when their churches, synagogues, mosques, and temples get involved in community outreaches *because their faith, patriotism, and sense of civic duty compel them to.*

Johnson was not referring to these millions of faith-filled Americans who quietly bring their values into public life every day. Like his mentor Barton, he was referring to evangelicals with dominionist leanings who want to see their way of life championed in public policy. *Their* view, *their* way of life, is under assault. So goes Johnson's and Barton's reading of Christian nationalism, and the only solution is to enshrine their views into government policy. As part of that solution, Johnson has spent countless hours litigating against the rights of queer people, declaring that doing so is necessary to protect the freedoms of dominionist-minded evangelicals.

Some of the founders and luminaries of the ADF and the CNP were signatories to a dominionist document from 1986 called "A Manifesto for the Christian Church." Those names included D. James Kennedy along with Tim LaHaye, who helped run Jerry Falwell's Moral Majority, cofounded the CNP, and later cowrote the mega-bestselling *Left Behind* series. Michael Farris, the founder of the Home School Legal Defense Association and Patrick Henry College, and who eventually became CEO and general counsel of the ADF. Farris also founded the Convention of States in 2013. Endorsed by a retinue of conservative politicians and right-wing operatives, including James Dobson, his goal is to use Article V to call for a "convention of states" to amend, if not rewrite entirely, the US Constitution.

"Forgive us for failing to occupy our proper position as servants in the affairs of law, government, economics, business, education, media, the arts, medicine, and science,"[8] reads "A Manifesto for the Christian Church." It contained a rudimentary form of what became the 7MM, listing what Loren Cunningham and Bill Bright were referring to as spheres of influence. The manifesto also professes to oppose "statist-collectivist theft from citizens through devaluation of their money and redistribution of their wealth," with the term "statist" coming directly from Rushdoony's views of public enterprises that did not originate with the church; the statement regarding "statist-collectivist theft" could have come directly from him or his son-in-law and economic protégé, Gary North. Both North and Rushdoony signed the manifesto.

The document that shaped the trajectory of the ADF, CNP, and much of the rest of the dominionist movement came from a small group that few people had heard of, the Coalition on Revival, and it did not draw much attention among scholars or journalists. Perhaps the text was too extremist to be taken seriously in 1986, despite being signed by a "Who's Who" of evangelical politics: Harold O.J. Brown, who had helped spearhead the antiabortion movement and cofounded Christian Action Council; Harold Lindsell, who helped found Fuller Seminary before becoming editor of *Christianity Today*; Josh McDowell, the well-known Christian apologist who worked with Bill Bright's Campus Crusade for Christ; Mark Siljander, a former Congressman who worked extensively with The Family; Adrian Rogers, who had led a conservative insurgency within the Southern Baptist Convention in the late 1970s and was elected the convention's president in 1979; Edith Schaeffer, wife of the late Francis Schaeffer; C. Peter Wagner, who systematized the dominionist theology of the New Apostolic Reformation; and Don Wildmon, who founded the American Family Association that sponsored Rick Perry's 2011 "The Response" prayer rally. There was also Ern Baxter, who had worked with William Branham during the Latter-Rain revival and went on to lead in the Shepherding Movement, along with Bob Mumford and Charles Simpson, fellow Shepherding leaders. And of course, Gary North, R.J. Rushdoony, Tim LaHaye, D. James Kennedy, and Michael Farris.

"We affirm that the Bible is not only God's statement to us regarding religion, salvation, eternity, and righteousness," "A Manifesto for the Christian Church" proclaims, "but also the final measurement and depository of certain fundamental facts of reality and basic principles that God wants all mankind to know in the spheres of law, government, economics, business, education, arts and communication, medicine, psychology, and science." Like the later 7MM, this document called on evangelical culture warriors to use the Bible as the absolute measure of all truth, not only of theology but also with regard to how the government and economy should function, what scientific theories are taught in schools, even how schools themselves operate. "All theories and practices of these spheres of life are only true, right, and realistic to the degree that they agree with the Bible. The Bible furnishes mankind with the only logical and verbal connection between time and eternity, religion and science, the visible and invisible worlds."[9]

Using language that was already in circulation among dominionists by the mid-1980s, "A Manifesto for the Christian Church" reads, "Those people or nations that live in opposition to biblical laws and commandments will, sooner or later, be cursed and destroyed." The document then makes clear what it means in using the Bible as the "final measurement" in the area of government: "It is, therefore, to the great benefit of all mankind, Christian and non-Christian alike, to bring every society's judicial and legal systems into as close an approximation to the laws and commandments of the Bible as its citizens will allow."[10] The manifesto may have garnered little outside attention at the time, but it was eerily prescient of how dominionist ideas would take over not only evangelicalism but eventually the Republican Party and, with the election of 2024, the entire federal government.

Johnson's election to the US House of Representatives and sudden ascent to Speaker of the House was a long time coming, in no small part because of the evangelical political operatives who stood behind him and the bigger dominionist movement that he was part of. And he is far from the only dominionist in Congress. He is joined by Senator Ted Cruz, a Republican from Texas whose father is a leader in the NAR. Cruz espouses

Christian-nationalist rhetoric while advancing what seems to be a secularized version of NAR policy goals. One popular NAR prophecy from the 2010s is called the End-Times transfer of wealth and claims that soon, God will take money and material resources away from ungodly, liberal organizations and funnel it toward churches that are working to build his kingdom on earth. Senator Cruz has not publicly endorsed this prophecy, but he has promoted economic policies that seem to support this goal. He advocates devolving material resources from the government and toward private organizations, especially churches, which can then use those resources to implement the 7MM. Before Cruz, Sam Brownback was a senator from Kansas with deep connections to Lou Engle, the International House of Prayer, and The Family.

Lauren Boebert and Marjorie Taylor Greene have also worked alongside Johnson in the House of Representatives to advance dominionist causes. Both have partnered with NAR organizations and leaders to advance the 7MM alongside the myth of the stolen election—that Trump, in fact, won in 2020 but was cheated. And Johnson is far from the only congressional representative who has staged the NAR's Appeal to Heaven flag right outside of his office. There is Senator Shelley Moore Capito from West Virginia, Senator Mike Lee from Utah, Representative Josh Brecheen from Oklahoma, Representative Eric Burlison from Missouri, Representative Michael Cloud from Texas, Representative Warren Davidson from Ohio, Representative Glenn Grothman from Wisconsin, Representative Barry Moore from Alabama, Representative Gary Palmer from Alabama, Representative David Rouzer from North Carolina, and Representative Pete Sessions from Texas.

Dominionism is alive and well in the US Congress.

◆

Too much scrutiny on politically active evangelicals and the organizations they serve betrays the core place that the dominionist movement has spread: America's churches. Evangelicals who attend Southern and Independent Baptist, Pentecostal, nondenominational, Presbyterian, and Bible churches do not see groups such as Focus on the Family, Alliance Defending Freedom, and Family Research Council as hate groups. Working-class members of these churches happily give money from their hard-earned paychecks to support these organizations and so many others like them, not for their hate-filled invective against queer people, but for their work in bringing to light issues that concern everyday evangelicals. Things like their fears of the government taking the position that Christianity should have no role in public life, concerns about their tax dollars funding the murder of unborn children, and angst over being coerced into supporting views about the LGBTQ+ community that they see as contradicting the Bible.

Notwithstanding, there are many Christians, including evangelicals, who do not see queer rights as incompatible with biblical views. There is only a handful of verses that seem to oppose gay rights, and most of these verses can be interpreted as far less punitive toward queer people than anti-gay ambassadors make them out to be. And given that Christ himself said that the greatest commandment is to love God and love neighbor, churches welcoming and even being led by queer people do not necessarily contradict the Bible.

Dominionist churches are overwhelmingly those that do teach an anti-queer approach to the Bible, in line with Dobson's Focus on the Family, Perkins's Family Research Council, and Johnson's work at the ADF. This bias primes members to believe that litigation against gay rights provides a crucial means of preserving the freedoms of Christians, including the right of a bakery owner or county clerk to not serve same-sex couples trying to get married. These same churches also tend to support David Barton's pseudohistory and his attempts to use his arguments about religious freedom to force the Bible into America's public schools. Evangelical celebrities like Barton and Johnson did not rise to prominence through mainstream news outlets and public forums. Their Christian-nationalist ideas and even careers began in churches, where they spoke to like-minded people who shared their concerns that were not being represented in government. Johnson, Barton, Perkins, Farris, and other powerfully connected dominionists were able to address everyday concerns with overblown, hyperbolic responses that would ultimately come to force much of America to adjust to laws based on dominionist ideals.

17

Project 2025

"To escape our current darkness, restore America's civic life, and take back our country for good, conservatives can't merely continue putting out fires," Kevin Roberts wrote in a book that came out a week after Donald Trump won the 2024 election. "We must be brave enough to go on the offense, strike the match, and start a long, controlled burn."[1] The original title of the book was *Dawn's Early Light: Burning Down Washington to Save America*, and it was slated for release about six weeks before the election. However, toward the end of that summer, the Heritage Foundation released a report called Project 2025, which envisioned a dramatic reshaping of the entire government along the lines of dominionism. Negative press about the goals of Project 2025 and its alignment with a second Trump administration led to the title being changed to *Dawn's Early Light: Taking Back Washington to Save America*, and its release date being postponed until a week after the election.

Roberts, the book's author, was the president of the Heritage Foundation, the think tank behind Project 2025. He went on to write in *Dawn's Early Light*,

> For America to flourish again, [our institutions] don't need to be reformed; they need to be burned. A nice start would include: Every Ivy League college, the FBI, the *New York Times*, the National Institute of Allergy and Infectious Diseases, the Department of Education, 80 percent of 'Catholic' higher education, BlackRock, the Loudoun County Public School System, the Boy Scouts of America, the Bill and Melinda Gates Foundation, the World Economic Forum, the Chinese Communist Party, and the National Endowment for Democracy.[2]

The language of burning everything down hearkens back to Sean Feucht's congressional run in 2020, when his catchphrase was Burn It Down. But Roberts had muscle behind his proposal that Feucht could not have imagined prior to the national fame he garnered when his Let Us Worship tour presaged the Capitol Riot. None other than J.D. Vance wrote the foreword to *Dawn's Early Light*. The Yale-trained lawyer had risen to national fame when his memoir, *Hillbilly Elegy*, became a bestseller during the summer of 2016, just before Trump's surprise victory over Hillary Clinton. Pundits came to see the book, which details and sometimes glamorizes his experiences growing up in an impoverished and abusive home, as explaining the America that had been so long forgotten that it finally rebelled in electing Trump. Vance's America was one in which not the government but his grandmother saved him, and he came to see the sphere of family as overriding any kind of government intervention in protecting and nurturing children. The best-selling author initially opposed Trump, but he changed his tune and became a MAGA senator from Ohio in 2022. And in the summer of 2024, Trump tapped him to be vice president.

In *Dawn's Early Light*, Roberts included accounts of his own upbringing, not entirely dissimilar to Vance's. His grandfather stepped in and provided him with love and stability after his parents' divorce, a revolving door of stepparents, and his brother's suicide left him stunned and gasping for air. Roberts and Vance have something else in common: their Catholic faith, with Roberts growing up Catholic and Vance converting after growing up in fundamentalist Protestantism. Not that Catholics are dominionists; far from it. Dominionism emerged on the cult-like fringes of Protestantism, with British Israelism, faith-healing, Frank Sandford's Shiloh community, John Alexander Dowie's city of Zion, and Charles Fox Parham's emergent Pentecostalism. Yet Roberts and Vance both subscribe to a right-wing approach to Catholicism known as integralism, which insists that the church and state are supposed to be united, as they were in medieval Europe. Though Catholic integralists tend to have an appreciation for intellectualism and high culture that dominionists not only lack but aggressively despise, Vance and Roberts have made common cause with supporters of the 7MM, Reconstructionism, and Neo-Confederacy.

"Men and women should marry (and do so younger than most do today),"[3] Roberts wrote about the role of family in his idealized society. "They should marry for life and should bring children into the world (more than most do today)." In making these claims, he ignored a primary reason why, ever since Women's Liberation during the 1960s and 1970s, the age of marriage and divorce rates have gone up: domestic violence. Prior to Women's Liberation, single women had very limited options in caring for themselves, and those options were even fewer for those who needed to take their children and leave an abusive husband. Many women did not even have their own bank accounts, much less education or job skills. Increased levels of self-determination have given women the ability to leave emotionally and physically abusive relationships, oftentimes leading to divorce. Attaining the level of education, job skills, and life experience necessary to achieve this self-determination has meant, among other things, that women get married older and have fewer children.

Roberts ignored the reality of abuse, which is endemic to the entire world of dominionism. Instead, he wanted to burn down all of the government institutions that have contributed to a wide social safety net that allows people to leave abusive situations, especially when they do not have grandparents or other family members to fall back on. But unlike conservatives before him, he did not believe that burning everything down and then getting out of the way would automatically allow for a natural stabilization. "It's fine to take a laissez-faire approach when you are in the safety of the sunshine," he wrote, referring to a long-disproven economic theory that claims when the government gets out of the way, markets flourish. "But when the twilight descends and you hear the wolves, you've got to circle the wagon and load the muskets."[4]

In other words, America needed to bring out its ultimate weapon: Donald Trump. He would start a long burn in Washington that would destroy the government institutions that, in Roberts's and Vance's view, have kept America from flourishing. Trump 2.0 was to be the Second American Revolution.

◆

Project 2025 was built on the history of the Heritage Foundation and how, since its founding in 1973, it has guided America's conservative movement. When Franklin Delano Roosevelt became president at the height of the Great Depression, he instituted a series of reforms that he called the New Deal. These reforms included, to name only a few, social security so that older workers could retire and younger workers take their place; mortgage programs that helped distressed farmers keep their farms and homes; government-funded job programs that trained people with job skills and then put them to work; and the creation of the Securities and Exchange Commission to prevent the kind of practices that had crashed the stock market. The New Deal vastly increased the size of the government by providing social programs and business regulations that would protect people from what Roosevelt saw as abusive practices and an inherently unstable market.

The modern conservative movement began with business moguls working to overturn the New Deal and deregulate America's economy. Even though the New Deal helped pull the country out of the Great Depression, conservative leaders gave their movement a powerful message by saying that their plan would unleash American creativity and productivity. The New Deal would ruin the economy and lead the country down the path of communism; they had a plan to save America. Remove these programs and regulations, they claimed, and markets would naturally balance themselves, resulting in prosperity for all. This model of economics, commonly known as *laissez-faire*, is also referred to as Austrian economics, owing to the influence of Austrian intellectuals such as Ludwig von Mises and Friedrich Hayek. Their work inspired the economic thought of dominionists, beginning with Rushdoony and then Gary North, who saw Austrian economics as biblical.

The conservative movement to overturn the New Deal retained strong white-supremacist overtones as it hobbled through the 1940s, 1950s, and 1960s with no meaningful gains. The John Birch Society saw the nascent Civil Rights Movement as a communist plot by foreign agitators who wanted to sow racial discontent in America. Precipitating the "Great Switch," when Democrats would become the liberal party of civil rights and Republicans would become the conservative party of the Lost Cause, Barry Goldwater ran as the 1964 Republican presidential nominee on a platform of overturning the Civil Rights Act. Meanwhile, Rushdoony was writing a massive tome that would shape both the dominionist movement and, eventually, the Republican Party: *Institutes of Biblical Law*, which came out in 1973. His ideas would move conservative discourse so that, in addition to dismantling the New Deal, eventually his dominionist protégés would advocate replacing it with a church-based society governed by biblical law. That same year, 1973, the Heritage Foundation was born.

Paul Weyrich, the conservative pundit who cofounded the Heritage Foundation with Joseph Coors (of brewing fame), also cofounded Jerry Falwell's Moral Majority. In doing so, the Catholic Weyrich created common cause with conservative evangelicals, leading to a formidable alliance that would, forty years later, bring together evangelical dominionists and Catholic integralists. The Heritage Foundation was never Catholic or Protestant; it was a conservative, nativist think tank that absorbed ideas from various perspectives and turned those ideas into actionable policy goals. At the same time, the Heritage Foundation served as a big tent for anyone who wanted to see the government champion certain expressions of Christian faith that could be brought into the service of a conservative agenda. When Ronald Reagan assumed office in January 1981, the Heritage Foundation presented him with a document called *Mandate for Leadership*, which contained 2000 points of action that the conservative movement wanted to see implemented. Reagan followed through with half of them.

Even though Reconstructionism was on the ascendancy during the 1980s, it was far too extremist for the coalition of conservatives who came together in the Reagan Eighties. Falwell wrote an editorial for the Heritage Foundation's journal, *Policy Review*, denouncing Reconstructionism for wanting to execute "homosexuals and drunkards."[5] Rushdoony replied that Falwell was wrong; he did not want to execute drunkards. Even though Falwell disagreed with Rushdoony on various points, he agreed that Rushdoony's movement around education was a primary reason for the existence of the voting bloc that he was organizing. Francis Schaeffer also disagreed with components of Reconstructionism, but his ideas—which traveled through evangelicalism's intellectual circuits from the 1970s and beyond—were very much inspired by Rushdoony.

Despite views that included death by stoning for adulterers, blasphemers, apostates, heretics, and rebellious children, the influence of Reconstructionism at the Heritage Foundation grew as Rushdoony's extremist discourse shaped conservative dialogue. One reason why is simply the reactionary nature of opposing extremism. If Rushdoony wanted to stone queer individuals, then slightly more moderate approaches—such as imprisoning them—can quickly become more palatable. But in addition to shaping reactions, moderated approaches to Rushdoony's ideas came to embody the policy agenda embraced by the Heritage Foundation, ultimately leading to Project 2025.

This slow-but-steady embrace of Reconstructionism began with the same issue that Rushdoony wrote about in his first book, *The Messianic Character of American Education*: public schools, what he saw as the archetype of government overreach. In a foreshadowing of the nationwide war on school boards, parents in Kanawha County, West Virginia, fumed at the adoption of textbooks that they claimed promoted racial intermarriage and secular humanism. The year was not 2020 but 1974, and this first parents' revolt came to be known as the textbook wars. It culminated in conservative evangelicals dynamiting the building that housed the school board, attacking school buses, and firebombing two elementary schools. Neoconservatives from the newly formed Heritage Foundation rushed to the aid of parents now facing legal repercussions for their crimes. One of those who got involved was Connie Marshner, who had recently started her career on Capitol Hill by creating messaging around a bill that would create a federal network of daycares. While the bill had much support in the liberation movements of the 1970s, she insisted that it represented the government turning itself into a therapeutic state and taking over the home.

The Heritage Foundation picked Marshner up as its first director of education, where she developed less extreme versions of Rushdoony's ideas. One of those was parent-run educational cooperatives as an alternative to schools, an idea that she wrote about in her 1984 book, the Rushdoony-inspired *Blackboard Tyranny*. It was based on her experiences supporting beleaguered parents who had been part of the Kanawha County upheaval, a struggle that the Heritage Foundation presented in righteous terms, even though parents and local pastors had firebombed schools.

This model of the Heritage Foundation endorsing citizen violence against government institutions became evident again in the aftermath of the 2020 election. During the first Trump presidency, more than sixty employees and alumni of the Heritage Foundation served in his administration. When Trump raised alarms that if he lost the 2020 election, the only explanation would be fraud, advocates at the Heritage Foundation used a quasi-scholarly framework to promote the same view. Not only did the organization endorse the political violence seen at the Capitol Riot, but four members of the Trump cabinet who remained loyal to him went on to serve in leading positions.

Roberts took over in 2021, a time when the conservative movement was in crisis over responses to the dominionist-led Capitol Riot. During the Biden presidency, Roberts guided activists and intellectuals associated with the Heritage Foundation to create a document that would provide a roadmap for a second Trump presidency.

◆

On the campaign trail, Trump repeatedly tried to distance himself from the media-maligned Project 2025. Even after choosing as his running mate J.D. Vance, the senator who wrote the foreword to Roberts's book, Trump insisted that he had not even read Project 2025. But he did not need to, as he has long surrounded himself with dominionists and, for his second term, also entwined himself with a cadre of politically minded integralists. The evidence bore itself out during his first hundred days, when he vastly overhauled the federal government along the lines of Project 2025.

Against the gains of the Civil Rights Movement, Women's Liberation, and the Gay Rights Movement, on day one, President Trump issued a total ban on diversity, equity, and inclusion—what Project 2025 called the "DEI apparatus"—in the federal government. Dominionism began with British Israelism and the Ku Klux Klan; the ending of DEI resounded as a *coup de grâce* to liberal democracy.

In keeping with Rushdoony's thought and Falwell's original organizing aimed at overthrowing *Brown v. Board of Education*, Project 2025 called for abolishing the Department of Education. Within two months of resuming office, Trump issued an executive order that began exactly that process.

Project 2025 insists on devolving federal responsibilities, including disaster relief, to states and localities. Trump began efforts at dismantling the Federal Emergency Management Agency (FEMA) by March 2025, claiming that states should take over the duties previously overseen by FEMA. Those duties have included emergency relief for people impacted by hurricanes, wildfires, and floods—risks that will continue to compound with rising exposure to climate change.

With regard to climate change, Trump removed America from the Paris Climate Agreement the day that he returned to the Oval Office. He promised oil companies that if they donated to his campaign, he would remove regulations; upon retaking office, he made good on this promise. He went on to boost the fossil fuel industry while gutting environmental protections and freezing money for green initiatives. These anti-environmental programs are also in keeping with Project 2025, which set out to dismantle all environmental protections and green-energy projects. After all, the oil industry has long been funding the dominionist movement, especially David Barton's work in educating legislators and schoolchildren across the country into his understanding of American history.

Trump appointed Brendan Carr to lead the Federal Communications Commission, which oversees National Public Radio (NPR) and the Public Broadcasting Station (PBS), both of which are funded through the Corporation for Public Broadcasting. Carr had written parts of Project 2025 regarding the FCC and urged Congress to cease all funding for the Corporation for Public Broadcasting.

He appointed Russell Vought, who likewise wrote parts of Project 2025, as head of the Office of Management and Budget (OMB). Not long after Trump's 2025 inauguration, the OMB ordered a freeze on federal loans, grants, and assistance programs until the administration could review the use of all funds to ensure that they are being used according to his priorities.

Project 2025 was an unabashedly nativist document that sought to restore the power of a white patriarchy in America. To this end, it set out the policy goals of ending asylum claims for refugees fleeing their home countries and carrying out mass deportations, including for people who had immigrated to the United States legally. When Trump empowered Immigration and Customs Enforcement (ICE) to carry out this plan, legal immigrants with court protections, university students on lawful visas, and even American citizens were deported, many of them to a megaprison in El Salvador. When courts ordered a halt to the deportations and that people who had been wrongfully detained and/or deported be returned home, Trump did more than ignore these orders. He asked the president of El Salvador to build more megaprisons so that he could begin deporting citizens.

Perhaps most infamously, Trump created the Department of Government Efficiency (DOGE) to, as Roberts put it in the original title of his book, burn down Washington. With the president's blessing, tech billionaire Elon Musk shut down the United States Agency for International Development (USAID), which has long funded and implemented humanitarian programs around the world. "We spent the weekend feeding USAID into the wood chipper," Musk boasted on social media. "Could gone to some great parties. Did that instead."[6] Consistent with the origins of dominionism and its long-standing ties to hard antisemitism, at Trump's second inauguration, Musk had made a Sieg Heil salute. DOGE went on to slash the federal workforce, also a goal of Project 2025, whose overarching aim was to dismantle what Roberts referred to as the administrative state.

These moves represent only a handful of the changes Trump made in the first hundred days of his second term. Project 2025 was not about violently overthrowing the government. It was about subverting it from within so that the 7MM could be fulfilled, not just on the mountain of government but in every area of society: education, media, religion, the arts and entertainment, family life, and business.

◆

By the time Trump ran for reelection in 2024 and then reassumed office, dominionism had left the confines of its white-supremacist origins. NAR prophets and apostles had used promises of faith-healing and divine intervention in all areas of life to build a multiracial, diverse coalition of voters. These dominionist leaders had turned marginal dilemmas, such as whether trans athletes should be allowed to compete in school sports, into national hot-button issues while partnering with Turning Point USA to stoke the anger and terror of voters. They had used conspiracy theories that serve a political agenda, especially QAnon and the stolen election, to ignite fears of what might happen if Trump is not reelected. They continued to reach out to like-minded dominionists who might have different, even contradictory ideas about theology, to expand their base. By the time Trump was reelected, the big surprise was not how many white evangelicals had voted for him but rather how many minorities had. African American and Latino voters in particular turned out in large numbers to vote for Trump.

NAR messaging about divine intervention and doing politics God's way has worked. Dominionism is no longer confined to the boundaries of White Anglo-Saxon Protestants who felt left behind by the political establishment and found in NAR churches something that appealed to them. One can visit a NAR church today and see immigrants worshipping alongside white evangelicals and listening to a pastor talk about Christian nationalism using the language of spiritual warfare. What would have been unthinkable to the white supremacist Charles Fox Parham is now the norm.

The goal of the 7MM was to place a king on the mountains of culture. On February 19, 2025, Trump shared on Musk's platform X a picture of himself wearing a crown. The caption read, "CONGESTION PRICING IS DEAD. Manhattan, and all of New York, is SAVED. LONG LIVE THE KING!"[7] He unofficially crowned himself king, surrounded by a movement that wanted to see exactly that. However the rest of his second term plays out, how he responds to the courts, whether his voters will continue supporting him, and how much cultural capital dominionist churches can continue to gain, what seems abundantly clear is that Trump will not relinquish power easily.

And neither will the dominionists.

Conclusion

At the age of twenty-two, I got the miracle that I needed. I suffered greatly with scoliosis from the time I was a toddler until just before I graduated from college. And then one day, the scoliosis was gone. X-rays showed that the vertebrae in my spine had inexplicably shifted into place, and the nerves and muscles were following suit. Constant pain from pinched nerves, spasmatic muscles, and TMJ had been my normal for two decades, but just like that, I was able to do things like sit in a chair for more than fifteen minutes and then stand up without stumbling. God healed my back.

In the years since, I have had to reckon with the stories of people who never got their miracle. My college friend who was born with severe cerebral palsy and has never been able to stand but has the kindest heart and always knows how to make someone feel valued. My aunt who died of cancer after a lifetime of faithful devotion to Christ and the people around her. The victims of clergy sexual abuse who experienced such deep mental anguish that it had to have taken a physical toll. The parents of Olive Heilegenthal. That one kept me up at night. So did the horrifying stories told by the people who managed to escape Columbine High School on April 20, 1999.

I am glad that, in the haste of my early twenties, I never saved those X-rays that would have provided medical proof of my miracle. The last thing that I want now is for one of the best things that ever happened to me to become fuel for more of the faith-healing that continues to draw people into the dominionist movement. My miracle was not about Manifest Sons of God, or bringing God back into public schools, or the Seven Mountain Mandate. It was about, well, I don't really know. Because there are so many people that God does not heal, at least not in the way that we may want for God to heal them. What made me so special that I got my miracle, but Olive did not come back?

Dominionist theology is wrong. It is so, so wrong. It fills people with the hope and expectation that God is going to deliver on their behalf because God wants God's name to be great among the nations. And then God doesn't deliver because… well, this is now a problem of theodicy, the eternal struggle over why God does not remove evil and suffering from the creation that God so dearly loves. Theodicy and the 7MM cannot coexist. Theodicy begins with compassion for those on the margins of society, while the 7MM begins with taking over the halls of power. The root word of theodicy, "theo," means God. Theodicy is an apprehending of God's righteousness, worked out in how we respond to the evil and suffering that fills our world. The 7MM is nothing more than men seeking power to lord over others.

I first began this book with an optimistic naivete that insists *we can find our way back*. If we just understand the historical roots of our radicalized politics, we will reject all things Ku Klux Klan and Confederate and instead—here I am speaking to evangelicals, like myself—cling only to Christ.

But by the time I was halfway through with writing this book, that optimism was gone. Maybe we do not want to find our way back because, well, what if this is who we are now, as Americans, as evangelicals? Confederate sympathizers, slavery apologists, government insurrectionists? January 6 did happen, as did the reelection of the man who incited the attack on our Capitol. Maybe America in the 2020s really is a romanticized, nostalgia-driven resurrection of the Confederacy. Whatever the case may be, American dominion is a problem bigger than one book can solve. I began this book with hope, but I ended with a personal sense of despair.

If we are to do anything about this radicalized movement that has overwhelmed our political institutions, we need to get to where the funding is. Dominionist politics are overwhelmingly funded with oil dollars. This money does not merely drive climate change, pollute the air that we breathe, and cause lifelong health problems that range from asthma to terminal cancer. It is funding school curricula that glorify the Confederacy and teach that the church must have dominion over society. And it is funding politicians who seek to enact those aims.

This may sound underwhelming, but part of the way back begins with renewable energy. Its adoption cannot be limited to evangelicals who reject the dominionist program; our reliance on oil and subsequent funding of dominionism has to end. Replacing oil with renewable energy is about so much more than climate change. Far too many American voters make their choices at the polls based not on complex political, cultural, economic, and theological dilemmas, but rather on the cost of gas. This single-issue voting opens us up to exploitation by politicians who make promises about gas prices and then implement dominionist programs once elected. We can reverse this vulnerability for our elected leaders to exploit us if we support green-energy projects that reduce our need for gas altogether.

But for evangelicals, what do we do now? Where do we go? Do we keep listening to the catchy dominionist worship music that is sung in our churches? Do we keep attending the revivals held by faith healers? Do we sift through this whole mess to find what is worth keeping and discard everything else? Or do we just start all over again, throwing it all out and floundering for a new foundation?

There is a better foundation that has already been laid, and it does not rest on Christian nationalism, Neo-Confederacy, or any belief system connected to the Ku Klux Klan. That foundation is Christ and communities of faith that welcome in everyone: the homeless, the immigrant, the Republican, the Democrat, the queer, the neurodivergent. Because when we make space for all, we can see Christ in the eyes of everyone that the dominionist movement has, quite literally, demonized. The paraplegic who never got the healing miracle, the trans kid who is considering suicide, the Democrat who thinks the government has a role in consumer safety and preventing abuse. But we must remember that the cross of Jesus is not a call to take up arms against worldly powers and conquer the Seven Mountains but rather an invitation to lay down our rights.

While writing this book, I worked part-time in a community of adults with autism and other developmental challenges. The faith healers would have us believe that autism is a demonic spirit to be exorcised, but what I saw every day were people made in the image of God and desperate to know that they have a voice, even when they cannot speak. One of the ladies I worked with is an irrepressible cheerleader who constantly said to me, "You're awesome, Keri. You're so good at being awesome." Who was I to deserve her unconditional love? But that is precisely what she offered me, not because I deserved it, but because of how loving and kind she is. When I got neck-deep in Neo-Confederacy's connection to modern evangelicalism, her voice got stuck in my head. And I needed to hear what she had to say to me so much more than I needed to hear the hatred of demon-obsessed faith healers or Confederate sympathizers. I needed a community of people with developmental challenges to remind me of Christ and point me back to him, away from the noise of dominion and toward the message of the gospel.

Maybe that is what we need: to reject everything about faith-healing and embrace the things and the people, including our own selves, who are less than perfect. Because what people need is to be loved, not in some ephemeral sense where we link fingers around a metaphorical campfire and sing "Kumbayah," but where we live side by side with people who constantly reflect Christ back to us. And for the record, "Kumbayah" is not a passive song of woo-woo spirituality but rather a powerful hymn of resistance against oppression. "Well, we down in trouble, Lord, come by here," the Gullah Geechee people of South Carolina sang. "Well it's somebody sick, Lord, come by here."[1] In other words, *We have been kidnapped from our ancestral homes in Africa. We have been forced to toil for the white man and make him rich. We found our freedom in the Civil War and then lost it with the Ku Klux Klan and Jim Crow. God, if you do not act on our behalf, we cannot survive.* While their tormentors were singing hymns of praise, the Gullah Geechee were pleading to God for their existence. Worship was not their weapon; it was their act of holy rebellion, of disrupting the *status quo* by calling God's attention to their plight. Of calling God to their aid when they were being oppressed by people who were—in today's terms—dominionists.

My act of holy rebellion was looking at these young men and women with autism and seeing the image of God, because that is exactly what they were to me. I needed to see Christ when everywhere I looked, I saw Neo-Confederacy masquerading around as Christian nationalism and promises of miraculous cures for illness. This lady with special needs was Christ to me and showed me the way back.

I hope and pray that we can all find our way back, because the Confederacy cannot be the future of the United States.

Notes

Preface

1 Bill Johnson, *When Heaven Invades Earth: A Practical Guide to a Life of Miracles* (Shippensburg, PA: Destiny Image, 2003), 29.

2 Jack Jenkins, "January 6: A Timeline in Prayers," from *Religion News Service*, January 6, 2022.

3 "Full Statement from Bethel Leadership" regarding the death of Olive Heilegenthal, from www.bethel.com, December 20, 2019.

Introduction

1 Mike Johnson, "Justices Take Swipe at American Values," in *The Times*, Shreveport, LA: July 8, 2003, 7.

2 Jack Jenkins, "January 6: A Timeline in Prayers," from *Religion News Service*, January 6, 2022.

3 Dan MacGuill, "Fact Check: Did Trump Adviser Paula White Pray for All 'Satanic Pregnancies' to Be Terminated?" from *Snopes*, January 28, 2020.

4 MacGuill, "Satanic Pregnancies."

5 Women for a Great America, "Outside the US Capitol Praying for Peace," video on Facebook Live. https://www.facebook.com/watch/live/?v=401353424303676

6 Chuck Pierce and Dutch Sheets, *Releasing the Prophetic Destiny of a Nation*, 2nd edition (Shippensburg, PA: Destiny Image Publishers, 2024), 21.

7 Sheets and Pierce, *Releasing the Prophetic Destiny of a Nation*.

8 Dutch Sheets, "Dutch Sheets Tells Story behind Appeal to Heaven Flag," in *Charisma Magazine*, January 27, 2015. https://mycharisma.com/spiritled-living/prayer-devotion/dutch-sheets-tells-story-behind-the-appeal-to-heaven-flag/

9 Dutch Sheets, "This Flag Is Symbolic of an Emerging Move of God," in *Charisma Magazine*, February 25, 2015.

10 Sheets and Pierce, *Releasing the Prophetic Destiny of a Nation*, 537.

11 Dutch Sheets, "The Key to Governmental Authority," in Lighthouse of Christ, January 13, 2015.

12 Sheets, "The Key to Governmental Authority."

13 Danny Silk, *Culture of Honor: Sustaining a Supernatural Environment* (Destiny Image, 2009), 58.

14 Dutch Sheets, "Imparting Wisdom and Revelation to Apostles and Prophets," preached at King of Kings Worship Center, March 29, 2022. https://www.youtube.com/watch?v=I7OO09gYZgk

15 Dutch Sheets, "An Appeal to Heaven," preached at Bethany Church, July 2, 2016. https://www.youtube.com/watch?v=t_tOJCWKdKE

16 Dutch Sheets, "Give Him 15: America Shall Be Saved," April 9, 2021. https://www.youtube.com/watch?app=desktop&v=mLkiMvib2LE. Here he claimed to be quoting from the prophet Gina Goldstein.

Chapter 1

1 As recorded in: Shirley Nelson, *Fair, Clear, and Terrible: The Story of Shiloh* (Latham, NY: British American Publishing, 1989), 54.

2 Frank Sandford, "Judah First," in *The Everlasting Gospel*, ed. Frank Sandford (Vol. 2, Issues 36–9) (Shiloh, ME, September 1, 1902), 463.

3 Sandford, "Judah First," 469.

4 As recorded in: Nelson, *Fair, Clear, and Terrible*.

5 Charles Fox Parham, *A Voice Crying in the Wilderness*, 2nd edition (Baxter Springs, KS: Apostolic Faith College, 1910), 86.

6 Parham, *A Voice Crying in the Wilderness*, 70.

Chapter 2

1 John Alexander Dowie, *Leaves of Healing*, September 27, 1895.

2 Gordon Lindsay, *Alexander Dowie: A Life Story of Trials, Tragedies and Triumphs* (Dallas, TX: Christ for the Nations, January 1, 1980),140.

3   Hannah Whitall Smith, *The Christian's Secret to a Happy Life* (Chicago, IL: Christian Witness, 1875), Chapter 1.

4   Gordon Lindsay, *The Gordon Lindsay Story*, revised edition (Dallas, TX: Christ for the Nations, 2013), 94.

5   Aimee Semple McPherson, "This Is My Task," sermon, undated. Retrieved from https://resources.foursquare.org/audio/aimee-semple-mcphersons-classic-sermon-this-is-my-task/

6   George Warnock, *The Feast of Tabernacles* (originally self-published in 1951), 47.

7   Kris Vallotton, *Heavy Rain: How to Flood Your World with God's Transforming Power* (Grand Rapids, MI: Baker Publishing Group, 2016), 38.

Chapter 3

1   Mike Bickle, *Growing in the Prophetic* (Lake Mary, FL: Charisma House, 2008), 2nd edition (1st edition 1996), 79.

2   Franklin Hall, *Atomic Power with God through Fasting and Prayer* (Quicktime Press, 2020; originally published in 1946), 19.

3   Bickle, *Growing in the Prophetic*, 71.

4   Bickle interpreted the imagery of Revelation 12 differently than did Parham. Parham saw the "Man-Child" as a group of End-Time Anglo-Saxon Christians, while Bickle saw the "Man-Child" as Christ himself. Still, the contours of the idea itself, that of an End-Times breed of elite Christians, are consistent and can be traced historically from Parham through the Latter Rain and to Bickle.

5   "Paul Cain Interviewed by Mike Bickle 1990 His Life, Supernatural Miracles, Healings & Revelation," Part 2. https://www.youtube.com/watch?v=dN02HZIaZHU

6   Che Ahn, *When Heaven Comes Down: Experiencing God's Glory in Your Life* (Grand Rapids, MI: Chosen Books, 2009), 121.

7   Todd Bentley, *Journey into the Miraculous: Experiencing the Touch of the Supernatural God* (Shippensburg, PA: Destiny Image, 2008), 23.

8   Bentley, *Journey into the Miraculous*, 23.

9   Bentley, *Journey into the Miraculous*, 22.

10 Bentley, *Journey into the Miraculous*, 83.

11 *Nightline*, ABC News, July 9, 2008.

12 *Nightline*, ABC News, July 9, 2008.

Chapter 4

1. "Rick Perry Speaks at The Response," August 6, 2011, full version, shared by Bruce Wilson on YouTube. https://www.youtube.com/watch?v=4gyQjWDjRs4

2. "Rick Perry Speaks at The Response," August 6, 2011, full version, shared by Bruce Wilson on YouTube. https://www.youtube.com/watch?v=4gyQjWDjRs4

3. Jennifer LeClaire, "The New Apostolic Reformation Is Not a Cult," from *Charisma News*. August 24, 2011.

4. C. Peter Wagner, *Churchquake! How the New Apostolic Reformation Is Shaking Up the Church as We Know It* (Ventura, CA: Regal Books, 1999), 6.

5. Terry Gross and C. Peter Wagner, "A Leading Figure in the New Apostolic Reformation," on Fresh Air. Aired on National Public Radio, October 3, 2011.

6. Lance Wallnau, "The Seven Mountain Mandate," in *Invading Babylon*, ed. Bill Johnson and Lance Wallnau (Shippensburg, PA: Destiny Image, 2013), 54.

7. Lance Wallnau, *God's Chaos Code: The Shocking Blueprint That Reveals Five Keys to the Destiny of Nations* (New York, NY: Killer Sheep Media, 2024), 95.

8. Grace Wyler, "Meet the Radical Evangelical Army Behind Rick Perry," in Business Insider. July 21, 2011.

9. Lou Engle and James Goll, *The Call of the Elijah Generation*, (Destiny Image Publishers, 2011), Kindle loc. 2822.

10. Engle and Goll, *The Call of the Elijah Revolution*, Kindle loc. 285.

11. Engle and Goll, *The Call of the Elijah Revolution*, Kindle loc. 1290–1298.

Chapter 5

1. David Mikkelson, "Darrell Scott's Testimony on the Columbine Shooting," from Snopes.com, July 29, 2001.

2. Mikkelson, "Darrell Scott's Testimony."

3. Dutch Sheets, *Watchman Prayer: How to Stand Guard and Protect Your Family, Home, and Community* (Ventura, CA: Regal Books, 2000), 21, 22.

4. Bruce Porter, *The Martyr's Torch: The Message of the Columbine Massacre* (Shippensburg, PA: Destiny Image, 1999), 25.

5. Porter, *The Martyr's Torch*, 53.

6. Video from The Call DC, accessed from YouTube at https://www.youtube.com/watch?v=83lh6m93ZKw

7   Che Ahn and Lou Engle, *The Call Revolution: A Radical Invitation to Turn the Heart of a Nation Back to God* (Colorado Springs, CO: Wagner Publications, 2001), 35.

8   Ahn and Engle, *The Call Revolution*, 19.

Chapter 6

1   Frank Sandford, *The Great Warfare* (Durham, ME: Kingdom Christian Ministries, 1935), 21.

2   Sandford, *The Great Warfare*, 19.

3   C. Peter Wagner, *Confronting the Queen of Heaven* (Colorado Springs, CO: Wagner Institute for Practical Ministry, 1998), 13.

4   Wagner, *Confronting the Queen of Heaven*, 13.

5   Wagner, *Confronting the Queen of Heaven*, 13.

6   Wagner, *Confronting the Queen of Heaven*, 34.

7   Thomas Muthee Sermon, "Why Sarah Palin?" October 16, 2005 at Wasilla Assemblies of God.

8   C. Peter Wagner, et al., *Wrestling with Dark Angels: Toward a Deeper Understanding of the Supernatural Forces in Spiritual Warfare* (Ventura, CA: Regal Books, 1990), 6.

9   C. Peter Wagner, "Who Is Allah?" accessed from John Mark Ministries, dated July 2, 2003.

10 Bill Johnson, *When Heaven Invades Earth* (Shippensburg, PA: Destiny Image, 2003), 27–8.

11 Bill Johnson, *God Is Good: He's Better than You Think* (Shippensburg, PA: Destiny Image, 2018), 31.

12 Kris Vallotton, *Spirit Wars: Winning the Invisible Battle against Sin and the Enemy* (Bloomington, MN: Chosen Books, 2012), 28.

13 Kris Vallotton, *Heavy Rain: How to Flood Your World with God's Transforming Power* (Grand Rapids, MI: Baker Publishing Group, 2016), 223.

14 *Rediscover Bethel Episode 4: The Church, the Ministry, and the New Apostolic Reformation* from https://www.youtube.com/watch?v=TVAVfD5OSkU

15 The Watchman with Erick Stackelbeck, "Part 1: Pastor John Hagee on President Trump's Support for Israel + Need to Keep Jerusalem Unified<https://www.youtube.com/watch?v=kq74JO-dTZc>," The Watchman, March 10, 2017, YouTube video, 4:23.

Chapter 7

1   Roger Ross Williams, *God Loves Uganda* (Variance Films, 2013).

2. Williams, *God Loves Uganda*.

3. Loren Cunningham, *The Book That Transforms Nations: The Power of the Bible to Change Any Country* (Seattle, WA: YWAM Publishing, 2007), 29.

4. Loren Cunningham, "The Seven Spheres of Influence," undated. Accessed from YWAM Podcast Network, posted on January 12, 2016 by Bill Hutchison.

5. Cunningham, *The Book That Transforms Nations*, 107.

6. Loren Cunningham, "The Dominion Mandate," originally preached in 1985. Accessed from YWAM Podcast Network, posted on January 12, 2018, by Bill Hutchison.

7. Cunningham, "The Dominion Mandate."

8. YWAM Tyler Facebook post from April 10, 2016.

9. "Touched by God—The Story of Rolland and Heidi Baker," from GlobalAwakening.com. https://globalawakening.com/touched-by-god-the-story-of-rolland-and-heidi-baker/

10. Quote from Heidi Baker in "How Heidi Baker's Supernatural Encounter with Holy Spirit Is Changing Nations," by J.D. King in *Charisma* Magazine, May 11, 2017.

11. "Heidi Baker's Supernatural Encounter."

12. Heidi Baker, "The Power of Yielding," from IHOP-KC, May 13, 2022.

13. See Virginia Pereira, "The Simplicity of Love," in Revive Nations; Heidi Baker Facebook post from September 6, 2016, shared from her devotional *Reckless Devotion*, Day 250: True Forgiveness.

14. Quote from Bonnke on page 64 in "'Africa Shall Be Saved': An Appraisal of Reinhard Bonnke's Pan-African Crusade," by Paul Gifford in *Journal of Religion in Africa*, February 1987, 63–92.

15. "'Africa Shall Be Saved': An Appraisal of Reinhard Bonnke's Pan-African Crusade," 69.

16. One notable exception is William Carey (1761–1834), a missionary to India who agitated against the practice of *sati*, or the self-immolation of widows on their husbands' funeral pyres. However, the government official who outlawed *sati* was actually Lord William Bentinck, the British governor of India, which was then a British colony. Carey faced much local opposition in his effort to end the practice of *sati*, but he was actually advocating for his own government—the British—to do so.

17. Jeff Sharlet, *C Street: The Fundamentalist Threat to American Democracy* (New York: Little, Brown, 2010), 133.

18. From Warren Throckmorton, "The True Story of the False Origins of the Seven Mountains," from the *Telling Jefferson Lies* podcast, April 1, 2024. Quote from Lance Wallnau, as depicted in a clip of him speaking.

Chapter 8

1 From 14 Kids and Pregnant Again.

Chapter 9

1 Steve Wilkins and Douglas Wilson, *Southern Slavery as It Was* (Moscow, ID: Canon Press, 1996), 7.

2 Wilkins and Wilson, *Southern Slavery as It Was*, 8.

3 Quoted from Southern Poverty Law Center, "Doug Wilson's Religious Empire Expanding in the Northwest," from *SPLC Report*, April 20, 2004. From *Southern Slavery as It Was* page 25.

4 Alexander Stephens, "Cornerstone Speech," March 21, 1861.

5 Molly Worthen, "Onward Christian Soldiers," in *New York Times Magazine*, September 30, 2007.

6 Rousas John Rushdoony, *The Institutes of Biblical Law* (Craig, CO: The Craig Press, 1973), 60. Quoted from Julie Ingersoll, *Building God's Kingdom: Inside the World of Christian Reconstruction* (Oxford: Oxford University Press, 2015), 18.

7 Doug Wilson, "God and Governments," from Blog and Mablog, April 18, 2020.

8 Cite from Stone Lectures.

9 Doug Wilson interview with Toby Sumpter, "Kuyperian?" by Canon Press, May 3, 2019.

10 "Introductory and Foundational Information," Patrick Henry College Course Catalog 2024–2025.

11 "The Boniface Award," from Association of Classical Christian Schools. https://classicalchristian.org/the-boniface-award/

12 Doug Wilson, "What's Your View of Southern Slavery?" video interview, Canon Press, June 24, 2011.

13 Doug Wilson, "The Bait Lies Before You Now. Do Not Take It," from Blog and Mablog, September 5, 2022.

Chapter 10

1 David Barton, *Separation of Church and State: What the Founders Meant* (Aledo, TX: WallBuilders, 2007), loc. 130.

2   *Time* Staff, "Influential Evangelicals: David Barton," February 7, 2005.

3   "Influential Evangelicals: David Barton."

4   Barton, *Separation of Church and State*, loc. 130.

5   Francis Schaeffer, *A Christian Manifesto* (Wheaton, IL: Crossway. Books, 1981), 33.

6   Schaeffer, *A Christian Manifesto*, 24.

7   Schaeffer, *A Christian Manifesto*, 31.

8   Schaeffer, *A Christian Manifesto*, 31–2.

9   David Barton, *America's Godly Heritage*, 3rd edition (Aledo, TX: Wallbuilders, 2009), 48. Originally published in 1993.

10 Barton, *America's Godly Heritage*, 49.

11 Barton, *America's Godly Heritage*, 50.

12 David Barton, *The American Heritage Series* Season 1, Episode 23, "The Civil Rights Movement" (Wallbuilders, 2008).

13 Barton, "The Civil Rights Movement."

14 David Barton, *The Jefferson Lies: Exposing the Myths You've Always Believed about Thomas Jefferson* (Washington, DC: WND Books, 2016), 2nd edition after Thomas Nelson withdrew the 2012 edition. 147.

15 Barton, *The Jefferson Lies*, 120.

16 David Barton, 2009 TEKS Review. https://tea.texas.gov/system/files/Bartoncurrent.pdf

17 Gerald A. Danzer, J. Jorge Kior De Alva, Larry S. Krieger, Louis E. Wilson, and Nancy Woloch, *The Americans: United States History since* 1877 (Boston, MA: Houghton Mifflin Harcourt, 2016), 188. Note that while the publication date is officially 2016, the book went into circulation in Texas classrooms in the fall of 2015.

Chapter 11

1   Sarah Palin, *Going Rogue: An American Life* (New York: Harper Collins, 2009), 1.

2   Quoted from "Palin's Speech at the Republican National Convention," from *The New York Times*, September 3, 2008.

3   "Palin's Speech at the Republican National Convention."

4   "Palin's Speech at the Republican National Convention."

5   Michael Joseph Gross, "Is Palin's Rise Part of God's Plan?" in Vanity Fair, September 17, 2010.

6 David Barton, "What Does the Bible Say about Taxes?" January 29, 2018. https://www.youtube.com/watch?v=vyB9MAE5Wsk

7 Dale Steinreich, "The Tea Party, Fifteen Years Later," from The Mises Institute, December 16, 2022.

Chapter 12

1 Jessica Glenza, "Paula White: The Pastor Who Helps Trump Hear 'What God Has to Say,'" in *The Guardian*, March 27, 2019.

2 "Changing Boundaries," by the staff of Ebony, Ebony magazine, December 2004, Vol. 60, No. 2, 153–5.

3 The original article was deleted, but Warren Throckmorton quoted extensive pieces of it on his blog. See Warren Throckmorton, "Donald Trump Shall Become the Trumpet: My Entry for Best Article in the 'Wait, This Isn't Parody?' Category," from wthrockmorton.com. July 29, 2015.

4 Lance Wallnau, "My Take on Donald Trump, Part 2," from lancewallnau.com. Undated, but based on dates in the comments, this article was written around October 7, 2015.

5 Glenza, "Paula White: The Pastor Who Helps Trump Hear 'What God Has to Say.'"

6 Quoted from *The QAnon Deception: Everything You Need to Know about the World's Most Dangerous Conspiracy Theory* by James Beverley (Concord, NC: Equal Time Books, 2020), 31.

7 "QAnon's Antisemitism and What Comes Next," from American Defense League, September 17, 2021.

8 Peter Montgomery, "Trump 'Prophet' Lance Wallnau Uses QAnon Rhetoric to Promote Preelection Spiritual Warfare Rally," from People For, October 30, 2020.

9 Montgomery, "Trump 'Prophet' Lance Wallnau Uses QAnon Rhetoric."

10 Candace Owens, "Tristan Tate x Candace Owens," Episode 45 of *Candace*, August 14, 2024.

11 The Anglo-Saxons actually lived in Britain, not Germany. Saxony is a region in Germany, but the "Anglo" in Anglo-Saxon indicates that the term refers to Saxons who settled parts of Britain.

12 Quoted from "Kanye West Suggests African-American Slavery Was a 'Choice,'" from BBC News, May 2, 2018.

13 Jeremiah Johnson, *Trump and the Future of America* (Lakeland, FL: Jeremiah Johnson Ministries, 2020), 36.

14 Quoted from Joel Shannon, "After Backlash, Conservative Pundit Candace Owens Clarifies Viral Hitler Comment," from USA Today, February 8, 2019.

15 Quoted from "Unpacking Kanye West's Antisemitic Remarks," from Anti-Defamation League, October 14, 2022.

16 "Unpacking Kanye West's Antisemitic Remarks," from Anti-Defamation League, October 14, 2022.

17 Tommy Barnett, *What If? My Story of Believing God for More ... Always for More* (Birmingham, AL: Association of Related Churches Publishing, 2020), 236 (Kindle).

Chapter 13

1 David Barton, Gateway FIRST Conference 2012, produced by Daystar.

2 Ralph Reed, *For God and Country: The Christian Case for Trump* (Washington, DC: Regenery Publishing, 2020), 6.

3 Reed, *For God and Country*, 43.

4 Michelle Goldberg, "Why the Right Loves Public School Culture Wars," from *The New York Times*, May 3, 2021.

5 From the song "For the Love of Money" by the O'Jays. Ironically, the song that introduced the billionaire champion of conservative evangelicals tells of the evils and pitfalls of seeking after money.

6 Betsy DeVos at "The Gathering" 2001, uploaded to YouTube by Bruce Wilson on February 23, 2015.

7 Quote by Peter Bohlinger, recorded in "Inside the Secret Right-Wing Plan to 'Take Down the Education System as We Know It,'" from Documented, October 17, 2023.

8 Quote by Robert Morris, recorded by Mike Hixenbaugh and Antonia Hylton in "Christian Activists Are Fighting to Glorify God in a Suburban Texas School District," from NBC News, October 4, 2023.

9 The extent of Robert Morris' engagement at CFNI is impossible to determine following the revelation of his pedophile history, as records of him have been completely scrubbed from the websites of both CFNI and Gateway Church.

10 Quote by Lance Wallnau, recorded by Mike Hixenbaugh and Antonia Hylton in "The Seven Mountains," episode two of the podcast *Grapevine*, October 4, 2023.

11 David Barton, "History of Public Schools in America," at Patriot Mobile. Video uploaded by PatriotMobile, April 10, 2023.

Chapter 14

1. Sean Feucht, "Worship Is Our Weapon," podcast for Hold the Line, July 5, 2022.
2. Sean Feucht, *Brazen: Be a Voice, Not an Echo* (NewType Publishing, 2020), 74.
3. Feucht, *Brazen*, 153.
4. Feucht, *Brazen*, 167.
5. Sean Feucht posts on Instagram, December 16, 2019.
6. "Let Us Worship, Washington DC," from October 25, 2020. Uploaded to YouTube by Sean Feucht. https://www.youtube.com/watch?v=i3p8oPrn-Cg
7. Feucht, "Worship Is Our Weapon."
8. Sean Feucht, *Bold: Moving Forward in Faith, Not Fear* (Washington, DC: Salem Books, 2022), 18.
9. Feucht, *Bold*, 19.
10. Feucht, *Bold*, 42–3.
11. Sean Feucht and Andy Byrd, *Fire and Fragrance: From the Great Commandment to the Great Commission* (Shippensburg, PA: Destiny Image, 2010), 44.
12. Sean Feucht, recording taken from "The Freedom to Worship," Season 2, Episode 1 of the *Heaven Bent* podcast by Tara Jean Stevens.
13. "Bethel Church Casts Out Demon of Racism with Wizard Staff," video uploaded to YouTube by Chelsi Bedell in 2020. https://www.youtube.com/watch?v=LF7yCs1sZfU
14. "Let Us Worship, Washington DC," from October 26, 2024. Uploaded to YouTube by Sean Feucht. https://www.youtube.com/watch?v=_ocS4qXCDNE

Chapter 15

1. "'Hail Trump!': Richard Spencer Speech Excerpts," uploaded to YouTube by *The Atlantic*, November 21, 2016.
2. Tweet from Donald Trump, recorded by Jeremy Diamond in "Trump Calls Removal of Confederate Monuments 'So Foolish,'" from CNN, August 17, 2017.
3. "User Clip: Paula White Prophetic Word to the President," from C-Span, May 7, 2020. https://www.c-span.org/clip/white-house-event/user-clip-paula-white-prophetic-word-to-the-president/4874847
4. Quoted from Pat Robertson, recorded by Josh Peter in "Televangelist Pat Robertson predicts Trump Win, Then Chaos, Then the End of the World," in *USA Today*, October 20, 2020.

5. Jeremiah Johnson in "Prophetic Dream Concerning Trump and the 2020 Election—Jeremiah Johnson," from *Encounter Today*, hosted by Alan Didio, August 26, 2020. https://www.youtube.com/watch?v=DhZ3RqSGLbk

6. Michael Grenholm, "These 12 Church Leaders Prophesied That Trump Would Win," from *Pentecostals and Charismatics for Peace & Justice*, December 15, 2020.

7. Quote from Bill Johnson, recorded by Annelise Pierce in "Bethel's Bill Johnson Calls Biden's Election 100% Fraud," in *Shasta Scout*, January 3, 2021.

8. Quote from Beni Johnson, recorded by David Benda in "Bethel Church Pastor Who Prophesied Trump Win Posts Apology Video, Then Takes It Down," in *Redding Record Spotlight*, November 10, 2020.

9. Quoted from Kris Vallotton, recorded by David Benda in "Bethel Church Pastor Who Prophesied Trump Win Posts Apology Video, Then Takes It Down," in *Redding Record Spotlight*, November 10, 2020.

10. "Oath Keepers' Stewart Rhodes Calls for 'Bloody War' at Jericho March," posted on YouTube by Right Wing Watch on December 14, 2020.

11. "Pastor Che Ahn in Freedom Plaza at a Prayer Rally for President Trump," uploaded to UGETube on January 6, 2021. https://ugetube.com/watch/pastor-che-ahn-in-freedom-plaza-at-a-prayer-rally-for-president-trump_llj2aCCMvRPAUn7.html

12. "Outside the US Capitol Praying for Peace," video shared on Facebook by Women for a Great America, January 6, 2021.

13. "Outside the US Capitol Praying for Peace."

14. "Outside the US Capitol Praying for Peace."

15. "Paula White Jan 6 Prayer," from C-Span, January 6, 2021.

16. Jack Jenkins, "January 6: A Timeline in Prayers," from Religion News Service, January 6, 2022.

17. Jenkins, "January 6: A Timeline in Prayers."

18. Jenkins, "January 6: A Timeline in Prayers."

19. "Che Ahn's Perspective on the Events of January 6, 2021," uploaded to YouTube by Che Ahn on January 12, 2021.

20. Dutch Sheets, "God's Plans Will Be Accomplished," from *Give Him 15*. Uploaded to YouTube by Dutch Sheets, January 12, 2021.

Chapter 16

1. Mike Johnson Speaking at the Council for National Policy, October 2019, video uploaded to Documented on October 21, 2020.

2. "Liberty Counsel Cases," from Liberty Counsel website. https://lc.org/cases
3. Mike Johnson Speaking at the Council for National Policy, October 2019, video uploaded to Documented on October 21, 2020.
4. Quote by Mike Johnson, recorded by Luke Broadwater and Steve Eder in "Johnson Played Leading Role in Effort to Overturn 2020 Election," from *The New York Times*, October 25, 2023.
5. David Barton, Tim Barton, and Rick Green, "The Making of a Speaker: Mike Johnson's Commitment to Conservative Values," from the WallBuilders podcast, October 26, 2023.
6. Quote by Mike Johnson, recorded by Annie Karni, Ruth Graham, and Steve Eder in "For Mike Johnson, Religion Is at the Forefront of Politics and Policy," from *The New York Times*, October 27, 2023.
7. Mike Johnson, "How to Stand for Religious Freedom & Address the 'Separation of Church and State,'" from *Truth Be Told*, September 8, 2023.
8. Jay Grimstead and Calvin Beisner, "A Manifesto for the Christian Church: Declaration and Covenant." (Murphys, CA: Coalition on Revival, 1986).
9. Grimstead and Beisner, "A Manifesto for the Christian Church."
10. Grimstead and Beisner, "A Manifesto for the Christian Church."

Chapter 17

1. Kevin Roberts, *Dawn's Early Light: Taking Back Washington to Save America* (New York: Broadside Books, 2024), 2.
2. Roberts, *Dawn's Early Light*, 2.
3. Roberts, *Dawn's Early Light*, 18.
4. Roberts, *Dawn's Early Light*, 10.
5. Quoted by Jerry Falwell, recorded by Walter Olson in "Reasonable Doubts: Invitation to a Stoning," from *Reason*, November 1998.
6. Quote by Elon Musk, recorded by Taylor Giorno in "We Are Terrified: Musk Puts USAID through Wood Chipper," from *The Hill*, February 3, 2025.
7. The White House, post on X, February 19, 2025.

Conclusion

1. https://blogs.loc.gov/folklife/2018/02/kumbaya-history-of-an-old-song/

Sources

Chapter 1

Anderson, Allan, "The Azusa Street Revival and the Emergence of Pentecostal Missions in the Early Twentieth Century," in *Transformation* by Sage Publications, Vol. 23, No. 2, April 2006, 107–18.
Anderson, Allan, "The Dubious Legacy of Charles Parham: Racism and Cultural Insensitivities among Pentecostals," in *Pneuma*, Vol. 27, No. 1, Spring 2005, 51–64.
Anderson, Allan, "The Origins of Pentecostalism and Its Global Spread in the Early Twentieth Century," in *Transformation*, Vol. 22, No. 3, July 2005, 175–85.
Barkun, Michael, *Religion and the Racist Right: The Origins of the Christian Identity Movement* (Chapel Hill, NC: University of North Carolina Press, 1997).
Burgess, Stanley and Gary McGee, eds., *The New International Dictionary of Pentecostal and Charismatic Movements* (Grand Rapids, MI: Zondervan, 2002).
Creech, Joe, "Visions of Glory: The Place of the Azusa Street Revival in Pentecostal History," in *Church History* by Cambridge University Press, Vol. 65, No. 3, September 1996, 405–24.
Martin, Larry, *Charles Fox Parham: The Unlikely Father of Modern Pentecostalism* (New Kensington, PA: Whitaker House, 2022).
McFarland, Michael and Glenn Gottfried, "The Chosen Ones: A Mythic Analysis of the Theological and Political Self-Justification of Christian Identity," in *Journal for the Study of Religion,* Vol. 15, No. 1, 2002, 125–45. Published by Association for the Study of Religion in Southern Africa.
Nelson, Shirley, *Fair, Clear, and Terrible: The Story of Shiloh* (Latham, NY: British American Publishing, 1989).
Sandford, Frank, *The Everlasting Gospel*, Vol. 2 Iss. 36–9 (Shiloh, ME, 1902).
Wacker, Grant, "The Functions of Faith in Primitive Pentecostalism," in *The Harvard Theological Review*, Vol. 77, No. 3/4, July–October 1984, 353–75.
Williams, Joseph, "The Pentecostalization of Christian Zionism," in *Church History*, Vol. 84, No. 1, March 2015, 159–94. Published by Cambridge University, American Society of Church History.
Wilson, John, "British Israelism: A Revitalization Movement in Contemporary Culture," in *Archives de sociologie des religions,* Vol. 13e, No. 26, July–December 1968, 73–80.

Chapter 2

Baer, Jonathan, "Redeemed Bodies: The Functions of Divine Healing in Incipient Pentecostalism," in *Church History*, Vol. 70, No. 4, December 2001, 735–71.

Barkun, Michael, *Religion and the Racist Right: The Origins of the Christian Identity Movement* (Chapel Hill, NC: University of North Carolina Press, 1997).

Bebbington, David, *Holiness in Nineteenth-Century England* (Carlisle, Cumbria: Paternoster Press, 2000).

Collins, John, "Joel's Army: The Manifested Sons of God," published by San Diego State University, undated.

Dowie, John Alexander, *Leaves of Healing*. September 27, 1895.

Faupel, David William, "Theological Influences on the Teaching and Practices of John Alexander Dowie," in *Pneuma*, Vol. 29, No. 2, November 2007, 226–53.

Harlan, Rolvix, *John Alexander Dowie and the Christian Catholic Apostolic Church in Zion* (PhD Thesis, University of Chicago, 1906).

Harrell, David Edwin Jr., *All Things Are Possible: The Healing and Charismatic Revivals in Modern America* (Bloomington, IN: Indiana University Press, 1975).

Johnson, Bill, *When Heaven Invades Earth: A Practical Guide to a Life of Miracles* (Shippensburg, PA: Treasure House Publishers, 2003).

Lindsay, Gordon, *The Gordon Lindsay Story*, revised edition (Dallas, TX: Christ for the Nations, 2013).

Lindsay, Gordon, *Alexander Dowie: A Life Story of Trials, Tragedies and Triumphs* (Dallas, TX: Christ for the Nations, January 1, 1980).

McPherson, Aimee Semple, "This Is My Task," sermon, undated. Retrieved from https://resources.foursquare.org/audio/aimee-semple-mcphersons-classic-sermon-this-is-my-task/

"Protests Winrod Appearance," *The Sentinel*. July 24, 1938.

Sutton, Matthew Avery, *Aimee Semple McPherson and the Resurrection of Christian America* (Cambridge, MA: Harvard University Press, 2007).

Vallotton, Kris, *Heavy Rain: How to Flood Your World with God's Transforming Power* (Grand Rapids, MI: Baker Publishing Group, 2016).

Warfield, Benjamin Breckenridge, *Counterfeit Miracles* (New York: Charles Scribner's Sons, 1918).

Warnock, George, *The Feast of Tabernacles* (self-published in 1951).

Chapter 3

Ahn, Che, *When Heaven Comes Down: Experiencing God's Glory in Your Life* (Grand Rapids, MI: Chosen Books, 2009).

Bentley, Todd, *Journey into the Miraculous: Experiencing the Touch of the Supernatural* (Shippensburg, PA: Destiny Image, 2008).

Beverly, James, *Holy Laughter and the Toronto Blessing: An Investigative Report* (Grand Rapids, MI: Zondervan, 1995).

Deere, Stephen, "IHOPKC Figure Aided Other Abusers, Sought to Buy 'Forgiveness,'" from *Divine Detour*. May 16, 2024.
Eckholm, Erik, "Where Worship Never Pauses," *The New York Times*, July 9, 2011.
Falls, Daniel, *The Life and Legacy of Pat Bickle and a History of the Kansas City Prophets*, 3rd edition (self-published in 2019).
Geivett, Doug and Holly Pivec, *Reckless Christianity: The Destructive New Teachings and Practices of Bill Johnson, Bethel Church, and the Global Movement of Apostles and Prophets* (Eugene, OR: Wipf and Stock, 2023).
Jackson, Bill, *The Quest for the Radical Middle: A History of the Vineyard* (Cape Town: Vineyard International Publishing, 1999).
Nightline, ABC News. July 9, 2008.
Roberts, Troy, "Fall From Grace," CBS News 48 Hours. August 1, 2015.
Sanchez, Casey, "Todd Bentley's Militant Joel's Army Gains Followers in Florida," from *Intelligence Report* by Southern Poverty Law Center. August 29, 2008. Montgomery, AL.

Chapter 4

Engle, Lou and James Goll, *The Call of the Elijah Generation* (Shippenburg, PA: Destiny Image Publishers, 2011).
Gross, Terry and C. Peter Wagner, "A Leading Figure in the New Apostolic Reformation," on *Fresh Air*. Aired on National Public Radio. October 3, 2011.
Gross, Terry and Rachel Tabachnik, "The Evangelicals Engaged in Spiritual Warfare," on *Fresh Air*. Aired on National Public Radio. August 19, 2011.
Johnson, Bill and Lance Wallnau, eds., *Invading Babylon: The Seven Mountain Mandate* (Shippensburg, PA: Destiny Image, 2013).
"Rick Perry Speaks at The Response, August 6, 2011, Full Version," shared by Bruce Wilson on YouTube. https://www.youtube.com/watch?v=4gyQjWDjRs4
Wallnau, Lance, *God's Chaos Code: The Shocking Blueprint That Reveals Five Keys to the Destiny of Nations* (New York: Killer Sheep Media, 2024).
Wyler, Grace, "Meet the Radical Evangelical Army behind Rick Perry," in *Business Insider*. July 21, 2011.

Chapter 5

Ahn, Che and Lou Engle, *The Call Revolution: A Radical Invitation to Turn the Heart of a Nation Back to God* (Colorado Springs, CO: Wagner Publications, 2001).
Cullen, Dave, *Columbine* (New York: Twelve Books, 2009).
Mikkelson, David, "Darrell Scott's Testimony on the Columbine Shooting," from Snopes.com. July 29, 2001.
Nimmo, Beth and Darrell Scott, *Rachel's Tears: The Spiritual Journey of Columbine Martyr Rachel Scott* (Nashville, TN: Tommy Nelson, 1999).

Porter, Bruce, *The Martyr's Torch: The Message of the Columbine Massacre* (Shippensburg, PA: Destiny Image, 1999).

Rosin, Hanna, "Columbine Miracle: A Matter of Belief," in *Washington Post*. October 13, 1999.

Sheets, Dutch, *Watchman Prayer: How to Stand Guard and Protect Your Family, Home, and Community* (Ventura, CA: Regal Books, 2000).

Video from The Call DC, accessed from YouTube at https://www.youtube.com/watch?v=83lh6m93ZKw

Chapter 6

"Briefs: The World," in *Christianity Today*, May 21, 2001.

Clark, Randy, et al., "A Response to New Apostolic Reformation Critics, Revised and Expanded August 2022," published by Oral Roberts University.

Durbin, Sean, "Christian Zionism in the United States, 1930–2020," in *Oxford Research Encyclopedia of Religion*. September 2023.

Jackson, Bill, *The Quest for the Radical Middle: A History of the Vineyard* (Cape Town: Vineyard International Publishing, 1999).

Johnson, Bill, *God Is Good: He's Better than You Think* (Shippensburg, PA: Destiny Image, 2018).

Johnson, Bill, *When Heaven Invades Earth* (Shippensburg, PA: Destiny Image, 2003).

"The Lausanne Story," from www.lausanne.org.

"A Leading Figure in the New Apostolic Reformation," from NPR's *Fresh Air*. Interview between Terry Gross and C. Peter Wagner. October 3, 2011.

Moore, Art, "Spiritual Mapping Gains Credibility among Leaders," in *Christianity Today*. January 12, 1998.

Pivec, Holly and Doug Geivett, *Reckless Christianity: The Destructive New Teachings and Practices of Bill Johnson, Bethel Church, and the Global Movement of Apostles and Prophets* (Eugene, OR: Cascade Books, 2023).

Rediscover Bethel Episode 4: The Church, Ministry, and the New Apostolic Reformation from Bethel. 2021. https://www.youtube.com/watch?v=TVAVfD5OSkU/

Sandford, Frank, *The Great Warfare* (Durham, ME: Kingdom Christian Ministries, 1935).

Sermon, Thomas Muthee, "Why Sarah Palin?" October 16, 2005 at Wasilla Assemblies of God.

Stott, John, "The Lausanne Covenant." 1974.

Vallotton, Kris, *Heavy Rain: How to Flood Your World with God's Transforming Power* (Shippensburg, PA: Destiny Image, 2016).

Vallotton, Kris, *Spirit Wars: Winning the Invisible Battle against Sin and the Enemy* (Bloomington, MN: Chosen Books, 2012).

Van Biema, David, "Religion: Missionaries under Cover," in *Time* Magazine. June 30, 2003.

Wagner, C. Peter, *Confronting the Queen of Heaven* (Colorado Springs, CO: Wagner Institute for Practical Ministry, 1998).

Wagner, C. Peter, "Who Is Allah?" accessed from John Mark Ministries, dated July 2, 2003.

Wagner, C. Peter, et al., *Wrestling with Dark Angels: Toward a Deeper Understanding of the Supernatural Forces in Spiritual Warfare* (Ventura, CA: Regal Books, 1990).
The Watchman with Erick Stackelbeck, "Part 1: Pastor John Hagee on President Trump's Support for Israel + Need to Keep Jerusalem Unified<https://www.youtube.com/watch?v=kq74JO-dTZc>," The Watchman, March 10, 2017, YouTube video, 4:23.

Chapter 7

"Analysis of the History and Spread of HIV-1 in Uganda Using Phylodynamics," in *Journal of General Virology* (2015 July; 96 (Pt 7): 1890–1898).
Anderson, Allan, "New African Initiated Pentecostalism and Charismatics in South Africa," in *Journal of Religion in Africa*, Vol. 35, No. 1, February 2005, 66–92.
Baker, Heidi, "The Power of Yielding," from IHOP-KC. May 13, 2022.
Bowler, Kate, *Blessed: A History of the American Prosperity Gospel* (Oxford: Oxford University Press, 2013).
Brown, Candy Gunther, et al., "Study of the Therapeutic Effects of Proximal Intercessory Prayer (STEPP) on Auditory and Visual Impairments in Rural Mozambique," in *Southern Medical Journal*, Vol. 103, No. 9, September 2010, 864–9.
Cunningham, Loren, *The Book That Transforms Nations: The Power of the Bible to Change Any Country* (Seattle, WA: YWAM Publishing, 2007).
Cunningham, Loren, "The Dominion Mandate," originally preached in 1985. Accessed from YWAM Podcast Network, posted on January 12, 2018 by Bill Hutchison.
Cunningham, Loren, *Is That Really You, God? Hearing the Voice of God* (Seattle, WA: YWAM Publishing, undated).
Cunningham, Loren, *Making Jesus Lord: The Dynamic Power of Laying Down Your Rights* (Seattle, WA: YWAM Publishing, 1988).
Cunningham, Loren, "The Seven Spheres of Influence," undated. Accessed from YWAM Podcast Network, posted on January 12, 2016 by Bill Hutchison.
Gifford, Paul, "'Africa Shall Be Saved': An Appraisal of Reinhard Bonnke's Pan-African Crusade," in *Journal of Religion in Africa*, Vol. 17, No. 1, February 1987, 63–92.
Green, Lynn, "What Happened in Kansas City," from YWAM News. September 20, 2016.
Gusman, Alessandro, "HIV/AIDS, Pentecostal Churches, and the 'Joseph Generation' in Uganda," in *Africa Today*, Vol. 56, No. 1, Special Issue: *Christianity and HIV/AIDS in East and Southern Africa*, Fall 2009, 66–86.
Jjuuko, Adrian and Monica Tabengwa, "Expanded Criminalisation of Consensual Same-Sex Relations in Africa: Contextualising Recent Developments," in *Envisioning Global LGBT Human Rights: (Neo)colonialism, Neoliberalism, Resistance and Hope*, edited by Nancy Nicol, Adrian Jjuuko, Richard Lusimbo, Nick J. Mulé, Susan Ursel, Amar Wahab, and Phyllis Waugh, 63–96 (London: University of London Press, 2018).
Kaoma, Kapya, *Globalizing the Culture Wars: U.S. Conservatives, African Churches, and Homophobia* (Somerville, MA: Political Research Associates, 2009).
King, J.D., "How Heidi Baker's Supernatural Encounter with Holy Spirit Is Changing Nations," in *Charisma* Magazine. May 11, 2017.

Pivec, Holly, "What Churches Should Know about YWAM Part 2: Partnering with the New Apostolic Reformation," from hollypivec.com. June 7, 2019.

A Question of Miracles documentary, written and directed by Anthony Thomas, 2001.

Rice, Xan, "Uganda Considers Death Sentence for Gay Sex in Bill before Parliament," in *The Guardian*. November 29, 2009.

Roig-Franzia, Manuel, "Politicians' Scandals Elevate the Profile of a Spiritual Haven on C Street SE," from *Washington Post*. June 26, 2009.

Sharlet, Jeff, *C Street: The Fundamentalist Threat to American Democracy* (New York: Little, Brown), 2010.

Throckmorton, Warren, "Chrisma Magazine Reports on 7Mountains Teaching and Anti-Homosexuality Bill," from wthrockmorton.com. December 14, 2009.

Throckmorton, Warren, "The True Story of the False Origins of the Seven Mountains," from *Telling Jefferson Lies* podcast. April 1, 2024.

Throckmorton, Warren, "What Would Dominionists Do with Gays?" from wthrockmorton.com. Part 1, August 29, 2011. Part 2, August 30, 2011. Part 3, September 1, 2011.

Williams, Roger Ross, *God Loves Uganda* (Variance Films, 2013).

Wilson, Bruce, "Documents Show Christian World Domination Group Paid for Bitarisan Congressional Hawaii Trip," from *Huffington Post*. September 11, 2009.

Chapter 8

Collins, John, "Bill Gothard and the Shepherding Movement," from William Branham Historical Research podcast.

Cooper, Andrea, "I Introduced the Duggar Family to the World. Am I Responsible for Their Rise to Fame?" in *Huffington Post*. May 24, 2022.

Deng, Boer and Sam Cabral, "Madison Cawthorn: Republicans Oust Trump-Backed Young Congressman," from *BBC News*. May 17, 2022.

Espada, Mariah, "The True Story behind the Duggar Family Docuseries *Shiny Happy People*," in *Time* Magazine. June 2, 2023.

Harrison, Laura and Sarah Rowley, "Babies by the Bundle: Gender, Backlash, and the Quiverfull Movement," in *Feminist Formations,* Vol. 23, No. 1, Spring 2011, 47–69.

Ingersoll, Julie, *Building God's Kingdom: Inside the World of Christian Reconstruction* (Oxford: Oxford University Press, 2015).

Marshall, K.L., *Faith and Oil: How the Alaska Pipeline Shaped America's Religious Right* (Eugene, OR: Wipf and Stock, 2020).

Resane, Kelebogile, "The Influence and Legacy of the Shepherding Movement on the Current Neo-Pentecostal Movement in South Africa," in *Journal for the Study of Religion,* Vol. 34, No. 2, December 2021, 1–18.

Shiny Happy People documentary series.

Stasson, Anneke, "The Politicization of Family Life: How Headship Became Essential to Evangelical Identity in the Late Twentieth Century," in *Religion and American Culture: A Journal of Interpretation*, Vol. 24, No. 1, Winter 2014, 100–38.

Veinot, Don and Joy A. Veinot, Ron Henzel, *A Matter of Basic Principles: Bill Gothard and His Cultish Teachings* (Wonder Lake, IL: MCOI Publishing, Second Edition), 2023.

Chapter 9

Alexander Stephens, "Cornerstone Speech." March 21, 1865.
American Battlefield Trust, "Patrick Henry," undated. https://www.battlefields.org/learn/biographies/patrick-henry
Charles Reagan Wilson, "The Religion of the Lost Cause: Ritual and Organization of the Southern Civil Religion, 1865–1920," in *The Journal of Southern History*, Vol. 46, No. 2, May 1980, 219–38.
Charles Reagan Wilson, "Robert Lewis Dabney: Religion and the Southern Holocaust," in *The Virginia Magazine of History and Biography*, Vol. 89, No. 1, January 1981, 79–89.
Doug Wilson, "The Bait Lies before You Now. Do Not Take It," from *Blog and Mablog*. September 5, 2022.
Doug Wilson, "God and Governments," from *Blog and Mablog*. April 18, 2020.
Doug Wilson, "Philosophy and Me," from *Blog and Mablog*. December 3, 2005.
Doug Wilson interview with Toby Sumpter, "Kuyperian?" by Canon Press. May 3, 2019.
Doug Wilson and Steve Wilkins, *Southern Slavery as It Was* (Moscow, ID: Canon Press, 1996).
"Doug Wilson's Religious Empire Expanding in the Northwest," from *Southern Poverty Law Center Report*. April 20, 2004.
Francis B. Simkins, "Robert Lewis Dabney, Southern Conservative," in *The Georgia Review*, Vol. 18, No. 4, Winter 1964, 393–407.
Julie Ingersoll, *Building God's Kingdom: Inside the World of Christian Reconstruction* (Oxford: Oxford University Press, 2015).
Nick Gier, "Doug Wilson's Religious Empire," undated. https://www.webpages.uidaho.edu/ngier/wilsonempire.htm

Chapter 10

Bailey, Fred Arthur, "The Textbooks of the 'Lost Cause': Censorship and the Creation of Southern State Histories," in *The Georgia Historical Quarterly*, Vol. 75, No. 3, Fall 1991, 507–33.
Barton, David, "2009 TEKS Review." https://tea.texas.gov/system/files/Bartoncurrent.pdf
Barton, David, *America's Godly Heritage*, 3rd edition (Aledo, TX: WallBuilders, 2009). Originally published in 1993.
Barton, David, "The Civil Rights Movement," *The American Heritage Series* Season 1, Episode 23 (WallBuilders, 2008).
Barton, David, "This Is the Enemy," short video produced by WallBuilders. March 5, 2014.
Danzer Gerald A., J. Jorge Kior De Alva, S. Larry Krieger, E. Louis Wilson, and Nancy Woloch, *The Americans: United States History since 1877* (Boston, MA: Houghton Mifflin Harcourt, 2016).
Dean, Adam Wesley, "'Who Controls the Past Controls the Future': The Virginia History Textbook Controversy," in *The Virginia Magazine of History and Biography*, Vol. 117, No. 4, 2009, 318–55.

Editors of Encyclopedia Britannica, "Democratic-Republican Party," from *Encyclopedia Britannica*. Last updated March 26, 2025. Accessed March 31, 2025.
Hankins, Barry, *Francis Schaeffer and the Shaping of Evangelical America* (Grand Rapids, MI: Eerdmans, 2008).
Hu, Elise, "Publisher Pulls Controversial Thomas Jefferson Book, Citing Loss of Confidence," from NPR. August 9, 2012.
Schaeffer, Francis, *A Christian Manifesto* (Wheaton, IL: Crossway. Books, 1981).
Shorto, Russell, "How Christian Were the Founders?" in *The New York Times* Magazine. February 11, 2010.
Stephens, Randall and Karl Giberson, *The Anointed: Evangelical Truth in a Secular Age* (Cambridge, MA: The Belknap Press of Harvard University Press, 2011).
Stille, Alexander, "Textbook Publishers Learn: Avoid Messing with Texas," in *The New York Times*. June 29, 2002.
Texas Education Agency, "Social Studies TEKS: TEKS for Social Studies, Adopted 2010." https://tea.texas.gov/academics/curriculum-standards/teks-review/social-studies-teks
Time Staff, "Influential Evangelicals: David Barton." February 7, 2005.

Chapter 11

Barton, David, "What Does the Bible Say about Taxes?" January 29, 2018. https://www.youtube.com/watch?v=vyB9MAE5Wsk
Boedy, Matthew, "Ten Years of Turning Point USA: From Free Markets to Freedom Square," from Political Research Associates. January 28, 2022.
Brockman, David, "Christian Americanism and Texas Politics Since 2008," from Rice University's Baker Institute for Public Policy. March 2020.
"David Barton," Southern Poverty Law Center.
Gross, Michael Joseph, "Is Palin's Rise Part of God's Plan?" in Vanity Fair. September 17, 2010.
Hague, Euan, Heidi Beirich, and Edward Sebesta, *Neo-Confederacy: A Critical Introduction* (Austin, TX: University of Texas Press, 2008).
Hixenbaugh, Mike and Allan Smith, "Charlie Kirk Once Pushed a 'Secular Worldview.' Now He's Fighting to Make America Christian Again," from NBC News. June 12, 2024.
Ingersoll, Julie, *Building God's Kingdom: Inside the World of Christian Reconstruction* (Oxford: Oxford University Press, 2015).
Ingersoll, Julie, "Meet the Tea Party's Evangelical Quack: David Barton Is Glenn Beck's Favorite 'Historian,'" from Salon.com. August 23, 2015.
"Inside Obama's First Budget", from National Public Radio. February 26, 2009.
Kofman, Ava, "A Pair of Billionaire Preachers Built the Most Powerful Political Machine in Texas. That's Just the Start," from *ProPublica*. October 2, 2024.
Marshall, K.L., *Faith and Oil: How the Alaska Pipeline Shaped America's Religious Right* (Eugene, OR: Wipf and Stock, 2020).
Palin, Sarah, *Going Rogue: An American Life* (New York: Harper Collins, 2009).

Palin, Sarah, "Sarah Palin's Keynote Speech at the National Tea Party Convention," by C-Span. February 8, 2010.

"Palin's Speech at the Republican National Convention," from *The New York Times*. September 3, 2008.

Silliman, Daniel, "Died: Gary North, Who Saw Austrian Economics in the Bible and Disaster on the Horizon," in *Christianity Today*. March 3, 2022.

Steinreich, Dale, "The Tea Party, Fifteen Years Later," from the Mises Institute. December 16, 2022.

Worthen, Molly, "The Chalcedon Problem: Rousas John Rushdoony and the Origins of Christian Reconstruction," in *Church History*, Vol. 77, No. 2, June 2008, 399–437.

Chapter 12

Barnett, Tommy, *What If? My Story of Always Believing God for More ... Always for More* (Birmingham, AL: Association of Related Churches Resources, 2020).

Bim, Mara Richards, "How Charlie Kirk Went from College Dropout to Trump influencer," from Baptist News. April 15, 2025.

"Changing Boundaries," by the staff of Ebony. *Ebony* Magazine, Vol. 60, No. 2, December 2004, 153–5.

Draper, Robert, "How Charlie Kirk Became the Youth Whisperer of the American Right," from *The New York Times*. February 10, 2025.

Duin, Julia, "She Led Trump to Christ: The Rise of the Televangelist Who Advises the White House," from *The Washington Post*. November 14, 2017.

Glenza, Jessica, "Paula White: The Pastor Who Helps Trump Hear 'What God Has to Say,'" in *The Guardian*. March 27, 2019.

Graham, Ruth, "Conservative Activist Charlie Kirk Leaves Liberty University Think Tank," from *The New York Times*. March 16, 2021.

Huff, Ian, "QAnon Beliefs Have Increased since 2021 as Americans Are Less Likely to Reject Conspiracies," from Public Religion Research Institute. June 24, 2022.

Johnson, Jeremiah, *Trump and the Future of America* (Lakeland, FL: Jeremiah Johnson Ministries, 2020).

Jones, Ja'han, "Trump Smooching Joe Arpaio Was MAGA Masculinity in a Nutshell," from MSNBC News. June 10, 2024.

"Kanye West Suggests African-American Slavery Was a 'Choice,'" from BBC News. May 2, 2018.

Malone, Clare, "The Gospel of Candace Owens," from *The New Yorker*. April 22, 2023.

Montgomery, Peter, "Trump 'Prophet' Lance Wallnau Uses QAnon Rhetoric to Promote Preelection Spiritual Warfare Rally," from People For. October 30, 2020.

Owens, Candace, "Tristan Tate x Candace Owens," Episode 45 of Candace. August 14, 2024.

The QAnon Deception: Everything You Need to Know about the World's Most Dangerous Conspiracy Theory by James Beverley (Concord, NC: Equal Time Books, 2020).

"QAnon's Antisemitism and What Comes Next," from American Defense League. September 17, 2021.

Shannon, Joel, "After Backlash, Conservative Pundit Candace Owens Clarifies Viral Hitler Comment," from USA Today. February 8, 2019.

Staff, Hatewatch, "What You Need to Know about QAnon," from Southern Poverty Law Center. October 27, 2020.

Taylor, Matthew, *The Violent Take It by Force: The Christian Movement That Is Threatening Our Democracy* (Minneapolis, MN: Broadleaf Books, 2024).

Throckmorton, Warren, "Donald Trump Shall Become the Trumpet: My Entry for Best Article in the 'Wait, This Isn't Parody?' Category," from wthrockmorton.com. July 29, 2015.

"Unpacking Kanye West's Antisemitic Remarks," from Anti-Defamation League. October 14, 2022.

Wallnau, Lance, "My Take on Donald Trump, Part 2," from lancewallnau.com. Undated, but based on dates in the comments, this article was written around October 7, 2015.

Chapter 13

Barton, David, Gateway FIRST Conference 2012, produced by Daystar.

Barton, David, "History of Public Schools in America," at Patriot Mobile. Video uploaded by Patriot Mobile. April 10, 2023.

Christ for the Nations Academic Catalog, Spring 2025. Christforthenations.org. https://resources.cfni.org/documents/academics/CFNI_AcademicCatalog.pdf

"Dick and Betsy DeVos at The Gathering 2001," video uploaded by Bruce Wilson. https://www.youtube.com/watch?v=qJYFPMLuVRE

"Dennis Lindsay," Christforthenations.org. https://cfni.org/ourhistory/drlindsay/

"Golan Lindsay," Christforthenations.org. https://cfni.org/ourhistory/golan/

Goldberg, Michelle, "Why the Right Loves Public School Culture Wars," from *The New York Times*. May 3, 2021.

Hart, Natalie, "Grand Rapids Pastors Explore the History of Our Education System," from G-Rap (Grand Rapids Pastors Blog). October 31, 2016.

Hixenbaugh, Mike, *They Came for the Schools: One Town's Fight over Race and Identity, and the New War for America's Classrooms* (Boston, MA: Mariner Books, 2024).

Hixenbaugh, Mike and Antonia Hylton, "Christian Activists Are Fighting to Glorify God in a Suburban Texas School District," from NBC News. October 4, 2023.

Hixenbaugh, Mike and Antonia Hylton, "The Seven Mountains," episode two of podcast Grapevine. October 4, 2023.

"Inside the Secret Right-Wing Plan to 'Take Down the Education System as We Know It,'" from Documented. October 17, 2023.

Kroll, Andy and Nick Surgey, "Inside Ziklag, the Secret Organization of Wealthy Christians Trying to Sway the Election and Change the Country," from ProPublica. July 13, 2024.

Michaelson, Jay, "The $1-Billion-a-Year Right-Wing Conspiracy You Haven't Heard Of," from *The Daily Beast*. September 25, 2014.

Reed, Ralph, *For God and Country: The Christian Case for Trump* (Washington, DC: Regenery Publishing, 2020).
Reitman, Janet, "Betsy Devos' Holy War," in *Rolling Stone*. March 8, 2017.
Rozell, Mark J. and Clyde Wilcox, "Second Coming: The Strategies of the New Christian Right," in *Political Science Quarterly*, Vol. 111, No. 2, Summer 1996, 271–94.
Shogren, Elizabeth and Douglas Frantz, "School Boards Become the Religious Right's New Pulpit: Education: Alliances of Conservative Christian Parents, Political Groups Take Control of Panels, Spark Battles," from *Los Angeles Times*. December 10, 1993.
Wilson, Bruce, "The Gathering: The Religious Right's Cash Cow," from Truth Wins Out Center against Religious Extremism (TWOCARE). April 30, 2014.

Chapter 14

"Bethel Church Casts Out Demon of Racism with Wizard Staff," video uploaded to YouTube by Chelsi Bedell in 2020. https://www.youtube.com/watch?v=LF7yCs1sZfU
Feucht, Sean, *Bold: Moving Forward in Faith, Not Fear* (Washington, DC: Salem Books, 2022).
Feucht, Sean, *Brazen: Be a Voice, Not an Echo* (Redding, CA: NewType Publishing, 2020).
Feucht, Sean, "Worship Is Our Weapon," podcast for Hold the Line. July 5, 2022.
Feucht, Sean and Andy Byrd, *Fire and Fragrance: From the Great Commandment to the Great Commission* (Shippensburg, PA: Destiny Image, 2010).
IHOPKC Staff, "IHOPKC's Expression of the Harp and Bowl Model," from IHOPKC.org. June 8, 2019.
"Let Us Worship, Washington DC," from October 25, 2020. Uploaded to YouTube by Sean Feucht. https://www.youtube.com/watch?v=i3p8oPrn-Cg
"Let Us Worship, Washington DC," from October 26, 2024. Uploaded to YouTube by Sean Feucht. https://www.youtube.com/watch?v=_ocS4qXCDNE
Ruth, Lester and Lim Swee Hong, *A History of Contemporary Praise and Worship: Understanding the Ideas That Reshaped the Protestant Church* (Ada, MI: Baker Publishing, 2021).
Sean Feucht post on Instagram. December 16, 2019.
Stevens, Tara Jean, *Heaven Bent* podcast series, Season 2: Bethel Church.

Chapter 15

Benda, David, "Bethel Church Pastor Who Prophesied Trump Win Posts Apology Video, Then Takes It Down," in Redding Record Spotlight. November 10, 2020.
Diamond, Jeremy, "Trump Calls Removal of Confederate Monuments 'So Foolish,'" from CNN. August 17, 2017.
Green, Emma, "A Christian Insurrection," in *The Atlantic*. January 8, 2021.
Grenholm, Michael, "These 12 Church Leaders Prophesied That Trump Would Win," from Pentecostals and Charismatics for Peace & Justice. December 15, 2020.

"Hail Trump!': Richard Spencer Speech Excerpts," uploaded to YouTube by The Atlantic. November 21, 2016.

Hawes, Jennifer Berry, *Grace Will Lead Us Home: The Charleston Church Massacre and the Hard, Inspiring Journey to Forgiveness* (New York: St. Martin's Press, 2019).

Katz, Andrew, "Clashes over a Show of White Nationalism in Charlottesville Turn Deadly," from *Time* Magazine. Undated.

Kenes, Bulent, "Richard B. Spencer: The Founder of Alt-Right Presents Racism in a Chic New Outfit," from European Center for Populism Studies. June 28, 2021.

Montgomery, Peter, "The Religious Right's Rhetoric Fueled the Insurrection, and It Continues to Fan Fear and Rage," in The American Prospect. February 8, 2021.

"Outside the US Capitol Praying for Peace," video shared on Facebook by Women for a Great America. January 6, 2021.

"Pastor Che Ahn in Freedom Plaza at a Prayer Rally for President Trump," uploaded to UGETube on January 6, 2021. https://ugetube.com/watch/pastor-che-ahn-in-freedom-plaza-at-a-prayer-rally-for-president-trump_llj2aCCMvRPAUn7.html

Peter, Josh, "Televangelist Pat Robertson Predicts Trump Win, Then Chaos, Then the End of the World," in USA Today. October 20, 2020.

Pierce, Annelise, "Bethel's Bill Johnson Calls Biden's Election 100% Fraud," in Shasta Scout. January 3, 2021.

"Prophetic Dream Concerning Trump and the 2020 Election—Jeremiah Johnson," from Encounter Today, hosted by Alan Didio. August 26, 2020. https://www.youtube.com/watch?v=DhZ3RqSGLbk

"Pro-Trump Rallies in DC Attract Extremists & Erupt into Violence," from American Defense League. December 13, 2020.

Select Committee to Investigate the January 6 Attack on the US Capitol, "Deposition of Charles Kirk," from US House of Representatives, Washington DC. May 24, 2022.

Sheets, Dutch, "God's Plans Will Be Accomplished," from Give Him 15. Uploaded to YouTube by Dutch Sheets. January 12, 2021.

[Shooter's Name Redacted] Jailhouse Notebook, 2015.

Taylor, Matthew, *The Violent Take It by Force* (Minneapolis, MN: Broadleaf Books, 2024).

"User Clip: Paula White Prophetic Word to the President," from C-Span. May 7, 2020. https://www.c-span.org/clip/white-house-event/user-clip-paula-white-prophetic-word-to-the-president/4874847

Chapter 16

"About Us," Alliance Defending Freedom.

Barton, David, Tim Barton, and Rick Green, "The Making of a Speaker: Mike Johnson's Commitment to Conservative Values," from WallBuilders podcast. October 26, 2023.

Beirich, Heidi and Mark Potok, "The Council for National Policy: Behind the Curtain," from Southern Poverty Law Center. May 17, 2016.

Bim, Mara Richards, "A Visual Guide to the Elected Officials Who Fly Christian Nationalist Flags at the Capitol," from *Baptist News Global*. April 3, 2025.

Blumenthal, Max, "Justice Sunday Preachers," from *The Nation*. May 9, 2005.

Broadwater, Luke and Steve Eder, "Johnson Played Leading Role in Effort to Overturn 2020 Election," from *The New York Times*. October 25, 2023.

CNN Editorial Research, "Mike Johnson Fast Facts," from CNN. March 20, 2025.

Cravens, R.G., "Judge Recommends Former ADF Attorney Be Disbarred, Law License Now Inactive," from Southern Poverty Law Center. April 3, 2024.

Dickinson, Tim, "Meet the Apostle of Right-Wing Christian Nationalism," from *Rolling Stone*. September 1, 2022.

Edmondson, Catie and Luke Broadwater, "Rallying behind Trump, Most House Republicans Joined Failed Lawsuit," from *The New York Times*. December 11, 2020.

Farris, Michael, "Defying Conventional Wisdom: The Constitution Was Not the Product of a Runaway Convention," in *Harvard Journal of Law and Public Policy*, Vol. 40, No. 1, 2016, 61–146.

Farris, Michael, "Michael Farris on 'What We Can Do through a Convention of States'. Pat 1—A Single-Subject Rule." January 10, 2023.

Grimstead, Jay and Calvin Beisner, "A Manifesto for the Christian Church: Declaration and Covenant," (Murphys, CA: Coalition on Revival, 1986).

H.R. 9197—Stop the Sexualization of Children Act, sponsored by Mike Johnson in America's 117th Congress, 2021–2022.

"Inside the Secret Right-Wing Plan to 'Take Down the Education System as We Know It,'" from Documented. October 17, 2023.

Johnson, Mike, "How to Stand for Religious Freedom & Address the 'Separation of Church and State'," from Truth Be Told. September 8, 2023.

Karni, Annie, Ruth Graham, and Steve Eder, "For Mike Johnson, Religion Is at the Forefront of Politics and Policy," from *The New York Times*. October 27, 2023.

Kristin Kobes du Mez, *Jesus and John Wayne: How Evangelicals Corrupted a Faith and Fractured a Nation* (New York: Liveright Books, 2020).

"Liberty Counsel Cases," from Liberty Counsel website. https://lc.org/cases

Mike Johnson Speaking at the Council for National Policy, October 2019, video uploaded to Documented on October 21, 2020.

Sollenberger, Roger, "The Profound Influence of Christian Extremists on Mike Johnson," from *The Daily Beast*. January 31, 2024.

Southern Poverty Law Center, "Alliance Defending Freedom."

Stephens, Randall and Karl Giberson, *The Anointed: Evangelical Truth in a Secular Age* (Cambridge, MA: The Belknap Press of Harvard University, 2011).

Talbot, Margaret, "Amy Coney Barrett's Long Game," in *The New Yorker*. February 7, 2022.

Woodruff, Chase, "Rep. Boebert Tells Churchgoers to 'Rise Up' at Far-Right Christian Conference," from Colorado News Online. September 10, 2022.

Chapter 17

Dans, Paul and Steven Groves, eds., *Project 2025: Presidential Transition Project* (*Mandate for Leadership: The Conservative Promise*) (Washington, DC: The Heritage Foundation, 2023).

Gelles, David, Lisa Friedman, and Brad Plumer, "'Full on Fight Club': How Trump Is Crushing U.S. Climate Policy," from *The New York Times*. March 2, 2025.

Giorno, Taylor, "We are Terrified: Musk Puts USAID through Wood Chipper," from *The Hill*. February 3, 2025.

Gultasli, Selcuk, "Professor Ingersoll: The Theocratic Blueprint of Christian Nationalism, Reconstructionism, and Catholic Integralism behind Trump's Agenda," interview with Julie Ingersoll, from European Center for Populism Studies. February 14, 2025.

Olson, Walter, "Reasonable Doubts: Invitation to a Stoning," from *Reason*. November 1998.

Perlstein, Rick, "The Heritage Foundation and Me," from *The Nation*. November 27, 2013.

Phillips-Fein, Kim, "The Mandate for Leadership, Then and Now," from *The Nation*. June 4, 2024.

Quinn, Melissa, "How Trump's Policies and Project 2025 Proposals Match Up after First 100 Days," from CBS News. April 29, 2025.

Rabey, Steve, "Heritage Foundation: Reagan's Favorite Think Tank Reborn for Trump 2.0," from *Baptist News*. January 26, 2024.

Roberts, Kevin, *Dawn's Early Light: Taking Back Washington to Save America* (New York: Broadside Books, 2024).

Skinner, David, "A Battle over Books," in *Humanities*, Vol. 31, No. 5, September/October 2010.

Weiss, Rebecca Bratten, "Faith at the Expense of Freedom," from *Christian Century*. August 22, 2024.

The White House, post on X. February 19, 2025.

Index

Note: Page numbers followed by "n" refer to end notes.

Abbott, Greg 183
Abington School District v. Schempp 76, 78
Advanced Training Institute (ATI) 115, 119
Affordable Care Act 156
Ahn, Che, *When Heaven Comes Down* 54–5, 83, 92, 192, 200–1, 204
AIDS crisis 99, 106
Alliance Defense Fund (ADF) 1, 208–9, 212–13, 216
American Psychological Association (APA) 207
Ames, Fisher 137–8
Angelus Temple 29, 37–8, 171–2, 191
Answers in Genesis 211
Appeal to Heaven flag 6–14, 136, 193–4, 215
Ark Encounter LLC v. Parkinson 1
Arnott, John 55
authoritarianism 16
Azusa Street Revival 29, 54, 88, 103

Bahati, David 99–100, 106–7, 109
Barnett, Tommy 171–2
Barton, David 137–9, 142–8, 157–9, 162, 172–4, 181–3, 209–12, 216, 224
  America's Godly Heritage 142
  The Jefferson Lies 144–5
Baxter, Ern 213
Bebbington, David 15, 142
Bentley, Todd 56–8, 60
Bethel Church xiv–xvi, xx, 12–13, 43, 55–6, 94, 105, 173, 185–6, 192, 198

Bethel School of Supernatural Ministry (BSSM) 94
Bickle, Mike 45–58, 60, 62, 66, 88–9, 103, 234 n.4
  The Pleasures of Loving God 188–9
Biden, Joe 6, 98, 135–6, 156–7, 193, 197–8, 200–1, 203–4, 210, 223
Black Entertainment Television (BET) 163
Black Hebrew Israelites (BHI) 170–1
Black Lives Matter movement 192–3
Blackstone Legal Fellowship 208
blanket training 116
Boebert, Lauren 215
Bohlinger, Peter 179
Bonnke, Reinhard 105
Branham, William 40–3, 45, 48, 50, 117, 134, 171, 187–8, 191–2, 202–3, 213
Bright, Bill 62–4, 101, 142, 202, 207, 213
British Israelism 22–9, 33–5, 37–8, 40–1, 45, 96–8, 133–4, 171, 180, 197, 199, 202, 218, 223
Brown, Harold O. J. 213
Brown v. Board of Education 75–6, 223
Bryan, Cameron 180–1
Buffalo Bill 31–2
Bush, George W. 7, 11, 83, 90, 92–4, 151, 153, 205

Cain, Paul 45, 50–1, 53, 56
Calvary Chapel 49–50
Campus Crusade 62–4, 101, 162, 177, 213
Capitol Riot 5, 7–8, 14, 78, 81, 83, 92, 136, 203–5, 218, 223

Index

Carey, William 237 n.16
Carr, Brendan 224
Cawthorn, Madison 122–3, 131
The Celebrity Apprentice show 174–6
Charisma magazine 9, 164–5, 197
Children's Protection Society of Maine 24
Christ for the Nations Institute (CFNI) 180–1, 241 n.9
Christian Coalition 175–6
Christianity xii–xiii, xvi, 1, 10, 25, 29, 31, 33–4, 48–50, 76, 78, 93, 97, 100, 105, 121, 130, 132, 138–40, 142–5, 147, 164, 170, 193, 213, 216
Christianity Today magazine 93, 97, 132, 164, 213
Christian nationalism xi–xiii, 8, 10–11, 14, 60, 67, 127, 137–9, 143, 147, 162, 178, 181–4, 193, 211–12, 215–16, 226, 229, 231
Christian Zionism 96–7, 152
Civil Rights Act 143–4, 220
civil rights movement 60, 64, 75, 90, 109, 119, 128, 143–4, 147, 151, 220, 223
civil war 26, 125–8, 132–3, 143, 147, 158, 196–7, 199, 230
Clark, Randy 52, 55, 103–4
clash of civilizations 93–4, 96
Clinton, Hillary 166, 168, 218
Columbine High School 73–4, 78, 227
Columbine martyrs 73–84, 99
Confederacy 126–30, 132–3, 136, 141, 143, 152, 160, 172, 178, 195, 203, 228, 231
conservative activism 60, 122
Cooper, Andrea 113
Council for National Policy (CNP) 208–10, 212–13
Covid-19 pandemic 129, 138, 187, 189–92, 201
Creation Museum 211
Cruz, Rafael 2, 183
Cruz, Ted 2, 158, 161, 183, 214
C Street House 107
cult 16, 20, 34–5, 43, 48, 53, 80, 86, 91, 94, 102, 120–1

Cunningham, Loren 62–4, 100–3, 105, 107–8, 142, 177–8, 202, 213
Cyrus 164–5

Dabney, Robert Lewis 127–30, 133
Dawson, John, *Taking Our Cities for God* 103
DEI apparatus 223
Department of Government Efficiency (DOGE) 225
DeVos, Betsy 176–8, 183, 204
Dobson, James 207, 213
dominionism xi–xii, xvi, xvii, xx, 4–6, 34, 60, 102, 105, 107, 118, 120, 136, 152, 162, 172, 177, 181, 185, 197, 203, 217, 219, 225, 229
dominion theology 39, 51, 88
Dowie, John Alexander 20, 31–5, 40, 43
   Leaves of Healing 32
   Voice of Healing 33, 43
Dream City Church 171–2
drug use 63, 67, 207
Duggar, Jim Bob and Michelle Duggar, *The Duggars: 20 and Counting* 3–4, 113–23, 153, 211
Duggar, Michelle 117

Eastman, John 208
ekklesia 12–14
Engel v. Vitale 76
Engle, Lou 60, 67–8, 81–4, 94, 99–100, 103, 107, 152–3, 156–7, 185, 193, 202, 215
Eos Mobile 182–3
evangelicalism xii, 3, 9–10, 15–16, 24, 36, 48–51, 56, 62–4, 82, 88–9, 94, 96, 100, 119, 136, 139, 165, 171–2, 176, 181, 207, 214, 221, 230

Faith and Freedom Coalition 174–7
Falkirk Center 170
Falwell, Jerry 10, 59–60, 66–7, 75–8, 82–3, 106, 122, 143, 151–2, 155, 170–1, 175, 212, 221, 223
Family Research Council 209, 215–16

Farris, Michael 131-2, 160-1, 212-13
Federal Emergency Management Agency (FEMA) 223-4
Feucht, Sean 185-94, 197, 202, 218
Finney, Charles 9
Floyd, George (murder of) 189-91, 195, 197
14 Kids and Pregnant Again (TV show) 113-15, 119, 122-3
Foursquare Church 36, 41, 49-50
Freud, Sigmund 169
Fuller Seminary 61, 63, 87-9, 213

Gateway Church 173-4, 180-1
The Gathering 176-8
Gay Rights Movement 67, 119, 143, 223
Gish Gallup method 174
Global Awakening 55
glossolalia (speaking in tongues) 25-9, 41, 188
GOP 143, 145, 154, 162
Gothard, Bill 4, 115-19, 123, 160
Graham, Billy 10, 16, 34-5, 67, 90, 93
Great Commission 101-2, 108
Great Depression 219-20
Great Recession 155, 157
Great Switch 144, 220
Greene, Marjorie Taylor 215
ground-level spiritual warfare 91
Gulliksen, Kenn 49

Hagee, John 98
Haley, Nikki 195-6
Hall, Franklin, *Atomic Power with God Through Fasting and Prayer* 39, 45
Ham, Ken 211
Harvest International Ministry (HIM) 55
Hawtin, George 188
Hayek, Friedrich 159-60
Henry, Patrick 130-1
The Heritage Foundation 177, 217, 219, 221-3
Hitler, Adolf 167
Holy Spirit 19, 25, 27-9, 34, 36-7, 49, 56-7, 88, 90, 92, 104-5, 117

Home School Legal Defense Association (HSLDA) 131
Huckabee, Mike 121-2, 153, 158

Immigration and Customs Enforcement (ICE) 224
Institute of Basic Life Principles (IBLP) 4, 115-23, 131-2
integralism 218
International House of Prayer in Kansas City, Missouri (IHOP-KC) 45-8, 53, 56, 67, 103, 105, 107, 189

Jakes, T. D. 164
January 6 195-205, 210, 228
Jefferson, Thomas 144-5
Jericho March 98, 199-200
The Jesus Film (movie) 62, 64
Jesus Freaks 79
Jesus Movement 48-9, 82
Joel's Army 45-60, 83, 191-4
John Birch Society 220
Johnson Amendment 2, 175-6
Johnson, Bill xv, 43, 55-6, 58, 94-6, 103, 105, 162, 166, 181, 192, 198
Johnson, Jeremiah 164-5, 170, 197
Johnson, Mike 1-2, 10, 14, 106, 138, 207-16
Jones, Jim 20

Kansas City Fellowship 50-1
Kennedy, D. James 207-8, 212
Kennedy v. Bremerton 183
Keswick movement 16, 34-5, 102
King, Martin Luther Jr. 9, 15, 82
Kirk, Charlie 161-2, 169-72, 196, 201
Koresh, David 20
Ku Klux Klan 26-7, 37-8, 40, 43, 133-4, 136, 146-7, 171-2, 197, 209, 223, 228-9
Kuyper, Abraham 101, 129-30, 160, 177-8

LaHaye, Tim 143, 212
laissez-faire approach 219-20
Lake, John G. 35

Lakeland Outpouring 56–8
Latter Rain 27, 31–43, 45, 48, 50–7, 59, 61–2, 65, 85, 88–9, 116–17, 137, 171, 180–1, 188, 191, 213
Lawrence v. Texas 1, 106
Layzell, Reg 187–9, 191
Lee, Robert E. 196
Lenin, Vladimir 169
Let Us Worship 185–94
LGBTQ+ community 106, 207–9, 212, 216
Lindsay, Dennis 181
Lindsay, Gordon 33, 35, 45, 180
Livingston, Donald 158
Locke, John 8
Lost Cause 133–6, 146–7, 172, 220

"Man Child" doctrine 26–7, 29, 38, 42, 48, 234 n.4
Mandate for Leadership 221
Manifest Sons of God 19–29, 42–3, 48, 55, 58, 94, 191–3, 202, 227–8
Maranatha 49–50
Marshner, Connie 222
McCain, John 3, 15, 60, 122, 154–7
MC510 course 88–9
McDowell, Josh 213
McPherson, Aimee Semple (also known as Sister Aimee) 29, 36–8, 40, 49, 102, 171
Mendez, Ana 86–7
Millerism 121
Mises, Ludwig von 158–9
Moore, Russell 164
Moral Majority 76–7, 152, 171, 175, 212, 221
Morris, Robert 173–4, 180–1, 241 n.9
Musk, Elon 225–6
Muthee, Thomas 3, 91–2, 156

National Public Radio (NPR), *Fresh Air* 61, 64, 86, 224
Nazism 209
Nelson, Thomas 145
Neo-Confederacy 6, 126, 132, 136, 141, 152, 158–9, 195–7, 202–3, 218, 229–30
Network Ekklesia International 12

New Apostolic Reformation (NAR) 55, 60–5, 74, 80–2, 84–6, 91–2, 94, 96–8, 101, 103–5, 117–18, 122, 136, 152, 156–7, 159, 161, 164–8, 170, 173, 175, 180–1, 183, 194, 197–200, 202–5, 214–15, 225–6
New Deal 118, 219–20
Newsom, Gavin 189–90
New Testament 12, 25–6, 89, 102
9/11 attack (September 11) 93, 96–7, 151
North, Gary 158–9, 178, 220

Obama, Barack 67, 97, 154–7
occult-level spiritual warfare 91
Office of Management and Budget (OMB) 224
Oklahoma City Bombing 135–6
Old Testament 13–14, 21–3, 32, 68, 160, 164
Owens, Candace 169–70

Palin, Sarah 2–3, 6, 60, 66, 91–2, 122, 152–8, 160–1
Parham, Charles Fox, *A Voice Crying in the Wilderness* 24–9, 31–2, 34–5, 38, 42, 48, 88, 133, 218, 226
Patrick Henry College (PHC) 131–2, 136
Pearl, Michael and Debi, *To Train Up a Child* 116
Pentecostalism 27–9, 35, 38, 40, 48–9, 53, 82–3, 88, 103, 188, 218
People magazine 113, 121–3
Perkins, Tony 209
Perry, Rick 59–62, 64, 66–8, 83, 86, 213
  The Call 67, 82–4, 94, 97, 99, 103, 107, 152, 162, 185–6, 191
  The Response 60–1, 64, 66–8, 83, 162, 213
Pierce, Chuck 7
Porter, Bruce, *The Martyr's Torch* 81
presuppositional history 141–2
Project 2025 217–26
Public Broadcasting Station (PBS) 224

QAnon 167–9, 200, 203–4, 225
Q drops 166–7
Queen of Heaven 86–7, 92–3

Reagan, Ronald 10, 175, 221
Reconstructionism xi–xii, 4, 6, 10, 118–20, 128, 134, 136, 152, 159, 218, 221–2
Reed, Ralph 174–6, 182
religious liberty 1, 180
Religious Right 10, 59, 64, 66, 68, 76, 139–40, 143, 151–2, 155, 164, 170–1, 174, 177, 179, 208
Republican National Convention 153, 169
Republican Party 144–6, 152–4, 161, 172, 176, 214, 220
Rhodes, Stewart 200
Roberts, Kevin, *Dawn's Early Light* 217–19, 223, 225
Robertson, Pat 175, 181, 197–8
Rogers, Adrian 213
Roosevelt, Franklin D. 118, 219–20
Ruby Ridge 134–5, 202
Rushdoony, Rousas John xi, 4, 6, 10–11, 118–19, 127–32, 134, 141, 143, 147, 158–60, 162, 172, 178, 202, 210, 213–14, 220–3
The Messianic Character of American Education 118, 222

same-sex marriage 99
Sandford, Frank 19–26, 31, 33–5, 40, 43, 85, 92
Satanic Panic 87–9, 91
Schaeffer, Edith 213
Schaeffer, Francis 10, 139–42, 144, 147, 208, 213, 221
A Christian Manifesto 139, 141
Scott, Rachel 74, 77–8, 80, 83
Second World War 27, 40, 88
The Sentinel Group 92
17 Kids and Counting (TV show) 3–4, 115–16, 122
Seven Mountain Mandate (7MM) 59–69, 77, 85, 95, 99–109, 142–3, 157, 159, 164–6, 178–9, 194, 202, 213–15, 218, 225–6, 228
Seventh-Day Adventism 120–1
The 700 Club (show) 197
sexual revolution 63, 67, 207

Seymour, William 29, 88
Sheets, Dutch 7–8, 10–13, 21, 27, 33, 74, 78, 81–2, 98, 180, 204
Shepherding Movement 116–17, 213
Shiloh 19–27, 32, 35, 92, 218
Siljander, Mark 213
Silk, Danny 12–13
Simmons, Brian, *The Passion Translation* 11
Simpson, A. B. 35–6
Smith, Hannah 180–1
Smith, Michael W. 79
Social Gospel 118–19
Southlake Families PAC 179–82
Spencer, Richard 196–7
spiritual mapping 92–3
Stalin, Josef 169
Stephens, Alexander, "Cornerstone Speech" 127–8
strategic-level spiritual warfare 85, 89, 92–6, 98, 103–4

Tate, Tristan 169
Tea Party 67, 151–62, 168, 174
Teen Mania 79, 82
10/40 Window 86–7, 90–4, 97
Texas Education Agency 145–6, 183
Texas Essential Knowledge and Skills (TEKS) 145–6
Third Wave of the Holy Spirit 88–90
Toronto Airport Christian Fellowship 53–4, 104
Toronto Airport Vineyard Church 52–3
Toronto Blessing 52–6, 58, 82–3, 94, 103–4
Trump, Donald xvii–xviii, 4–9, 11, 15, 45, 59, 66, 69, 84, 97–8, 122, 136, 154, 161–72, 174–6, 179, 185–6, 192–205, 208–9, 215, 217–19, 222–6
Turning Point USA 161–2, 169–72, 183, 194, 196, 203, 225

Uganda 99, 106–7, 109, 122, 209
umbrellas of authority (concept of) 115–17
United States Agency for International Development (USAID) 225

Vallotton, Kris 95–6, 162, 192, 198–9, 204
  Heavy Rain 43
  Spirit Wars 95
Vance, J. D. 218–19, 223
Van Til, Cornelius 10, 141
Vineyard church 49–57, 82, 89
Voting Rights Act 143–4
Vought, Russell 224

Wagner, C. Peter 61–2, 64–6, 74, 85–94, 96–7, 103, 156, 199, 213
WallBuilders 138, 157–8, 174, 210–11
Wallnau, Lance 63, 65–6, 108, 164–5, 168, 178–83
Welsh Revival 29
West, Kanye 169–71
Weyrich, Paul 221
Whitall Smith, Hannah 19, 25–6, 33–4
  The Christian's Secret to a Happy Life 33–5

The White House 98, 157, 172, 175, 186–7, 194, 197, 199–200
White, Paula xvii, 4, 163, 166, 175, 197, 199, 203
Wildmon, Don 213
Williams, Roger 9–10
Wilson, Doug and Steve Wilkins, *Southern Slavery As It Was* xii, 125–7, 129, 132–3, 135, 178, 202
Wilson, John, *Our Israelitish Origins* 22
Wimber, John 49–55, 88–9

xenolalia 27–8

Youth with a Mission (YWAM) 62–3, 100–3, 107–8, 177, 181, 191

Ziklag 178–9
Zion 32
Zionist-occupied government (ZOG) 167–8

About the Author

Keri Ladner, PhD, is an expert on fundamentalist politics in America and the radicalization of the conservative movement. She specializes in the religious beliefs of the American right, and her work illuminates how those beliefs have become part of American power structures. She is the author of *End Time Politics: From the Moral Majority to QAnon* (2024), and her publications have been featured in a number of media outlets, including *Christian Century*, Religion Dispatches, and Good Faith Media.